the sea vegetable book

the seavegetable book

Judith Cooper Madlener

Drawings
by the author

Clarkson N. Potter, Inc. / Publishers   NEW YORK
DISTRIBUTED BY CROWN PUBLISHERS, INC.

Published simultaneously in Canada
by General Publishing Company Limited
First edition
Printed in the United States of America

Library of Congress Cataloging in Publication Data

Madlener, Judith Cooper.
  The sea vegetable book.

  Bibliography: p
  Includes index.
  1. Marine algae as food.   2. Cookery (Marine algae)
I. Title.
TX402.M3   641.6′5   76-58389
ISBN 0-517-52905-X
ISBN-0-517-52906-8 pbk

Photographs on jacket/cover:
(From right front to left back)
1) Kombu *(Laminaria)*
2) Grapestone *(Gigartina)*
3) Irish moss *(Chondrus)*
4) Elephant grass *(Uridaea)*

Contents

Foreword

It is both timely and significant that in this year 1977, as we are becoming ever more aware of the limitations of our land resources for both energy and food, along comes a book that will open many eyes to the possibilities of the sea as a source of food. Just as we are seeking to conserve the earth's *nonrenewable* resources, so we are also striving to develop and make optimum use of our *renewable* resources. Fortunately, marine algae fall into the renewable category. But what use have we made of them?

Few people realize they have been eating seaweeds in one form or another for many years. Extracts of marine algae are found in practically every type of prepared food item from ice cream, puddings, salad dressings, and bread to diet foods, cheeses, sauces, fruit juices, dehydrated mixes, and toppings. Most of these foods contain thickeners or stabilizers derived from one of three seaweed extracts: algin from the Brown algae and from the Red algae, carrageenan and agar.

Knowing this, perhaps it is not such a big leap to think of switching from the extract to the whole plant after all, and we of the Sea Grant Program applaud this attempt to awaken interest in marine algae as a foodstuff in the United States.

The Sea Grant Program has been one of the principal sponsors of seaweed research in the United States for nearly a decade. Much of our work has been directed toward the culture of various types of valuable marine algae to provide reliable high-quality supplies. This research has been conducted by university scientists in New Hampshire, Florida, California, Washington, Hawaii, and the Virgin Islands, in cooperation with seaweed processing companies. Other studies have been made on marine algae as a fertilizer and soil conditioner and as a source of food for edible marine animals being grown in aquaculture operations; significant programs are under way to extract drugs from these weeds. To date, there has been almost no work done on growing marine algae for human food in the United States. This is in direct contrast to the situation in many Asiatic countries where thousands of acres of coastal waters are devoted to this use. Increasing demand for foods of all types may well cause us to turn to the sea frontier and its marine algae, as our arable land resources are fully utilized.

Mrs. Madlener has skillfully combined the scientific and culinary aspects of this subject to produce a valuable practical work. Filled with thought-provoking material, the book includes historical notes on the use of algae as food, how they grow, where they are sold, how they are prepared and used, how they are or are not affected by pollution, what affects their flavor, what nutrient values they possess, and an extensive collection of recipes containing sea vegetables.

Welcome to the world of the sea vegetable. If I may be excused for the use of a cliché—try it, you'll like it.

ROBERT D. WILDMAN
National Sea Grant Program
Washington, D.C.

Preface

Perhaps it is important to mention that I would not consider myself a food faddist. As a wife and mother of two small children, proper nutrition is of prime concern to me. As a woman who loves cooking and its gastronomic rewards, I know that experiencing new foods is always exhilarating. I've always enjoyed browsing in the marketplaces of large cities, noticing the configurations of unfamiliar fruits and vegetables, their smells and tastes an unexpected pleasure. So much foreign produce is available now in local markets that it is common for the homemaker to serve exotic vegetables with the daily fare. In terms of practicality, it is simply good sense to make use of something which is highly nutritious, readily available, and inexpensive. With new commercial interest in the merchandizing potential of algae and new technology to facilitate it, processed forms of edible algae will no doubt soon be a common commodity on the American grocer's shelf.

JUDITH COOPER MADLENER
Berkeley, California
December, 1976

Acknowledgments

I could not have written a book of this nature without the advice and encouragement of numerous members of the scientific community. However, I must accept responsibility for any shortcomings which might be evident in the text.

I am particularly indebted to Dr. Paul Silva of the University of California at Berkeley for his invaluable help and for the many courtesies which he has shown me; and to Dr. D. P. Rogerson of the New York Botanical Garden for the research privileges which I enjoyed.

I wish to express special thanks to Mr. Tom DeCew of the University of California at Berkeley, for giving so freely of his time and energies to counsel me in the field of phycology.

For all the time graciously taken out of busy schedules I would like to express my deep gratitude to Dr. A. D. Boney, University of Glasgow, Scotland; Dr. David Coon, University of California, Santa Barbara; Dr. Michael Coon, Department of Recreation and Conservation, Vancouver, British Columbia; Dr. Emil Chi, University of Washington Medical School, Seattle; Dr. Y. M. Chiang, National Taiwan University, Taipeh; Professor A. H. Dizerbo, Roscoff Biological Station, France; Dr. Soewondo Djojosoebagio, National University of Malaysia, Kuala Lumpur; Dr. E. M. Donaldson, Fisheries Research Board, West Vancouver, British Columbia; Dr. Sylvia A. Earle, California Academy of Sciences, San Francisco; Dr. William Fenical, Scripps Institution of Oceanography, La Jolla, California; Dr. Louie Hanic, University of Prince Edward Island, Charlottetown; Dr. Max Hómmersand, University of North Carolina, Chapel Hill; Dr. Stephen Hsiao: Environment Canada, Quebec; Dr. Harold Humm, University of South Florida, Tampa; Dr. Charles Hunter, Northwest Fisheries Center, Seattle, Washington; Dr. Hideo Iwasaki, Mie University, Japan; Dr. David Jamison, Washington State Department of Natural Resources, Olympia; Dr. D. H. Kim, Conception University, Chile; Dr. Tetsuo Koyama, New York Botanical Garden; Dr. Min Jai Lee, Seoul National University, Korea; Dr. William O. McLarney, The New Alchemists Institute, Woods Hole, Massachusetts; Dr. Thomas Mumford, Department of Natural Resources, Olympia, Washington; Dr. A. K. Murray, Agriculture and Fisheries Department, Hong Kong; Dr. Michael Neushul, University of California, Santa Barbara; Dr. Wheeler J. North, California Institute of Technology, Corona del Mar; Dr. Luigi Provasoli, Yale University, New Haven, Connecticut; Dr. Robert A. Rasmussen, Humboldt State University, Arcata, California; Dr. John Ryther, Woods Hole Oceanographic Institute, Falmouth, Massachusetts; Dr. Richard Searles, Duke University, Durham, North Carolina; Dr. Toshio Segi, Mie University, Japan; Dr. Nicholas Shoumatoff, Ward Pound Ridge Reservation, Cross River, New York; Dr. G. H. Sidrak, University of the West Indies, Jamaica; Dr. R. H. Simmons, Department of Sea Fisheries, Republic of South Africa; Ms. Karen Steidinger, State Department of Natural Resources, St. Petersburg, Florida; Ms. Sarah Tanner, Moss Landing Marine Laboratory, California; Dr. Nancy J. Turner, Provincial Museum, Victoria, British Columbia; Dr. Gregorio T. Velasquez, University of the Philippines, Manila; Dr. Robert Wildman, National Oceanic and Atmospheric Administration, Office of Sea Grant, Washington, D.C.; and to Dr. Jacques Zaneveld, Old Dominion University, Williamsburg, Virginia.

And in appreciation for generous contributions to my culinary research, I thank Mr. Ted Shiramatsu of the Japan Trade Center, New York City and Tokyo; Mrs. Toshiko Sugai of Bayside, New York; Mrs. Hwa Cha Page of Queens Village, New York; Mr. Robert Felt of Boston; chef Hiroshi Hiashi of Boston; Mr. and Mrs. Ben Tsutsumoto of Seattle, Washington; Dr. Lynda J. Goff, University of California, Santa Cruz; Mr. Richard Moe, University of California, Berkeley; Dr. Joy Morrill, Academy of Natural Sciences, Philadelphia; Ms. Tay Hashimoto of the Japan American Society Inc., Seattle, Washington; Ms. Myung Cha Lim of the Korean Consulate, New York City; Ms. Marilyn Chilvers of Canada Safeway, Public Relations; Mr. Russell Ziemba of Amsterdam, New York; Mr. Charles Gibbs of Florida; Mr. Glanville Penn of Tortola, Virgin Islands; The Japanese-American Citizens League, San Francisco, California; The Japanese Consulate Information Service, San Francisco, California; The Japan Society, Los Angeles, California; The National Library of Australia; Mr. Giuseppe Cardillo of the Italian Cultural Institute, New York City; the Malaysian Consulate General, New York City; and The Pinellas County Science Center, Florida.

All about sea vegetables

SEAWEEDS ARE NOT WEEDS!

In the English language the suffix *weed* has for centuries served to describe the marine algae, defining their value and framing the way in which we look at them. But in many parts of the world the edible seaweeds are appreciated for what they truly are, *sea vegetables*.

Among the many definitions of *weed* found in the Oxford dictionary, only "wild plant" seems at all appropriate. The edible, wild plants of the oceans are the sea vegetables which form the lush, natural, underwater "gardens" proliferating along most of our continental shelves.

For those who might feel squeamish at the thought of eating weeds, there is comfort in the fact that many of our coveted esoteric spices, like thyme, mint, sage, and oregano, are in fact weeds. Certain algae, like *Codium fragile,* might, according to their use, be considered herbs or spices, but in general, the sea plants are more akin to land vegetables. It is my feeling that *seaweed* is no longer an appropriate term for the varieties of edible marine algae visible to the naked eye and that the term *sea vegetable* might supplant it as the proper designation.

What is a sea vegetable?   Sea vegetables are algae, marine algae to be exact. They are primitive, photosynthesizing plants without true leaves, stems, or roots. Although they are not differentiated by tissue or function into leaf, stem, and root, they do possess, in terms of shape, a blade which is leaflike, a stipe which is stemlike, and a holdfast which is rootlike. They range in size from barely visible to massive. The algae are not seed-bearing but reproduce by spores, gametes, and fragmentation. They are distinctive in shape and readily recognizable when found growing or washed ashore. The sea grasses, often mistaken for algae, are not seaweeds. They are considered marine angiosperms; seed-bearing, flowering plants living among the seaweeds.

The habitat of sea vegetables is the ocean and its brackish coastal waters. They fasten themselves to the sea floor by means of disc-shaped or tendril like holdfasts. These rootlike systems are not nutrient-gathering as is the case with land plants. Instead, the plants take nourishment through the entire surface of their leaflike blades or fronds directly from the seawater which bathes them. In this way the algae extract from the sea and assimilate inorganic substances and convert them into organic compounds which the human body is able to utilize.

Sea vegetables fall into five groups, each categorized not by its appearance but by its food reserves and chemical substances, its reproductive patterns, and also by its cell structure. Though these categories still bear their original designations according to pigment (Rhodophyta, Red algae; Chlorophyta, Green algae; Phaeophyta, Brown algae; Cyanophyta, Blue-green algae; and Xanthophyta, Yellow-green algae), their color is not a reliable indicator for classification. For instance, many algae in the Rhodophyta, or Red algae category contain overlying green pigments or range from one end of the spectrum to the other in color variation, making identification on the basis of hue alone impossible.

A rose by any other name   It is possible the names bestowed on foods produce certain attitudes toward them. The thought of starting the meal with an aspic of *star jelly,* dining on sautéed *heaven* *vegetable,* relishing a *fairy's butter* sauce, refreshing the palate with a tossed sea salad of delicate *green ocean leaves* and *water leaf,* finishing with a shimmery dessert of *red ribbons* or *cold sky* or perhaps just a small bowl of *sea grapes,* encourages gustatory experimentation.

Delicacies, not survival foods   The mistaken idea that sea vegetables are eaten only in impoverished sections of the world or in times of famine has for a long time colored the way in which Americans view the prospect of incorporating these plants into their diets. It is possible that a taste for some of the individual flavors in the algae might have to be acquired, but no more so than for say, broccoli, cabbage, Brussels sprouts, or any other of the stronger-tasting land vegetables.

In Asian countries sea vegetables are part of the daily diet. Although the degree to which they are utilized in the West does not compare to the extent of their use in places like Japan, the Philippines, Indonesia, and the Hawaiian Islands, these algal vegetables are nonetheless ever-present in world cuisine wherever the coast will support algal growth and marine grazers will allow it to flourish. Algae show up in basic cooking and haute cuisine from the subarctic to the subtropics around the globe. It is true, necessity has decreed that countries whose landmass is either too small or too poor to support large-scale agriculture or animal husbandry have in the past relied heavily on algae as a foodstuff. Areas where the climatic conditions are harsh have relied on marine algae as a year-round source of fresh vegetables. Granted, peoples have depended on algae in times of dearth, but to call sea vegetables survival food and equate them with reindeer moss or to classify them only as food for the camper would be a mistake!

Easy to use   For Americans sea vegetable cookery is a very new area of culinary expression, but one with immense possibilities for discovery and innovation. Sea vegetables can be used to create dishes which are not only nutritious and satisfying but pleasing to the palate and to the eye. They can be cooked with the same ease and comfort with which we prepare our everyday foods. They can be boiled, baked, steamed, sautéed, fried, blanched, dried, salted, brined, or prepared in any way in which their terrestrial counterparts, the land vegetables, are prepared. Most can be eaten raw and many can be successfully frozen. Many species possess unique characteristics of taste and texture which elevate them to the level of fine foods, appreciated the world over.

THE ALGAL GOURMET—PAST AND PRESENT

Taking individual taste into consideration, I find it remarkable that such a vast number of algae seem to be universally appreciated. The enormous body of literature concerned with sea vegetables eaten by man is astounding. Hundreds of species have been eaten since the beginning of history, by peoples who relished the different tastes and textures and were fascinated by their beauty and diversity of form, in much the same way we have appreciated land vegetables.

The oldest law book in Iceland makes reference to the rights and concessions involved before one might collect and/or eat fresh sol *(Palmaria palmata)* on a neighbor's land. The alga has been eaten there since the year 961 B.C.

Some of the earlier records, in the Chinese *Book of Poetry,* for example, which document the esteem in which sea vegetables were held, date to about 800 to 600 B.C. So as far back as the time of Confucius, algae were thought of as something very special. Elegance and fine composition are implicit in the Chinese character for algae, suggesting deep appreciation for the delicate nature and physical shape of the plants.

It is interesting to note that the renowned and ancient Chinese delicacy Birds' Nest Soup is popularly thought to be prepared from a nest made of algae. This is actually not the case at all. Passerine birds from the caves along the coast of Java use a gel-forming red alga *(Gracilaria spinosa)* to rebuild all or parts of their damaged nests. The original nests, made of the birds' congealed saliva, have a sugar-coated appearance, and it is the original nests which constitute the coveted delicacy. No self-respecting Chinese chef would confuse the two or substitute one for the other.

In the writings of Aristotle reference can be found to the "weedy sea." Scholar and scientist, having set down the original rules of biological classification, he was seemingly unaware of any culinary purpose these plants might serve. Virgil, his reputation as an epicure notwithstanding, refers to seaweed as "vile," designating it a useless commodity. It would seem that the rest of the ancient world did not share this view. Porterfield, in *References to Algae in the Chinese Classics,* refers to algae as exceptional fare—"some algae are a delicacy fit for the most honorable guest, even the king himself."

Japanese court poetry reflected modes of appreciation unequaled in the West. Expressions like "gemlike seaweed" and "seaweed glows like gems" were commonly used. Here, one of the most beautiful examples shows clearly the associations.

Love

Tamamo
Ama to wa nashi ni
Kimi kouru
Va gu koromode no
Kawaku toki naki

Although no fisher
Reaping the gemlike seaweed,
I yearn for you
So deeply that the salt spray
Never dries upon my sleeves.

Anonymous

Ancient Hawaiian nobility kept limu (edible algae) gardens. It was considered imperative that a variety of fresh plants be instantly available for eating at all times. The site was usually outside the royal beach home. The gardens were cultivated with utmost care. Basically, limu gardening consisted of transplanting the rare and choice varieties to a protected location and weeding out the less esoteric species, leaving the more desirable ones to flourish. Until the 1940s, a limu garden was maintained in Honolulu at the residence once belonging to Queen Liliuokalani. Today gardening and harvesting of limu is facilitated with the aid of "look boxes," rectangular containers with glass bottoms.

After World War I the eating of algae seemed to fall out of favor in the Hawaiian Islands. Later, with the advent of fast foods, age-old traditions were abandoned in favor of the expedient. The culinary traditions involving the use of algae by the Hawaiians, still alive and rich in the 1800s, became almost extinct. However, in recent years Hawaii has experienced a cultural renaissance. The near loss of almost all of the knowledge relating to limu has promoted much interest in studying and reincorporating the diverse forms of sea vegetables into the diet. Out of the seventy-five species documented as edible in the last century, knowledge of only twenty or so is extant, twelve to eighteen of which are in common use by the population today. This represents an incalculable loss. Unfortunately, the Hawaiian culture is not the only culture to have sustained this sort of loss. Knowledge of the uses of edible algae has fast fallen out of use and been lost to time in many countries throughout the world.

An offering to the gods　Not only in the Hawaiian Islands but also in Japan alga was considered a delicacy fine enough to serve as an offering to the gods. In Japan it is still possible to sit down to a meal and find seven or eight different kinds of algal foods served. Some of the most subtle and deft uses of algae in cooking developed by the Japanese through the centuries have stood the test of time and are still popular today. Etchings in Japanese museums depict the Ainu, a primitive race living on the island of Soya (present-day Hokkaido). These bearded fishermen, rendered so elegantly, crouched in their shallow boats, sporting long undulating black beards as they twisted long hooked poles into the waters to harvest the curly kelp, practiced the rudiments of Japanese algal cuisine.

The world-famous ama divers of Japan, who would plunge to the bottom of Tokyo Bay to harvest select food items, gathered the Red alga, *Porphyra tenera,* as one of the most prized sea vegetables. The folk name ama nori designated it a delicacy.

Primitive coastal societies almost universally appear to have gathered vegetables from the sea. From the Siberian Indians to the Aborigines of Tasmania, algae have had a place in the daily diet. Remnants of what seem to have been algal repasts have recently been excavated from the seaside dwellings of Stone Age South Africans.

The algae are primary producers of the food that ultimately sustains all sea life. There are herbivorous fish which eat only algae. The marine iguanas in the Galapagos Islands feed exclusively on one Red species. The abalone, sea urchin, and many invertebrates feed on marine algae as does the brant goose. Alaskan seals enjoy a diet of Green algae and the Eskimos enjoy the contents of the seal's stomach boiled up as a delicious and nourishing soup!

Dulse vs. the potato chip   In the British Isles laverbread made from *Porphyra leucosticta* is still considered a breakfast treat, while in Scotland the tougher species, *Porphyra umbilicalis,* is peddled to unsuspecting tourists as the real thing. In the Canadian Maritimes dulse, *Palmaria palmata,* is sold in the pubs and nibbled with beer as an improvement on the potato chip. In Southeast Asia, substantial quantities of sea vegetables are eaten daily. In the Philippines, marine algae are cultivated and harvested for the fresh vegetable market. Sea vegetables still form a good portion of Malaysian trade commodities and are eaten throughout the thousands of islands which make up Indonesia. In China, Japan, and Korea the cultivation of sea vegetables goes on in practically every bay and stretch of usable coast. Cultivation techniques are the most sophisticated in the entire world, and still the demand for these vegetables and food products made from them far outreaches the supply.

Liquor from sea vegetables   In Russia today a particular species of algae is prepared with beets, tomatoes, etc., and canned for sale throughout the USSR under the folk name sea cabbage. It is a very popular commodity and the sea vegetable used is believed by the older citizens to prevent cirrhosis of the liver. In the Siberian northlands, on the Kamchatka Peninsula, present-day Russian inhabitants ferment the Red alga *Palmaria palmata* into an alcoholic beverage.

Good appetite!   A delightful story was told me by a woman prominent in the field of phycology (as the study of seaweeds is known). It seems that on a recent junket to the islands in the western Pacific, the assembled group of scientists paused for a picnic lunch by the sea. Part of the group, including the lady, donned scuba gear and proceeded to dive for research specimens. The others set about making ready to dine. The diving went on, and soon a respectable pile of seaweeds lay on shore beside the luncheon cloth. One last dive and the lady surfaced only to find to her chagrin that her cache was being eaten as an appetizer. Not only that but individual plants were being passed around by the assembled group of Oriental aficionados and enjoyed with appropriate commenting and approbation! One small unacceptable sprig was all that was left of a morning's work. There was obviously not much to say in a situation like this except, perhaps, *bon appétit!*

Trying out the local algae   From an ethnobotanical standpoint the migration of peoples across the face of the earth molds culinary habits and tastes and affects the selection of food sources. Ethnic groups have for a very long time been experimenting in their new environs, testing by trial and error the local algae. Acceptable species resembling or identical to those found on their native shores are soon incorporated into the cuisine.

   This phenomenon is especially evident on the West Coast of the United States and Canada, where in the Russian, Philippine, Japanese, Korean, Chinese, and Hawaiian communities, local sea vegetables are used extensively in cooking. Indigenous species are constantly being discovered as "good eating." The use of the leafy Red alga *Polyneura latissima* by the Filipino and Chinese inhabitants of the San Francisco Bay area is a striking example of this sort of adaptation. Methods of preparing and eating it reflect a mixing of cultures and traditions. Since in the Philippines algae are eaten fresh in most instances, freezing of the plants for storage reflects American methods; sun drying of the plants is more typically Chinese. Blanching the algae before eating is popular both in the southern parts of the Philippines and in Japan.

Postelsia palmaeformis, the sea palm, is another alga recently recognized as edible. Both of these species are endemic to the North American West Coast.

The genus most often sampled in a new environment is *Porphyra*—nori to the Japanese, kim to the Koreans, and chi choy to the Chinese. Separating this genus from others is extremely easy, much easier than determining the individual species. But species determination is not all that important in the beginning, for *Porphyra* is the most universally delicious of all the genera. All of the species of *Porphyra* are edible, and most are exceptionally delicious. Oriental peoples on the West Coasts of the United States and Canada make extensive use of numerous species, many of them unique to that particular area. The practice of sampling local marine algae is also carried out on the East Coast of America. Small pockets of sea vegetable gatherers and users are to be found in the Boston area and parts of Maine. The utilization of *Laminaria longicruris* and *Ascophyllum mackaii* as food originated in these groups.

Are there poisonous varieties?   Normal apprehension, fear of poisoning oneself and others, might logically seem the main deterrent to experimentation. In the case of marine algae there are only a few species which are toxic if eaten in quantity and only one, *Lyngbya,* which is dangerous to consume. With algae even more so than with land plants, it is highly unlikely that the careful observer would confuse a toxic species with an edible variety. The difficulties experienced by the novice forager for mushrooms and other fungi do not arise in the case of the algae. There are not deadly look-alikes to ensnare the beginner. With the exception of an unsubstantiated, probably mythical, reference to a lethal species of *Caulerpa* growing only in one solitary spot in the Hawaiian Islands, there is nothing in the literature to show that anyone has ever been lethally poisoned by a seaweed.

Pure, wholesome foods   Logic would have to preempt prejudice against wild food on the grounds of cleanliness. The sticky mucilages found on the surface of most species are constantly being dissolved by the surrounding seawaters, so that impurities like silt suspended in the water, which might settle on the plants, cannot easily adhere to the algae's constantly renewing exterior. In terms of natural goodness, foraged sea vegetables are fresh growing plants, bathed by the sea and nourished by the earth's minerals; they are not sprayed with insecticides or touched by human hands. They are occasionally nibbled by fish and other marine creatures, just as land vegetables are eaten by insects. Small snails leave tiny holes in the fronds of many of the sea lettuces and even some of the larger tougher Laminarias. Sea vegetables which bear these perforations are rejected by commercial harvesters in Japan, just as in the United States land vegetables bearing the marks of insects are considered undesirable. We, so removed from the land, prefer to ingest pesticide rather than risk a worm in our apple!

The natural foods movement   At this point in time sun-dried sea vegetables can be bought in health food stores and ethnic markets in all major cities and most towns in North America. One need not forage on the shores to enjoy fresh sea vegetables. Frozen, blanched, or salted fresh sea vegetables are often available in the larger stores.

Western interest in cooking with sea vegetables has been on the upsurge in the last ten years. The flood of algal products which reaches our international markets from Japan has stirred public interest. Courses in ethnic cooking, offered everywhere today, have served to familiarize people with a diversity of culinary traditions. People are open to trying unfamiliar foods. It is realized that all things foreign need not be adapted to the American taste, whatever that is!

Awareness of the availability of fresh sea vegetables through foraging has played an important part in arousing interest, but the single most important factor affecting the popularity of sea vegetables has been the public movement toward natural foods and much of the feeling which it embraces, including the social phenomenon loosely termed the counterculture. This return-to-the-land experimentation fostered in the last decade has served to amass a treasury of original and sophisticated recipes using vegetables from the sea.

SEA VEGETABLES AND NUTRITION

As one might logically expect, sea vegetables are among the most nutritious plants on earth. Nutrients in seawater are constantly renewed by nature, and the plants themselves have the ability to concentrate particular elements present in the surrounding waters, several thousand times over. As is the case with land plants, these nutritive values vary from genus to genus and also with the season and growing environment.

The nutritive values of many sea vegetables greatly exceed those found in any existing food source. Algae are an excellent source of vitamins and possess the full range of vitamins known to man. But more sophisticated equipment is needed before these elusive entities can be isolated and studied properly. For reasons of simplification, algal vitamins may be equated with those of land vegetables because they fill the same dietary requirements. However, they are structurally different.

Vitamins   Almost all of the algal vitamins owe their origin to bacteria living on the plants or growing in the seawater immediately surrounding them. The amount of any vitamin concentrated by the particular alga depends upon the type of bacteria involved and the alga's ability to concentrate that vitamin. It is possible that vitamin B_{12} is one of the few Bs which is synthesized by the plants themselves, as it is essential to algal growth. This is true of the microscopic plants and probably the macroscopic as well.

In general, marine algae are rich in vitamins A and E. Niacin and vitamin C content are about the same in the Red (Rhodophyta), Green (Chlorophyta) and Brown (Phaeophyta) algae. Concentrations of vitamins B_{12}, B_1, pantothenic acid, and folic and folinic acids are generally higher in the Greens and Reds than in the Browns. Animal organs, especially liver, which are richest in vitamin B_{12}, contain a lesser amount in grams dry weight of this vitamin than do some of the Green algae. The concentrations of algal B vitamins are, in fact, comparable to those in many common fruits and vegetables.

The genus *Porphyra* appears to be the richest source, among the algae, of vitamins B and C. In fact, the Red algae *Porphyra perforata* and *Porphyra naidum,* various species of the Green algae *Ulva,* the Brown alga *Alaria valida,* and the Red alga *Gigartina papillata* share the distinction of possessing, pound for pound, vitamin C values comparable to that of lemons. Species of *Porphyra* have also been found to contain 36,000 to 50,000 IU per gram of vitamin A, far more than chicken eggs (850 IU) or chicken liver (10,000 IU).

Extraordinary amounts of vitamin A are found in the marine algae generally. Oils from various sea vegetables contain a thousand times more vitamins A and D than are contained in equal amounts of cod-liver oil. This might tend to support the scientific view that vitamins found in herbivorous fish originally come from the sea vegetables on which they feed Growth-promoting vitamins, such as A, are found in the algae in exceedingly large quantities (larger than butterfat of the best summer butter). The vitamin A content in cabbages is matched by the Green algar *Codium tomentosum* and *Ulva lactuca* and the Brown alga *Laminaria digitata.*

The Red alga *Palmaria palmata* contains half as much vitamin C (weight for weight) as is found in oranges. Some species of *Fucus* (Brown algae) and *Porphyra* (Red algae) are even richer. Interestingly enough the Angmagssalik Eskimos get 50 percent of their dietary vitamin C from sea vegetables.

The concentration of most algal vitamins changes markedly with the season, so it is hard to give rules to facilitate harvesting for high vitamin concentration. Some vitamin concentrations, like that of B_{12} and folic acid, are at their highest in spring and summer, and some, like niacin and folinic acid, are highest in winter. Spring and autumn seem to be times of high C concentration in certain algae. In terms of palatability, the only data apparent at this time show the Red algae thickest and best for eating from the end of winter through the summer.

Water   Most sea vegetables are largely water when fresh, as are land vegetables. Tougher species, many growing in the upper tidal zone, contain less water. Water content varies slightly with the portion of the plant sampled and with the season.

Protein   The proportion of protein in the algae accounts for as much as 25 percent of the dry weight. Soluble nitrogen compounds provide organic nitrogen in addition to the regular protein content. In many algae, free nitrogen content is higher in winter than in summer and higher in spring than in fall. The level of crude protein depends on the species, season, habitat (including depth at which plant grows), age of the plant, and the part sampled. So crude protein content is at its maximum in spring, as in land crops, diminishing with maturity and with the diminution of nitrate in the water as it is utilized by the algal vegetation. In the Phaeophyceae (Brown algae), two-thirds of the way up the frond from the stipe seems to be the highest in protein.

The algae contain, on the whole, highly digestible proteins. *Palmaria palmata* (Red algae), various species of *Porphyra* (Red algae), and various species of *Nostoc* (Blue-green algae) all contain proteins with a digestibility factor in excess of 75 percent.

The marine algae are similar to oats in both protein and carbohydrate value. The Red algae and the Green algae appear highest in crude protein in the species thus far tested. Variation in the protein content among the genera is about 4 percent to 25 percent. Highest in protein are *Nostoc* species (Blue-green algae) with 20 percent, *Enteromorpha linza* (Green algae) at 20 percent, *Analipus japonicus* (Brown algae) at 22 percent, and various species of *Porphyra* at 20 percent or more. Three ounces (100 grams) of dried *Porphyra tenera* (nori) supplies one-half the daily adult protein requirement. *Prophyra* is therefore higher than rice or soybeans and very close to horsemeat in protein value.

Carbohydrates   All algae contain carbohydrates (sugars and starches), and only in the case of the carbohydrate does algae differ nutritionally from any other food. The algal carbohydrate is called a polysaccharide. It is a natural nontoxic colloidal substance—the sticky, mucilaginous material referred to as gel. Until recently the complex components of its makeup were thought to be "unavailable" to the human system, that is, their structure was not readily broken down by the digestive processes and therefore they were of little use to us nutritionally. The fact that in certain areas like Polynesia, digestion of algae seemed apparent, was explained as a hereditary capability built up by the body over centuries. However, what now seems to be the case is that this capability is real, is not genetically linked, and can be acquired by any human digestive tract when algae is constantly present in the diet for only about a week's time. That is to say, conditioning can increase digestive efficiency by developing new enzymes, intestinal flora, or organisms to deal with the new food.

Gels Algin, one of the gel substances of the Brown algae, has recently been shown to have considerable nutritive value rather than, as was previously thought, being simply a source of roughage in the diet. Carrageenan, the gel produced by many of the Red algae, contains easily assimilated plant phosphorus, calcium, and other elements. Some sea vegetable extracts (gels) contain the elements iodine and bromine.

Sea vegetable gels can be used similarly to animal gels. Gelatin made from the hoofs and cartilage of animals is most commonly sold in powdered form, as is, or combined with artificial fruit flavoring. The product depends upon a constant supply of higher animals like cows to keep up with demand. Algal gels, on the other hand, come from a vast untapped resource, sea vegetables! The gels agar and carrageenan are water soluble and are extracted by boiling.

In cooking, algal gels can produce any effects which animal gels are capable of producing, and more. Algal gels have a much wider range of properties. Agar, for instance, will set at room temperature in a matter of minutes. It can be bought in "powdered" form (sometimes called agar-agar) or in dried-frozen strand, stick or flake form (kanten). Dried Irish moss *(Chondrus crispus)* can also be purchased. Carrageenan-producing and agar-producing species can also be gathered fresh and boiled in a variety of liquids from milk to fruit or vegetable juices, to produce distinctive gelatins.

Sea vegetable gels are not at all alien to our kitchens. We all eat these algal gels, most times unaware of their presence in our prepared foods. They are used as stabilizers and gelatins in everything from diet yogurt, chocolate milk, ice cream, marshmallows, and candies to bread, flours, and coatings for canned meats and fish.

Fats and oils Many sea vegetables contain substantial amounts of fats and oils, yet calories and cholesterol remain negligible. Fat content in sea vegetables ranges from 1 percent in the Laminarias to 8 percent in the rockweed, *Pelvetia canaliculata.* Algae which are exposed at low tide tend to be high in fats and oils. It is speculated that these high contents are necessary for plants like *Ascophyllum* to withstand long periods of drying out between tides.

Minerals All species of marine algae are rich in both minerals and essential trace elements. Proportions of minerals in seawater are found to be almost identical to those in human blood. Seawater contains all elements necessary to sustain health but not in a completely balanced complement. Seawater is low in both calcium and phosphorus. However, the algae's ability to concentrate to an extraordinary degree particular elements found in seawater renders this lack fairly meaningless. For example, one tablespoon of cooked hijiki *(Hizikia fusiforme)* a Brown alga, is approximately equal in calcium to one glass of whole milk. Some species contain as much iron as is found in whole wheat.

Organically combined iodine is present in most sea vegetables. Many contain iodine in concentrations unheard of in any land plant. The Browns possess organic iodine in the greatest amounts. Green algae are generally in the low range, and the Red algae are in the medium range. Two to three grams of dried algae per day will supply the adult with a sufficient dose of iodine to keep the thyroid gland functioning normally. Large amounts of iodine are, however, toxic, and care should be taken not to continually overdose one's system. Tea made from *Fucus vesiculosis* (bladderwrack) is called slimming tea because the high iodine content in the plants will act to stimulate the thyroid to regulate the metabolism. Curiously enough, the tea is recommended only for the obese, since the constant or prolonged use of it is found to be debilitating to the normal body.

Trace elements   All sea vegetables contain trace elements. These elements are part of the blood's chemistry and are necessary to the human body's well-being. Since our blood contains all of the elements found in seawater, there is no better way of providing the body with the full complement of trace elements than by consuming sea vegetables. Gold, aluminum, zinc, copper, and more than one hundred other elements are present in varying degrees in our blood. Even a substance like arsenic, toxic in large doses, is salutary in trace quantity.

Preventive medicine   The popularly enjoyed alga limu lipoa *(Dictyopteris plagiogramma)* is now being investigated in the Hawaiian Islands. It has been shown to degrade fats to highly unsaturated oils and may have been partially responsible for the low incidence of coronary occlusion in primitive Hawaii.

The alginic acid in kelp (certain large leafy members of the Brown algae) acts as binding agent in the intestines affecting the elimination of dietary radiostrontium, thus causing the absorption level in the human body to drop.

Through recent research, many sea vegetables have been found to possess antibiotic substances capable of deterring the growth of numerous pathological organisms. Certain extracts of the Red algae are known to affect regularity. Algar gel is recommended for its laxative qualities while the gel carrageenan is prescribed as an intestinal binding agent. In the Orient, the sea vegetable diet, high in potassium chloride, is believed to suppress hay fever.

Since in the fields of nutrition and preventive medicine, research on sea vegetables is very new, startling findings are sure to come.

WHAT MAKES A SEA VEGETABLE TASTY?

The Tuft of Kelp

All dripping in tangles green
Cast up by a lonely sea,
If purer for that, O Weed,
Bitterer, too, are ye?

Herman Melville

Years ago most algae had to be sun dried or prepared with great quantities of salt for preservation. Of course, foods prepared this way would last indefinitely without refrigeration. Few algae are naturally salty tasting. If a taste of sodium or potassium chloride is present, it is usually a delicate one. When plants are heavily salted for purposes of preservation, their natural flavors are often overpowered and lost. Modern means of refrigeration have rendered this means of preparation unnecessary.

For centuries in Japan the palate has been acclimated to this taste. Many products for export were stored in salt. It was hard for the Westerner to imagine these strange vegetable preparations as ever having been fresh, with a taste of their own. The fresh delicate sea vegetables eaten daily in Japan could not be transported across oceans in their natural state without decomposition. Today, frozen or blanched sea vegetables may be transported from Japan, the Hawaiian Islands, or the Philippines, and find their way to grocery stores in North America or anywhere else in the world.

Flavors all their own   The algal flavors are not salty or fishy as might be expected; some might be described as beanlike, nutlike, or even as reminiscent of celery, parsley, or even grapes. There are as yet no popularly recognized terms to describe the unique flavors produced by the algae. It is hard not to try to equate the tastes with those of the land plants. Tempting as it is, I feel it is a trap, and though it might serve to bolster the courage of the novice, the first trial is enough to satisfy one that comparison is not only futile but totally unnecessary. Sea vegetables can undoubtedly hold their own. Some are enticing and compete on the level of such delicacies as the abalone, the cloud ear and the truffle.

According to recent work on the genus *Porphyra,* desirable taste is affected by the concentration of isofloridoside (similar in taste to sucrose) and several free amino acids, among which are alanine (a lactic derivative), glutamic acid (glutamate), and glycine (a sweet amino-acid). The absence of substances which mask these taste producers or which impart an unpleasant odor is equally crucial. Air drying doesn't affect this taste, but environmental conditions such as sunlight and rainfall do affect the concentration, winter concentrations being generally higher and summer concentrations lower.

With the Porphyras, a souring of the plant body takes place in summertime. In the British Isles, laver *(Porphyra)* is not collected in months not containing an *r* in the spelling. Some species of *Porphyra* lack flavor or are distinctly unpleasant to the taste. Unpalatability in one particular species is not due to a lack of glutamate but rather to a strong fishy odor, possibly a volatile amine (ammonia-derived compound) present in the algae.

Each genus processes nutrients in its own way, concentrating some, building its own chemical substances and creating its own individual taste, the availability of nutrients and type of habitat in any given locality being all-important. It is thought that an alga growing epiphytically (not penetrating the host plant) on another alga will take taste-producing substances from its host.

Limu, Hawaiian sea vegetables   As with any food, criteria for judging the quality of an algal vegetable are set in terms of taste and texture. William Albert Setchell, famed algologist, wrote in 1905,

> The foreigner as a rule hesitates to eat raw seaweed, but when he tries the unaccustomed food, he finds a variety of flavors and a relish in some of the species which amply repays him for his courage in making the attempt.

He goes on to relate these important distinctions.

> I learned from a fisherman of Labaina [Hawaiian Islands] that there were specialties in "limu" [edible algae] and that while a certain kind obtained in most places might be unpalatable or tough, or in some other way undesirable for eating, when growing in some particular and apparently well-known locality, was highly esteemed, or some other universally eaten species was especially delicious in some particular locality. The connoisseurs of "limu" appear to distinguish them gastronomically as would the expert in the flavors of oysters or wine.

So plants of the same species may be delicious from one locale and completely unpalatable from another, this having to do with a variety of variables, such as available nutrients, light penetration, water conditions, and quality of the substrate sea floor.

Taste and classification   There is considerable variety of flavor among the sea vegetables, just as there is among land vegetables. Historically, varying species or even varying genera were lumped by phycophages or sea vegetable eaters, into categories designated by the same folk name. This was no doubt done on the basis of appearance and common usage determined by taste, without modern rules of taxonomy. Thus we find the genus *Porphyra* and the genus *Ulva* sharing a common folk name.

In Japan an attempt was made to classify two similar species of Brown algae, *Ecklonia cava* and *Ecklonia kurome,* according to the concentration of different substances by the plants—in other words classification through taste! *Ecklonia cava* contains bitter salts of potassium, sodium, and carbonic soda. *Ecklonia kurome* produces mannitol, a white powderlike substance which appears on the surface of the frond when it is dried, producing a good, sweet taste. Interestingly enough, the two algae when wet taste similar. However, when they are dried the concentration of different substances in each produces two opposite tastes.

Mucilage, a gummy carbohydrate secretion which many algae produce, affects both chewing pleasure and taste. Released on the surfaces of the frond and/or stipe through microscopic ducts, this viscose substance is highly desirable and sets apart the commercially important *Laminaria* and related genera, called kombu, from the inferior ones.

FARMING THE SEAS—FOOD OF THE FUTURE

In recent years it has become increasingly clear that man's eating habits have much to do with present and impending shortages of food and that man must therefore alter his use of the food chain. For example, grazing animals such as cattle and sheep, when fattened on grains in a feedlot, consume ten times their weight in edible foodstuffs. As a result, meat becomes absurdly expensive in terms of arable land use. The farming of the seas must soon become commonplace. In terms of proteins, the marine algae present interesting possibilities, since protein in many species can represent up to 25 percent of the dry weight. The staggering rate of algal growth means that an aqua farm could yield as much as eighty times as much protein per acre, per year, as a wheat field.

Sea gardens   The sea garden might well be a new embodiment of the victory garden. Sea gardens flourish winter and summer, need not be cared for, and have almost limitless acreage on which to grow. The gardener does not have to sow in order to reap. He will never go without nutritious and palatable food.

Marine crops   Research is sorely needed in the area of edible algae. Only in Japan is support forthcoming for scientists wanting to analyze marine algae for nutritive values. In the United States this sort of research has to be funded by large universities or big business. The small farmer wanting to raise crops of sea vegetables for food can receive loans from the United States Department of Agriculture under these categories which include The Sea Grant Program aquaculture projects. However, the financial feasibility of sea vegetable farming for profit is difficult (though not impossible) to show at this point. To foster the individual farmer, the government would have to fund the research necessary to develop agricultural techniques and knowledge to sustain crops against natural hazards. Understanding of the reproductive and growth patterns of the algae and of the ecological impact of harvesting would be necessary to continued success.

Japan has created in the United States a ready market for sea vegetables. Sea vegetable sales in million-dollar American-based Japanese companies are escalating, with sales in the United States accounting for 60% of the total. One has only to note the price per ounce of the best grades of Japanese Porphyra (nori), and multiply by sixteen to arrive at the mind-boggling figures of somewhere between forty-two and fifty-six dollars per pound, a price which puts smoked salmon to shame and for which, in edibles, there appear to be few equivalents.

Ecological impact   Increasing interest in marine algae as food will not necessarily upset the ecological balance of any given area. Public awareness has proven in the past to be a powerful force in the establishment of guidelines and protective measures to guard natural resources. With the amount of cultivated land itself becoming stable, we are best advised to look to the sea as a source of inexpensive vegetables. In so doing, we will find we are able to titillate our palates, serve our bodies, and promote a vital new ecology.

Foraging for sea vegetables

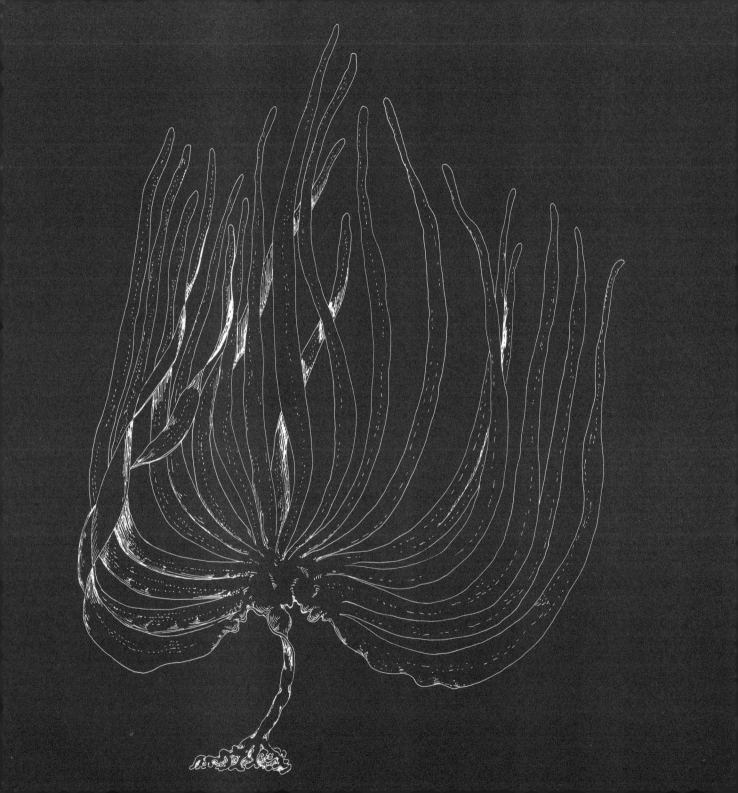

By the Moon's Ebb Tide

Must be our sensual nature that sends us into the
blustery dawn of the full moon's ebb tide to gather our
spring salad. Leave the hypnotizing heat of the chunk
stove. Strap up the hip boots. Sling the bushel baskets.
And fetch the hooks and sickles. The pure air takes
over all excess. Breathe in breathe out. Gingerly step
over the icy granite rocks. Past the slimy ones, tidal
pools lined with frizzy Irish moss, the leafy
fluorescence of sea lettuce, the swaying dulse palms,
delicate purple laver, down to the fleecy crashing
ocean roll: our cup overflows. Bending now. Wrist flick
of the stick looses the streaming fronds from their
holdfasts. Into the baskets. Swooping with the
sea-tattered wrack called wakame, honeyware,
murlins, marinkjarni, Alaria. Fresh breakers breaking.
The hour's come: another rakeload would be avarice.
The relentless sea's treacherous only toward the
greedy—she herself wu-wei. So now schlepping back
up the shore's incline.

    I am a pebble:
    make me the sea.
    Wave of the sea
    dissolve in the sea.

We unload the weed and ourselves into the VW and
head home from Schoodic Point to Hog Bay, town of
Franklin, Maine where stands our farmhouse banked
with eelgrass against the wind. Breakfast of Alaria miso
soup and creamy oat groats—how delicious!

    On for heaven and earth
    On for father and mother
    On for shelter and a bowl of rice.

Onto bamboo rods slides frond after frond of sea
vegetables. We stoke the Ashley with birch but mostly
oak. Suspend the rods above it and beside it open the
folding wooden racks. On them we drape the dripping
weed. (As the weather warms, the sun will replace the

stove.) Soon the room is alive with the sweet fragrance of burning logs and humid with the salty acrid smell of drying kelp. The drying must go quickly to prevent mold or fermentation. Once they're fully dried, the stiff now dark green blades go into an unheated room to relax a bit before we bend them into bundles. Do taste of this winter's green. Share with us the effortless energy of the sea.

ANNE FRANKLIN HARRIS

Reprinted with permission of the *East West Journal*.

UNLOCKING NEPTUNE'S LARDER

In these times of diminishing food supplies, foraging takes on a new importance. In terms of pleasure, the fulfillment involved in being able to sustain oneself outdoors, to recognize wild plants and obtain for the table an extraordinary source of fresh vegetables, is unequaled. For our children, gathering even a small part of the meal from the wild is what is aptly called a turn-on.

The seashore offers one of the very best environments for this sort of learning and enjoyment. Between the upper and lower tide marks exists a world of captivating complexity and beauty. Here the seaweeds grow, seeming to wrap around the rocks in various bands of subtle hue, alternately bathed and laid bare by the periodic ebb and flow of successive tides. It is here that the receding tide offers up the sea's bounty of growing vegetables and from its less accessible depths casts up still more.

One might well think of the sea floor as an immense vegetable garden yielding up pleasures heretofore unimagined in Western culture. If the covering seawaters could be rolled up all at once like a blanket, revealing the lush undersea gardens beneath, with their diversity of form and hue, it would be easy to imagine oneself standing in some foreign marketplace with the aromas and visions of unfamiliar edibles taking over the senses.

To those who think that collecting sea vegetables necessarily entails immersing oneself in the sea, I should say immediately that this does not have to be the case at all! In fact, it's not imperative to get so much as one's big toe wet in order to forage successfully between the tide marks.

When the tide is out, vast areas of rocky sea bottom are exposed, and the algae growing on these surfaces are as easy to collect as the vegetables in the local grocery. Sea vegetables can be gathered throughout the year by people of varying degrees of dedication. For those wishing to harvest species growing below the low tide mark it might be necessary to get wet, but it is also more than likely that some of these plants will wash in on the tide and be deposited at the feet of he who waits.

Equipment Before you start out, however, it's a good idea to assemble a few essentials. Depending upon the site, the climate, and the enthusiasm of the forager, the following items might come in handy.

1. warm clothes, hip boots, heavy shoes, or sneakers with corrugated soles
2. rock-scraping tool, heavy knife, short serrated knife
3. large pail, canvas bag, net bag, pillowcase, string, wide-mouthed jar

Improvised scraping tools might well include spackling knives of varying widths or paring knives. A blade with a toothed edge is often useful for sawing off woody stipes or inedible holdfasts. For collecting while wading, I find that a net bag works best. These bags have the advantage of an easy-to-use drawstring closing. Various sizes can be purchased in dive shops or sport shops, though orange or grapefruit sacks do nicely, as do pillowcases. The pillowcase can either be sewn with a drawstring closing, tied at the top with string, or simply tucked into the top of one's pants. Suspending the bags from a belt buckle or bathing suit strap will allow the plants to float in the seawater and thus remain fresh for the duration of the harvesting.

If wading isn't necessary, harvested plants can be kept fresh on the beach in a bucket of seawater. Placing the bucket in the shade and occasionally changing the water will help to keep plants crisp. Temperature, and not the amount of water, is important. Whether a bucket or a bag is used, the very delicate species are best placed in a separate jar of seawater so they won't be crushed by the larger, heavier ones.

Catching the tides   Sea vegetable foraging can be done at any time during the daylight hours, but since the greatest number of species are exposed at low tide, it is important to catch the turning tides. It is even more important to have sufficient knowledge of the times and character of the tides in order to avoid being trapped out on a boulder or a sandbar, or at the bottom of a cliff face, at the mercy of the inrushing tide!

Tides on the East and West Coasts of the United States reach high and low levels twice a day. Each succeeding day these ebbs and flows occur about fifty minutes later than the previous day.

Extreme high and low tides come monthly when the moon and sun are in conjunction, that is, at the new or full moon. These alternate with neap tides, which occur when the forces are in opposition, near the first and third quarters of the moon.

Tidal range is the difference between the highest tide and the lowest tide each day. That is to say, it measures the vertical drop, in feet, from highest tide to lowest tide. In the Atlantic the two lows are nearly alike, but this is not so in the Pacific. Tidal range varies from place to place all over the world. The size and configuration of any basin of water determines the variations in amplitude of its tides. In Anchorage, Alaska, there is a 33.0-foot differential between tides, whereas in Honolulu, only a 3.0-foot differential exists. What this means to the forager is that the greater the tidal range the larger the intertidal area.

Getting to the shore one hour before low tide will provide an extra hour of foraging while the water is at its low point, in addition to the hour or so after the tide has begun to flow. Early morning tides are best (low) for foraging. This is useful knowledge in cold weather when getting wet and cold isn't particularly desirable. It's a simple matter to check local newspapers for daily tide information. Long-range predictions can be found in tide tables.

Which plants to harvest   Taking growing plants directly from their places of attachment is the best way to ensure freshness. Although there is nothing wrong with gathering cast-up sea vegetables for food, it is sometimes difficult to determine just how long they have been floating on the tide. Old plants will not be nearly as tasty or as nutritious as fresh ones. With a little practice, however, it becomes easy to discern their wilted quality.

After a storm is a perfect time to forage for cast-up plants, the wind and wave action having just wrenched them from their places of attachment. Commercial Irish moss harvesting is often done directly after large storms. This way a substantial harvest of fresh plants is always ensured. Storms or high winds will often bring to shore many deep-water species not readily accessible without diving or using a dredge. For the individual harvester, it isn't even necessary to wait for a storm. A good wind will often create enough wave force to rip up plants enough for several meals.

Harvesting plants which are fruiting is ecologically unsound. There is also evidence which suggests that some sea vegetables are less palatable during their reproductive phases.

Which parts are good to eat   Contrary to what is the case with numerous land plants, when dealing with algae, if a species is edible then all its parts are likely to be edible; if a species is toxic then all its parts are probably toxic. However, individual parts of any given edible species may or may not be palatable. Of the three parts, blade, stipe, and holdfast, the blade portions are the most universally tender and tasty.

The most tender and nutritious part of a sea vegetable is the meristematic, or growth-producing, tissue. In the kelps, the area of the blade closest to the stipe is the part of the plant where new growth is taking place. The very tips of the longer plants, especially *Laminaria* and similar genera, are the oldest portions of the plant and are almost always tattered and thin from the ravages of currents and waves. About eight to ten inches up the blade from the point where it joins the stipe is the tenderest and most nutritionally valuable part of the Brown sea vegetables. In the Reds, the area of highest nutritional value can also be found near the margin or throughout the plant.

In terms of textural delicacy the small inconspicuous stipes and holdfasts of most of the Red and Green algae would not differ from that of the rest of the plant. It is really only in the Brown algae that the stipe or holdfast often becomes woody or leathery and might possess more alginic acid than the blade.

Some large kelps attach to any solid object. When the object is small, the holdfast then expands across the sedimentary bottom, the interstices filling with mud, and the whole acting as an anchor to the plant. I would venture a guess, in general, that holdfasts whose shapes are conical *(Postelsia)* rather than spreading *(Macrocystis),* whose upper portions would not come in contact with the sea floor, would be most suitable for eating. These upper portions would not contain the sand, rock chips, etc., which their lower portions would envelope. Among the sea vegetables with edible holdfasts are a few Brown algae including an undetermined species from the Pacific Northwest called "tall seaweed" by the Makah Indians. The stipes of many of the Brown algae are also eaten.

Diving for sea vegetables   For those of more adventurous spirit, skin diving is an excellent way of foraging for the different types of sea vegetables which grow too far below the low tide mark to be gathered by wading. Skin diving, although the word implies diving in one's skin, is commonly taken to mean diving without breathing apparatus. Certain kinds of minimal equipment, though not essential, will often serve to heighten the experience. Using a pair of fins facilitates movement and saves the swimmer's energy. Use of a mask allows for clarity of vision underwater, impossible to attain by simply opening one's eyes.

Snorkeling is very much akin to skin diving. With the aid of this simple breathing tube, the swimmer can receive air and not have to change position or lift his head to breathe as long as he remains on the surface of the water. The snorkel, used simultaneously with the face mask, enables one to make a systematic scanning of the sea bottom with minimal expenditure of energy. When a stand of sea vegetables is located, the swimmer has only to take a deep breath, block the snorkel's air passage with his tongue, and dive. Upon returning to the surface the diver exhales hard to clear the snorkel of water and then may continue to breathe through it or may slide it out of his mouth and breathe normally while he deposits his harvested plant.

How to secure the harvest   The forager will find using a net bag a convenient alternative to swimming back to shore with each plant. In this case a drawstring closing on the bag is essential to prevent the plants from floating out. Bags with metal clamp-closings are even easier to use and can also be bought where sports equipment is sold. These collecting bags come in a variety of sizes, and though the smaller bags are still manageable when full, they hold only a pound or two of plants. Alternatively, swimming underwater while towing a larger thirty-six-inch bag full of heavy sea vegetables can be cumbersome, to say nothing of tiring.

The time and effort involved in stuffing endless yards of *Laminaria* into a drawstring bag while holding one's breath underwater has led a few ingenious Bostonian friends to devise a simple but workable alternative.

All that is needed for this method is some nylon rope, empty plastic bottles (gallon size with handles), and plastic clothespins. The capped bottles are tied along the rope (a knot is made on each handle) at three-foot intervals. Clothespins are attached to the rope in the spaces between the bottles. Now the rope with clothespins and bottles attached is stretched across a portion of the cove or bay and fastened from one point on shore (a tree or bush, etc.) to another, with the floats (bottles) resting on the top of the water. As each sea vegetable is gathered, the forager surfaces, clips it with a clothespin, and returns for more. If the waters are cold and speed is desirable, a group of divers can work simultaneously

When the line is full, one end is detached from shore and allowed to float free while the diver climbs ashore at the other end and hauls in the rope with the attached sea vegetables. Care must be taken not to snag the rope on the rocks near shore, so the sea vegetables are best unclipped at the water's edge and placed in a bushel basket or other container. When sufficient numbers of plants are needed to feed large groups or for drying and storage, this type of harvesting is eminently suitable, while for the individual, foraging to fill limited or day-to-day needs, a small net bag (twelve inches) is ideal.

For most of us, skin diving and snorkeling mean shallow water diving, since the depth of the dive is a factor in how long the breath can be held. These skills don't call for great strength, endurance, or speed, though possessing a good pair of lungs does help things along. Anyone who can swim, can skin dive or snorkel. These are sports equally suited to man or woman. They are not dangerous, and after observing a few elementary precautions, one can safely relax and enjoy. This sort of endorsement requires some explanation.

Water safety Despite recent sensationalism, hazardous marine life is not the greatest danger to a person swimming or foraging. Panic is the most frequent cause of disaster and does not have to be the automatic response to peril. Knowledge of one's options is the best defense against panic in the water. The Red Cross's classes in swimming, water safety, and water rescue are unexcelled and the costs are minimal. Whatever one's skills, though, the rule observed by amateurs and professionals alike is: *Never swim alone.* Always have a buddy along, someone who is familiar with basic water skills.

When you are choosing a place to forage, it is of primary importance to pick a safe location. The safest places to collect plants are protected coves and shallow bays. Swimmers and divers should not venture into boating lanes or channels, underneath bridges, or out along exposed coasts. Anyone entering the water should know how to read its surface for runoffs, riptides, undertows, currents, and other phenomena.

What about pollution? Choice of the best foraging location along any seacoast should also be based upon the purity of the waters in which the harvest is to be carried out. Polluted waters can be just as harmful to the human body as they can be to plant life. A careful scan of the area is good insurance against foraging in polluted waters. A call to the local office of the Department of Conservation or Department of Fish and Game is an effective means of getting the facts on water quality and types of pollution in any given area.

Organic wastes Organic pollution like runoff from large farms and seepage from home cesspools usually remains at a tolerable level unless heavy rains cause these nitrogenous substances to be washed into adjacent waters in great quantities, thereby causing bacteria to multiply inordinately. Moderate amounts of organic wastes in the water merely serve as a natural fertilizer for the algae.

Toxic wastes Despite a raised public consciousness about water pollution, it is common to see a city's sewers emptying directly into its rivers, to observe factories pouring chemical wastes into waterways and dumps hundreds of feet high, leaking acids, herbicides, and other toxins into bays and estuaries. Obviously it is not advisable to swim in or to collect food plants from these waters. Though it hasn't been proven conclusively that chemical toxins present in the waters are absorbed or taken up by the algae, thus rendering the plants dangerous to health, it is a fact that close contact with thermal pollution and chemical toxins from distilleries, paper mills, and other similar factory operations eventually kills the algae. The question then becomes, are these dying plants toxic and at what point are they unfit for consumption? The question is yet unanswered.

Radioactive substances Radioactive heavy metals like cadmium, mercury, lead, strontium, etc. are taken up by the plants and concentrated to various degrees. But even the greatest levels of these residual pollutants thus far found in algae are still almost as low as the natural radioactivity which surrounds us. Interestingly enough, algae growing on calcium-rich rocks are not found to be contaminated with radiostrontium. Though continued consumption of contaminated plants might well endanger health, the consideration is relatively academic, since shipping lanes, busy harbors and other such polluted areas are not likely harvesting spots.

The algae will also adsorb radioactive substances on the surfaces of their fronds. But a freshwater cleansing will free the plants of any of these substances, and since these substances are concentrated up the food chain, man is infinitely better off eating the algae directly after he has washed it than he is eating the fish which has grazed on the algae. Processed sea vegetables, sea vegetable products and colloidal materials (gels) are constantly tested for radioactivity and show nothing out of the ordinary.

Toxic water blooms   The algae are not affected by toxic water "blooms," since they do not filter-feed or concentrate substances in any specialized organ. A bloom is an inordinate, abundant reproduction of microscopic organisms in the water. The red tides, though harmless to the algae, can be toxic to the bather. Certain algal blooms, though they do not affect the sea vegetables, may cause skin irritation to a person in the water. A rinse in fresh water will remove any traces of these organisms from the harvested sea vegetable, but it is safest for the forager to avoid these affected offshore waters. Waters affected by red tide organisms are posted as such with shellfish warnings. Algal blooms are easily recognized by the striking green or blue-green color which they impart to the water.

Oil spills   An oil spill will sterilize the sea surface, cutting off light so the algae cannot propagate and cutting off air so the plants suffocate. One quart of spilled oil uses the oxygen for one hundred thousand gallons of seawater. Though traces of oil slick can be washed from the surface of the sea vegetable, waters contaminated by oil would not yield the healthiest plants and should not be foraged.

Finding good locations   Sea vegetables grow in a variety of habitats. They grow anchored in sand, mud, gravel, or attached to rocks, shells, wood pilings, or coral. The type of sea bottom helps to determine the variety of species found and the extent to which they flourish.

The rocky shore is the best place for foraging because it supports the greatest variety of species. It's possible to find more than a dozen different species of algae clinging to a single large rock. The vertical sides of rocks are richer in plant life than are the tops. *Porphyra umbilicalis* plants found growing on the undersides of boulders, their free ends dangling in the water, are, in Europe, considered to have superior taste qualities as compared with those plants situated differently on the rocks. Often it is necessary to push away larger species in order to find smaller ones growing in among them.

Coves   Winds and currents tend to collect or localize rich harvests. Sheltered water areas, like shallow coves, are, at various times, excellent sources of freshly cast-up sea vegetables.

Bays   Bays of slow-moving water are good places to look for certain types of algae. Genera like *Enteromorpha, Ulva,* and *Monostroma* will flourish in sluggish, often organically polluted environs.

Beaches   Gravelly or sandy beaches, being somewhat unstable, don't usually support a wide range of algal life. Genera like *Caulerpa,* and certain of the agar-producing species like Gracilaria do, however, have holdfasts which anchor them to these types of sea bottoms. Very muddy areas are also places of sparse algal growth. Even if the plants could attach themselves to the oozy bottom, the waters in these areas are not usually clear enough to allow proper light to reach the plants and permit them to photosynthesize.

Rocky shores   On the rocky flats at low tide can be found innumerable pools and clefts filled with a diverse assembly of sea vegetables. The different types arrange themselves in horizontal bands which progress down the intertidal area and demarcate each's particular bounds. Toward the high tide mark can be found species of *Scytosiphon, Petalonia, Bangia, Fucus, Analipus, Palmaria,* and *Nemalion* are common throughout the midtidal area, while species of *Codium, Chondrus, Halosaccion, Alaria, Ascophyllum,* and *Gigartina* predominate in the lower tidal area.

Lying just below the low tide mark is the subtidal area. The plants growing here are exposed only at the very lowest of spring tides or in some cases not at all. Sea vegetables of the genera *Laminaria, Alaria, Chorda, Macrocystis,* and *Pleurophycus* populate this part of the sea, forming a junglelike growth. A species can inhabit one or a few adjacent tidal areas. Many species in the genera *Porphyra, Gelidium,* and *Gloiopeltis* are found growing throughout the tidal area, from upper tidal to lower tidal in many locations.

How to look   Predicting exactly where to find a particular sea vegetable growing, at any given time, is at best chancy. Finding a luxuriant growth of *Porphyra* in a certain location one year does not guarantee that it will be there the following year. This sort of variability among the annuals makes it necessary for the forager to have a general idea of the environmental factors which make knowing where to look directly dependent upon knowing how to look.

Species change   As one travels up or down the coast foraging, the appearance or disappearance of certain species becomes obvious even to the untrained eye. One can't help but notice the breathtaking carnival of colors, the proliferation of crimsons, fuchsias, and lavenders, which suddenly appears in the waters around the Monterey Peninsula, and the disappearance of the mammoth floating kelp beds as one travels northward along the Pacific Coast.

Variation in flora from north to south, warm water to cold water, is called species change and is nearly as radical as the vertical variation in species seen between the high tide and the low tide marks. At some points along the coast species changes will be very noticeable. At other places they will be more subtle.

Currents   A current will determine which species will thrive in its path. The cold water of the Japan Current brushing the Pacific Coast down as far as Point Conception, California, allows cold water species to flourish in what would otherwise be warmer waters. The Gulf Stream skirting Prince Edward

Island, Canada, warms the nearby waters and permits some south temperate species to proliferate.

Currents, winds, and the configuration of the sea floor produce phenomena called upwellings, thrusting upward nutrient rich cold water from the sea bottom. The surface waters, where the sea vegetables grow, are thereby enriched, and lush vegetation is always apparent. Upwellings occur along the West Coasts of Continents. Scientists are now attempting to create artificial upwellings.

Spore travel   The algae reproduce by spores, which are released to float in the water. Many variables affect the eventual success or failure of these vulnerable bodies in settling in a suitable location, where conditions are conducive to their growth. Because they affect spore travel, currents and jutting land-masses are fundamental factors in determining a species' range of distribution along any coast. Large stretches of deep water or unstable sea bottom, like sandbanks, leave no place for spores to settle. Lowered salinity at the mouths of large rivers or coastal temperature variations can be lethal to spores or may allow only certain species to thrive.

Temperature   In general, the factors determining which types of algae will predominate where, are the temperature of the water and how fast it moves. Red algae predominate in warm temperate and tropical waters. Brown algae prefer cold active waters (though some Browns, like Sargassum, prefer tropical and subtropical waters). The Greens are found chiefly in quiet waters and the Blue-greens in quiet waters and tidal salt marshes.

Interestingly, species growing outside the limits of their normal habitat will often undergo radical change in appearance. Cold water species of large leafy Brown algae will hybridize in warm, slow-moving bay waters. Many species when subjected to adverse conditions will grow as stunted forms. These variants are, however, recognizable and are just as edible as their normal counterparts.

Unequaled variety of species   Travel along the North American coasts in search of sea vegetables is a beautiful and rewarding experience. The ever-changing landscape is a constantly renewing source of pleasure and fascination. The forager will find Atlantic, Pacific, temperate, tropical, frigid, and subtropical species without ever having to leave the continental boundaries. In fact, within the continental borders of the United States alone there exists a variety of species probably unequaled in any other country.

East Coast foraging   The number and size of species is generally larger in the northern waters than in the southern waters. The large Brown algae, like *Laminaria* and other leafy genera, are most common in the arctic currents and cold waters of these rough, rocky coasts. From Long Island south, the continental shelf is sandy. Rocky coves almost entirely disappear in favor of beaches and shallow bays. Sea vegetables found between the tide marks become fewer. The large kelps disappear in favor of the sea lettuces and other Greens.

Farther south, around North Carolina, the silt from river deltas causes stunting of the intertidal algae. Subtidal vegetation, however, is lush and species are large. Winds often send the plants in to shore. Here the Brown and Green algae give way to a predominance of Reds. The sandy shore continues down the coast to Florida, and west around the Keys. And though rock outcroppings, lush with a variety of sea vegetables, are common around Biscayne Bay and the northern Keys, this seascape soon gives way to shallow waters, coral reefs, and mangrove swamps.

At this point, the fleshy Browns and Greens are seldom present, supplanted instead by numbers of gel-producing Red species, small or calcified Greens and some Reds and Blue-greens which grow on the roots of the ever-present mangrove trees. The western coast of the Keys is much the same as the eastern coast up to the area surrounding Tampa, where some rocky shores again appear and species are generally more diverse and plentiful.

Gulf Coast foraging   As one rounds the Gulf Shore toward Louisiana, however, the silt from the Mississippi Delta again has a stunting effect on the algae. The sandy sea floor supports few macroscopic species. The Brown sea vegetables dominate the area; and what little fleshy algae flourish are found mainly on wharfs and pilings. This phenomenon unfortunately persists throughout much of the Gulf.

West Coast foraging   The Gulf of California on the Pacific side, however, is as rich in edible marine algae as the Gulf of Mexico is poor. Reds, Browns, Greens, and Blue-greens proliferate in these quiet waters once known as the Sea of Cortes. Along the coast just south of the Mexican border, upwellings produce a rich flora. From Mexico to Point Conception vast stands of the giant Brown kelp, *Macrocystis,* occupy the shallow water offshore, their presence steadily diminishing toward Monterey, as water temperatures drop and rocky coves take the place of sandy beaches. In the waters around the Monterey Peninsula can be found species representative of the entire Pacific Coast. This unique distinction makes the area a forager's paradise. Much of the variety of species continues up the coast all the way to the San Juan Islands.The Porphyras become more abundant, draping the rocks with lettucelike forms.

North of San Francisco the shore becomes less sandy, progressively rockier, and often inaccessible all the way up into Oregon. Foraging a cove or beach often entails driving a few miles of twisting dirt road or scrambling down cliffsides in order to reach the water's edge. But with this, the joy of an early morning forage along miles of pristine coast is incomparable.

The cold waters of Washington State's Puget Sound foster the growth of numerous edible Brown species, as well as many species of Red algae. Superior species of *Porphyra* abound on the outer coast, and huge sheets of *Ulva* and *Monostroma* float in the quiet waters of the sound.

Don't be greedy!   As the eye feasts on the vast stands of sea vegetables uncovered by the ebb tide, one should be governed by the cardinal rule of foraging: *Don't take more than will be used*. The procuring of whole plants, including stipe and holdfast, is not necessary unless these portions of the plant are intended as food. Often just plucking the fronds will do.

HOW TO USE THE DATA PAGES

The fifty-two data sheet pages which follow cover only those sea vegetables growing on the shores of North America or those that can be readily purchased in health food stores, in ethnic markets, and through mail-order sources. (Foragable plants are marked with an asterisk.)

The use of the genus name, followed by the species name, is essential to any work whether scientifically or popularly oriented. Each pair of botanical names is decided by international agreement and is particular to one species. The genus name (always capitalized) and the accompanying species name (never capitalized) at the top of each data page are based on Latin or Greek roots which either describe the plant or honor a person in the field of study. The genus (plural = genera) is the smallest natural or related grouping of plants containing distinct species. The species then, is the basic unit of classification.

The pages listing plants alphabetically by genus and containing information about them are intended, along with accompanying drawings, to be used in combination with the recipes. The recipes are, in turn, keyed back by botanical name to the data pages. This easy-to-use system is intended to convey all the necessary information about the particular species in as concise a way as possible. One can start at any point and work forward or backward. Turn to a recipe, to note the botanical name of the plant best suited to the recipe and then find the plants listed alphabetically in the data pages. Or start with the botanical name of a plant listed in the data pages.

Having come home from the beach with a fresh plant of undetermined or suspected genus or having brought from the health food store a package of dried (perhaps unlabeled or mislabeled) plants, one can begin as follows: Dried plants will need to be soaked first in water. Then, using the drawings and species information, make an acceptable identification of the plant, at least by genus if not by species. In the majority of cases, recipes will serve for any number of edible species within the particular genus.

The book is thus set up so that those wishing to try recipes made with commercially sold sea vegetables can do so and those preferring to forage for the plants can do so, with equal ease.

All considered, the book should enable the novice not only to find and identify a particular plant but to prepare it for the table in a number of ways, with a good idea of how the alga has been used by different cultures through the ages and of the nutritional or other qualities it might possess.

The drawings serve a very important purpose, in addition to their use as a foraging tool. Renderings of entire plants will serve to put the purchaser of dried sea vegetables more at ease. There is nothing more disconcerting than having to buy dark, little, chopped-up pieces of who-knows-what, without knowledge of their original form. The knowledge of how truly beautiful and appetizing sea vegetables are in nature renders their unfamiliar names unimportant and encourages the beginner to accept them as easily as he does dried onions, celery flakes, mushrooms, shallots, and the innumerable raft of dehydrated edibles common to our kitchens.

PREPARING AND STORING FRESH SEA VEGETABLES

Since it is not always possible to eat exotic species of sea vegetables fresh out of the water and since in many cases certain methods of processing enhance palatability, it becomes necessary to prepare the algae in such a way that nutrients are preserved and plants retain a "fresh" quality even after drying.

Directly after picking, the plants should be refrigerated for immediate use or prepared for storage.

Refrigeration Most species, with the exception of very fragile ones, will remain fresh for a few days if they are kept refrigerated, sealed in plastic bags containing a little seawater. The Brown algae usually do very well if placed in a lettuce crisper.

Cleaning Rinsing in fresh water is not altogether necessary as long as the plants do not contain trapped sand within the folds of their fronds.

If freshwater washing is to be done, it should be done as quickly as possible. Running the plants under the tap, giving them no chance to soak, is best and quickest. Lukewarm water is best since cold water will not remove sand and rock chips as thoroughly. Warm or hot water will loosen valuable gel substances in the plants and make some gooey or shapeless.

The cell membranes of algae are not impervious to the density of fresh water, as they are to that of seawater. Seawater is the alga's natural medium. Soaking in fresh water causes many of the more delicate species to explode their cell walls and become waterlogged. This effect is called plasmolysis and causes vitamin loss into the surrounding liquid. Vitamin A is very susceptible to fresh water and suffers rapid breakdown, with losses up to 50 percent when subjected to rainwater.

In the case of nori *(Porphyra),* loss of soluble carbohydrates and possibly other soluble products (thus loss of taste) through rinsing in fresh water is inevitable, though loss through immersion for a minute or less is small.

Without any freshwater wash, dried Porphyra will have a slightly salty taste. Minimal freshwater washing will not only enhance the taste but will most certainly help retain certain vitamins. It is interesting to note that when nori is harvested after periods of little sunlight and much rainfall or when it has been soaked for long periods during preparation, the harvested product is low in taste-producing soluble carbohydrates. At this point the commercial outfits fortify the product with sucrose to restore flavor. The result, in terms of health and taste, is an undesirable refined product.

Freezing Many sea vegetables can be successfully frozen. *Laminaria* and related genera like *Pleurophycus* and *Alaria* do not freeze well. Freezing seems to alter in an undesirable way the properties of taste and texture. Plants of the more delicate genera can be rinsed, drained, and then arranged in convenient-sized portions and frozen in sealed plastic bags. With genera like *Polyneura* and *Gracilaria,* plants may be chopped while frozen and added to soups or they may be placed in a colander or strainer and blanched with boiling water, then used as a salad ingredient. Once defrosted, sea vegetables, like any other food, should not be refrozen.

Drying   Outdoor drying is the most common means of preserving sea vegetables and is in many ways the superior method in terms of ecology, simplicity, dollars, and the taste and textural qualities which drying produces.

Foraging on a dry, breezy day will ensure proper drying conditions for harvested plants. Shade drying seems to have advantages over sun drying for nutrient preservation. Plants which are sand-free can be dried immediately while those needing to be rinsed should be swished quickly in sand-free seawater before drying.

The sandy beach is not the best place to dry one's harvest. The plants will always manage to collect sand from the wind. I find grass the best place to dry sea vegetables. Hedges, terry-cloth towels, clotheslines, or chicken wire are also good. Avoid placing the plants on materials like rubber mats, cardboard, or paper because the algae will pick up unpleasant odors and tastes. Turn the plants every half hour or so to ensure even and thorough drying.

To maintain vitamin A values, drying is best completed within one twelve-hour period, and the plants should not be left out in dew or rain.

Indoor drying is by and large unsatisfactory. The slow drying process increases the possibility of mold and deterioration. Japanese factories make successful use of heated driers.

Sea vegetables can also be dried over a wood fire. Smoke drying produces a very beautiful nutty taste, especially in the edible kelps like *Alaria* and *Laminaria,* as Anne Franklin Harris writes in her poem "By the Moon's Ebb Tide." This process can be used to dry any species.

When the plants are crisp, store them in sealed containers or plastic bags to keep out moisture and ensure the preservation of freshness. Plants allowed to remain exposed on the shelf will absorb moisture, decompose, and lose nutritive values and flavor.

Storing   Dried plants should be stored in dry places where temperatures are low. High temperatures and high humidity facilitate breakdown of vitamin C (ascorbic acid). Under tolerable conditions vitamin C is 60 percent stable in sea vegetables, compared with 5 percent in most land vegetables. Prolonged storage (three to four months) will sometimes have a detrimental effect on vitamin A in some of the Brown algae. For some reason, *Fucus* is more than twice as vulnerable as *Ascophyllum.*

If plants should pick up a little moisture during storage, placing them in the oven at a low setting (100°F.) for a few minutes will quickly restore crispness. In the case of *Porphyra, Ulva, Monostroma,* and other relatively delicate genera, one may hold them over a flame (candle or stove) at a distance of about five to eight inches to toast the plants. This will impart a crisp texture and nutlike taste. Keep the plants well above the flame for no longer than a few seconds in order not to char the fronds.

Brining   Soaking sea vegetables in brine lowers nutritional value considerably. Soluble vitamins, minerals, and carbohydrates will dissolve into the brine solution, and unless the liquid itself is consumed, they will not, of course, reach the human system.

Salting Salting the fresh plants for purposes of nonrefrigerated storage is a workable alternative to drying; however, the amount of salt needed to ensure the algae against decomposition over long periods will, in most cases, overpower the plants' natural taste. Sometimes heavy salting is used in combination with freezing when plants are to be transported long distances. Thorough freshwater rinsing is almost always necessary to render plants prepared in this way suitable for eating. A light salting will keep most plants fresh for several days if they are refrigerated.

Blanching Plants can be blanched for limited periods of storage. Blanching involves dipping the plants into boiling water for a few seconds or placing them in some kind of sieve and pouring the boiling water over them. Blanched sea vegetables maintain very high vitamin A content. In Japan the processing of some of the Brown algae such as certain species of wakame and kombu often includes blanching, the blanching acting to precook the vegetables, shortening the time subsequently needed for home cooking, and producing an additional preservative effect.

Parboiling of hijiki followed by sun drying is done in order to produce a "fast-cooking" vegetable. If a minimal amount of water is used in this relatively rapid process, nutrients need not be lost.

Hydrating the dried plants For most dishes sun-dried sea vegetables call for a soaking in fresh water before they are ready to use. Although the process of hydration is necessary to most types of preparation, it does not have to cause loss of nutrients. Many genera, like *Palmaria,* need only a sprinkling of water. Others, like *Undaria,* need only a few seconds or a few minutes of soaking. And still others, like *Chondrus, Alaria,* and *Laminaria* need up to half an hour.

The large edible kelps, members of the genus *Alaria,* must be soaked overnight in fresh water to remove acrid taste producers.

With any of these processes, the more limited the contact with water, the better the plants fare, in terms of retaining their nutrients. The amount of soaking water used has only to be sufficient to cover the vegetable and should, except in the case of *Alaria,* afterward be added to the cooking foods or the accompanying sauces or gravies in order that the dissolved nutrients not be wasted.

Other methods of preparation Tenderizing processes are sometimes desirable as final steps in the preparation of certain algae.

Porphyra and *Enteromorpha* are sometimes allowed to ferment in order to tenderize them. The Haida and Kwakiutl Indian tribes of the Pacific Northwest employed a few unique methods of tenderizing *Porphyra,* but these practices have fallen out of use. (See *Porphyra perforata.*) Occasionally, privately collected *Porphyra* purchased in Chinatown, San Francisco, will have been roasted in soy sauce. This seasoning technique also serves to tenderize the plants.

In Japan tougher species of *Laminaria* are soaked in acetic acid or vinegar, pressed, and then shaved or shredded into a variety of thicknesses ranging from gossamer-thin transparent "kombu veils'' to paper-thin sheets. Some species of *Undaria* are even ''kneaded'' (their rough green outer coating rubbed off) as a preliminary tenderizing step to preparation.

Occasionally, it is desirable to effect certain taste changes in some of the stronger-tasting sea vegetables. In the Orient sun-dried *Gloiopeltis furcata* plants are hydrated in a water and rice vinegar solution. The subtle taste of the dilute vinegar is considered just enough to counteract the alga's slightly pungent flavor. In Southeast Asia sun-dried *Gelidium* is steeped in rose water in order to enhance palatability.

Sea vegetable data pages

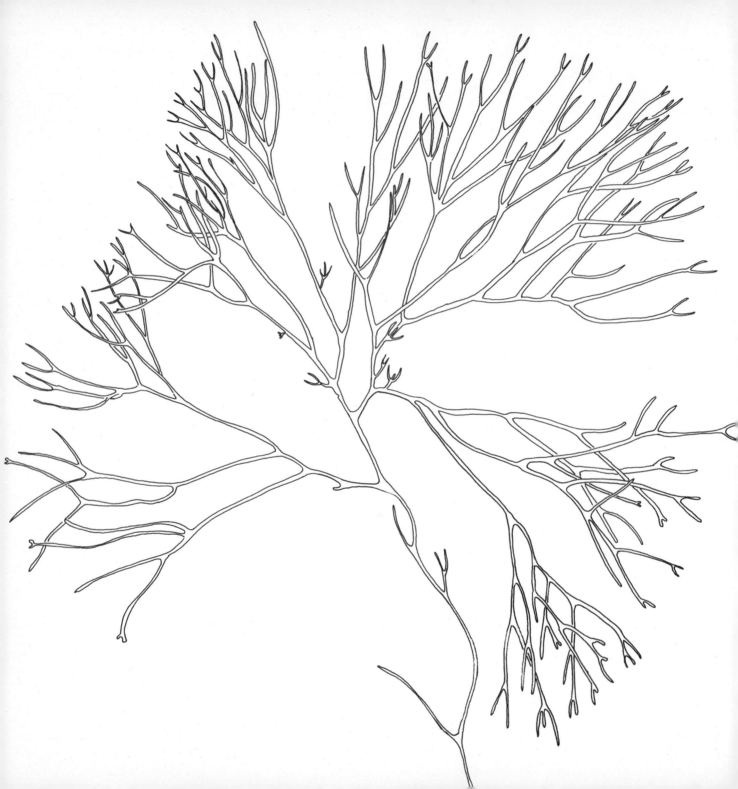

Phylum: Rhodophyta (Red Algae)

Ahnfeltia gigartinoides

Description: Plants golden brown to dark brown to almost black, bleaching white in the sun. Growing in thick, erect clumps, 6 to 12 inches tall, branching repeatedly in twos. Densely branched at top. Branches cylindrical with small cushionlike nodes on ends.

Habitat: Found in protected locations near and below the low tide mark, on sandy bottoms, in rock crevices, and on lava boulders. Large accumulations to be found drifting just above bottom along the continental shelf in coastal waters all over the world.

Foraging: A perennial. Peak harvest from early spring to early fall. Harvested by swimmers and divers, by means of dredging or by gathering cast-up or floating plants.

Preparation: Wash well, removing crabs and any other seaweed that might be clinging. Drain and chop well. Very resistant to decay.

Use: Hawaiian Islands—baked with chicken or fish; baked with ti leaves; added to chicken, beef, or pork dishes for flavor and thickening; eaten with raw limpets.
Japan—used in cooking and for making agar and karafuto kanten.
USSR—used to make agar.

Nutrients: Starch, sugar, and trace elements.

Gel: Agar.

Taste: Stiff texture.

Commercial Source: Japan (on Hokkaido and in Chiba and Mie Prefectures).

Recipes: Hawaiian Ahnfeltia (p. 250).

FOLK NAMES

Japan:

itanigusa saimi

Hawaiian Islands:

limu aki aki (trans. **nibbles) limu koeleele**

Phylum: Phaeophyta (Brown Algae)

Alaria esculenta

Edible Kelp

Description: Plants olive brown, 6 inches wide, up to 10 to 12 feet long with distinct flattened midrib, thin ruffled edges, and spatula-shaped reproductive blades (sporophylls) on stipe.

Habitat: Found in exposed locations near and below the low tide mark on rocky coasts, from the North Temperate to Subfrigid Zone of the Atlantic coastal waters.

Foraging: A perennial. Peak harvest from midsummer to midfall. Late spring harvest best for high vitamin C (ascorbic acid), late winter to late spring for high vitamin B_{12}, midwinter for high vitamin K (folinic acid), spring and summer for high vitamin K (folic acid). Harvested from boats by means of long-handled hooks or hooks attached to long ropes (unfortunately, this often rips out holdfasts and prevents regrowth). Collected by wading out in hip boots at very low tides and cutting algae from the rocks, using a sickle. Regeneration is ensured when stipe is cut just below the blade, leaving not less than 3 feet of stipe.

Preparation: Iceland—main fronds, excluding midribs, steeped in fresh water for two days before use. May be sun dried or used fresh. Store sun-dried Alaria in sealed plastic bags, to retain freshness.

Use: America—fresh midribs chopped and added to green salads or eaten like celery.
Scotland and Ireland—midrib and reproductive sporophylls eaten fresh. Greenland—eaten.
Iceland—main frond, excluding the midrib, prepared, chopped, and cooked in water or milk and flour, then eaten as thick pudding with milk or cream. Midribs are eaten separately and believed to be easily digested. Orkney Islands—midribs eaten fresh.

Nutrients: High vitamin B_6; high vitamin K; high iodine; high bromine. Also contains sugar, starch, vitamin B_{12}, vitamin C, nitrogen, boron, radium, rubidium, cadmium, cobalt, nickel, and trace elements.

Gel: Algin.

Taste: Main frond (excluding midrib and lateral blades), tends to be somewhat acrid unless soaked or dried and hydrated before use. Prepared plants have delicate texture. Reproductive sporophylls have a peanutlike taste; midrib is sweet tasting and crunchy.

Commercial Source: America—Alaria foraged and sold commercially in North America, is often labeled wakame. Scotland and Ireland—reproductive sporophylls and midribs were once hawked in the streets.

Recipes: Soup with Slivered Kombu (p. 171), Alaria Vegetable Soup (p. 171), Tossed Seaside Salad with Edible Kelp (p. 259), Alaria Vegetable Stew (p. 204), Boiled Alaria (p. 217), Alaria with Spring Greens (p. 218), Homemade Slivered Alaria (p. 256).

FOLK NAMES

Western usage:

edible kelp, honeyware, wing kelp

Scotland:

bladderlochs

Scotland, Ireland:

tangle

Greenland:

murlins

Faroe Islands:

henware

Iceland:

marinkjarni

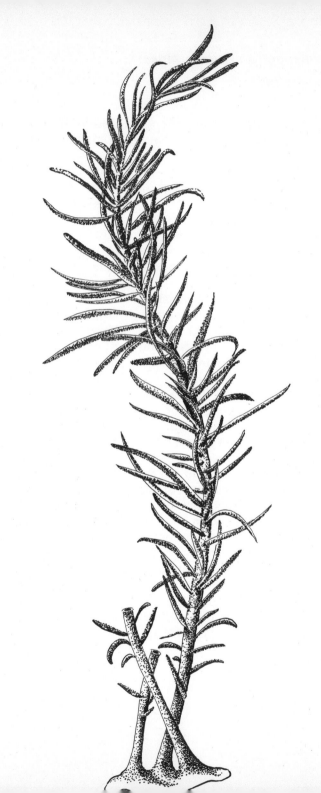

Phylum: Phaeophyta (Brown Algae)

Analipus japonicus

Fir Needle

Description: Plants light tan to deep olive to dark brown to forest green, with tall erect shoots 6 to 10 inches high resembling a spray of fir needles. Stipes and branches cylindrical but slightly flattened and pointed at tips. Crustlike holdfast.

Habitat: Found from the mid to the low tide mark on rocks from the Temperate to the Subfrigid Zone of the Pacific coastal waters.

Foraging: Peak harvest from late spring to late fall. Plants are cut from rocks at low tide.

Preparation: Japan—fresh young plants used as an ingredient in soup or as a garnish for sashime (raw seafood).

Use: Japan—used as foodstuff in its original form; sun dried, salted, and cooked with soy sauce; salted and made into sheets. Salted matsumo also used to preserve mushrooms. After mushrooms are washed in salt water, they are layered with the matsumo.

Nutrients: High protein, high fat, high calcium. Also contains sugar, starch, vitamin A, potassium, iron, sodium, phosphorus, nitrogen, sulfur, magnesium, molybdenum, selenium, and trace elements.

Commercial Source: Japan (Hokkaido): matsumo may be available salted, in markets in major cities.

FOLK NAMES

America:

fir needle, sea fir needle

Japan:

matsumo

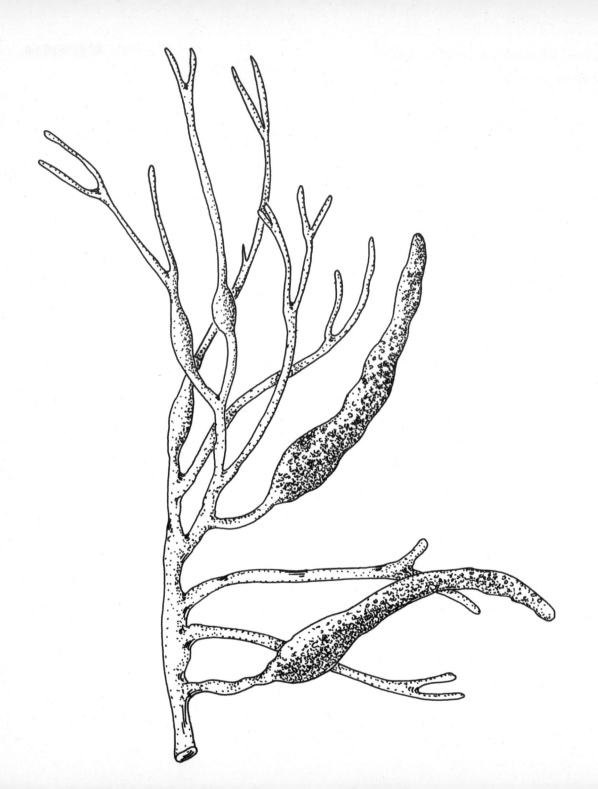

Phylum: Phaeophyta (Brown Algae)

Ascophyllum mackaii

Description: Plants olive green when fresh, black when dried, and emerald green when steamed. Plants grow entangled, with branches, freely dividing. Upper branches slender, simple or forked, often long, curved, or inflated. Holdfasts unknown.

Habitat: Found below the low tide mark on rocks, near or in mussel beds, in the North Temperate Zone of the Atlantic coastal waters.

Foraging: An annual. Harvest only young plants in late winter or early spring, before fruiting bodies appear. Collected by hand at low tide.

Preparation: America (Massachusetts)—used fresh.

Use: America (Massachusetts)—steamed, then sautéed with oil and soy sauce.

Nutrients: Sugar, starch, and trace elements. Probably very high in oil.

Gel: Algin.

Taste: Delicate texture and good taste when steamed.

Recipe: Sautéed Ascophyllum (p. 217).

FOLK NAME

America:

wrack

Phylum: Rhodophyta (Red Algae)
Asparagopsis taxiformis

Limu Kohu

Description: Plants dark red to violet, tannish-pink, brown, or olive, 3 to 5 inches tall. Creeping holdfast giving rise to erect blades. Stipe soft, smooth, and nude without branches or blades. All branches located at top of stipe. Branching plumelike appearing as soft feathery tufts.

Habitat: Found below the low tide mark on edges of reefs or in shallow pools, in locations with constant wave motion, from the Tropical to the Temperate Zone of Southern Pacific coastal waters.

Foraging: Annual shoots with a perennial holdfast. Usually collected by divers. Erect shoots are cut off to allow basal portion to reproduce.

Preparation: Hawaiian Islands—wash well in cold fresh water. Soak for half a day or overnight in fresh water, then, using a wooden mallet, salt lightly and pound upper branches. Roll entire plants into a ball. These will keep indefinitely without refrigeration. Small quantities can be used as required.

Use: Hawaiian Islands—small amounts cooked in beef stew.
Java—eaten.
Indonesia—cooked with fruit powder and pepper.

Nutrients: Iodine, trace elements. **This alga should not be consumed in large quantities** (see page 59).

Taste: Flavor, penetrating. Taste and fragrance of iodine developing when allowed to stand. Considered a delicacy.

Commercial Source: Hawaiian Islands: Sold in most markets. May be available in Hawaiian markets of West Coast cities in North America.

FOLK NAMES
Hawaiian Islands:

limu kohu (trans. **supreme limu), limu lipaakai, kohu lipehe** (trans. **light-colored kohu), kohu koko** (trans. **dark red kohu)**

Japan:

kagikenori

Phylum: Rhodophyta (Red Algae)

Bangia fuscopurpurea

Cow Hair

Description: Plants purplish-red to purplish-black to pale yellowish-brown to rust, bleaching to Mercurochrome color, are 1¾ to 6 inches long and grow in groups. Threadlike fronds resembling hair hang down from the rocks at low tide. Branchless single stipe, erect or curved, smooth at base, becoming slightly swollen at points. Disc-shaped holdfast.

Habitat: Found near the high tide mark on rocks or wooden pilings in coastal waters all over the world.

Foraging: Peak harvest from late fall to early spring. Harvested by scraping from the rocks with a sharp-edged tool.

Preparation: Taiwan—sun dried.

Use: China and Taiwan—dried plants added to salads.
Botel Tobago Island (Yami tribe)—eaten.
China (Fukien Province)—eaten.

Nutrients: Sugar, starch, and trace elements.

Taste: Dried plants have very fragrant smell and delicious taste. Considered a delicacy.

Commercial Source: Taiwan (coast of Ye Liu).

Recipe: Buddha's Delight (p. 206).

FOLK NAMES

Taiwan:

tou fah tsai (trans. **hair plant), tou mau tsai**

Botel Tobago Island:

damai

Japan:

ushi-ke-nori (trans. **cow hair nori)**

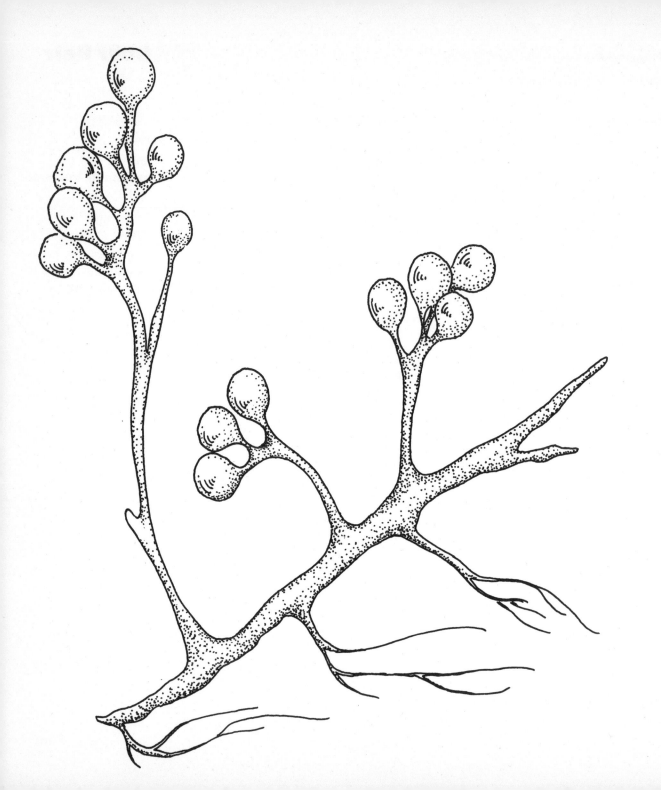

Phylum: Chlorophyta (Green Algae)

Caulerpa racemosa var. racemosa

Sea Grapes

Description: Plants are vibrant shades of green, sometimes having fluorescent appearance. Colorless basal portion creeps over the sea bottom and gives rise to green shoots that divide profusely around the axis.
Plastic-looking grapelike nodes borne on branches. Holdfast penetrates sandy bottom, forming a compact cushion.

Habitat: Found below the low tide mark, rooted in sandy, muddy bottoms or attached to rocks or dead coral. This radial form is suited to turbulent waters but also occurs in shallow quiet waters. Plants found in most tropical and some temperate seas.

Foraging: An annual basal portion, with a perennial holdfast. Lateral shoots are cut from rocks, leaving creeping basal portions to reproduce. Harvest just before use because plants deteriorate quickly.

Preparation: Japan—preserved in salt and often blanched. Always used fresh (not dried). Does not keep for more than a few hours after harvesting. Refrigeration helps.

Use: Philippines (Llocos Norte Province)—prominent in the local diet. Either eaten raw, dipped in vinegar, or as a salad combined with mashed tomatoes, onions, vinegar, salt, and red or black pepper.
Indonesia—eaten raw or blanched and dressed with an allspice sauce. Eaten sugarcoated, prepared as a relish, or cooked in palm sugar and soy sugar.
Japan—eaten raw as salad.
Micronesia—eaten raw as salad.
Eastern Malaysia (Java and Indonesia)—widely eaten.
Botel Tobago Island (Yami tribe)—eaten.
Taiwan—quick fried in lard or peanut oil or boiled with other foods.
China (Shantung Province)—added to boiling noodle soup.

Nutrients: Sugar, starch, and trace elements. **Caulerpa plants with a distinct peppery taste might best be avoided. Reports of toxicity are unsubstantiated.**

Taste: Crisp texture, pleasant taste, piquant and tangy.

Commercial Source: Philippines (Llocos Norte Province): Sold as a fresh vegetable in local markets.

Recipe: Seagrape salad (p. 195).

FOLK NAMES

Indonesia:

lelato

Australia:

sea grapes

Japan:

surikogidzuta

Philippines:

ararucip

Botel Tobago Island:

tahmuck

China:

mouse plant

Phylum: Chlorophyta (Green Algae)

Chaetomorpha crassa

Description: Plants yellowish to dark green to faint fluorescent green or blue. Composed of unbranched filaments. Plants twist together to form clumps or tangles. Cast-up plants often resemble cooked spaghetti. Tangles remain quite rigid when removed from water.

Habitat: Found near the high tide mark, growing on stones or wound around other algae (Sargassum) in warm, brackish waters with sandy or muddy bottoms, from the Temperate to Tropical zones of the Atlantic and Pacific coastal waters.

Foraging: Peak harvest, spring. Freshly cast-up plants are gathered.

Preparation: Philippines (La Union Province)—eaten fresh.
Taiwan—soaked in fresh water for several hours before use.
China (Chekiang Province)—plants are washed in fresh water to remove sand and salt, then sun dried, pulverized with stone implements to produce a powder, and stored in a well-sealed vessel. Mortar and pestle can be used to pulverize dried plants. Aroma should be very pleasing if the powder has been properly prepared.

Use: Tropical and Southeast Asia—commonly prepared as a gelatinlike sweetmeat or eaten as a salad.
Philippines (La Union Province)—eaten raw as salad.
China (Chekiang Province)—popular food of Buddhists. Prepared as tai tyau feen powder and baked into cookies.
Taiwan—fresh plants prepared, then fried in oil and eaten as a vegetable or cooked with fish, meat, etc.

Nutrients: High iron. Also contains sugar, starch, and trace elements.

Taste: Gelatinous texture.

Recipe: Tai Tyau Feen (Sea Vegetable Powder) (p. 253).

FOLK NAMES

Philippines:

kauat-kauat, ririppus

China:

tai tyau, hair-shaped green algae, big green algae

Phylum: Rhodophyta (Red Algae)

Chondrus crispus

Irish Moss

Description: plants dark red-purple to greenish to white, 2 to 4 inches tall, forming loose to dense clumps. Several blades arising out of a single holdfast. Stipes branching in twos. Blades slender, compressed, expanding above, narrowing sharply into wedge-shaped base. Blade tops rounded.

Habitat: Found near the low tide mark in pools and on rocks, shells, and wood pilings in the North Temperate Zone of the Atlantic coastal waters.

Foraging: A perennial. Peak harvest, spring and summer. Summer harvest best for high vitamin A. Raked by hand at low tide from small boats. Cut with sickles by wading out in shallow water. Storm-cast weed often harvested from the beaches.

Preparation: Plants can be sun dried, shade dried, or mechanically dried in heated drum dryers. Dried plants must be hydrated in fresh water, then picked clean of foreign matter before use.

Use: America (Boston area)—fresh or hydrated algae, cut up and added to soups and stews as a vegetable. America and Western Europe—fresh or hydrated algae is boiled and the gel sweetened, flavored, and used as a gelatin dessert (called blancmange) or used to make aspic dishes or jellies. Iceland—fresh or hydrated plants cooked in water or milk, with flour added to make thick pudding, then served with milk or cream.

Coast of Northern France—historically used with *Laminaria saccharina* to make a jelly called *pain des algues* (algae bread).

Nutrients: High vitamin A, high iodine. Also contains protein, sugar, starch, fat, vitamin B_1, iron, sodium, phosphorus, magnesium, copper, calcium, soluble nitrogen, bromine, potassium, chlorine, sulfur, boron, aluminum, arsenic, and trace elements.

Gel: Carrageenan.

Taste: Palatable only when cooked. Cartilaginous, bony texture when fresh.

Commercial Source: Scituate, Massachusetts; Nîmes; Brittany; Dublin; Canadian Maritimes.

Recipes: Irish Moss Soup (p. 182), Irish Moss Tomato Aspic (p. 188), Beets in Irish Moss Jelly (p. 186), Mixed Sea Vegetable Tempura with Shrimp Cakes (p. 200), Stir-fried Irish Moss (p. 220), Irish Moss Mousse (p. 228), Irish Moss Blender Pudding (p. 228), Irish Moss Blancmange Pie (p. 230), Skim Milk and Apple Blancmange (p. 233), Sweet Irish Moss Jelly (p. 244).

FOLK NAMES

Western usage:

Irish moss, carragheen, carragheen moss, carrageenan, Dorset weed, pearl moss, sea moss, sea pearl moss, jelly moss, rock moss, gristle moss, curly moss, curly gristle moss

Brittany:

bejin gwenn, white wrack, lichen, lichen carrageenin, pioca, goemon blanc

France:

mousse d'Irlande

Latin:

alga perlada

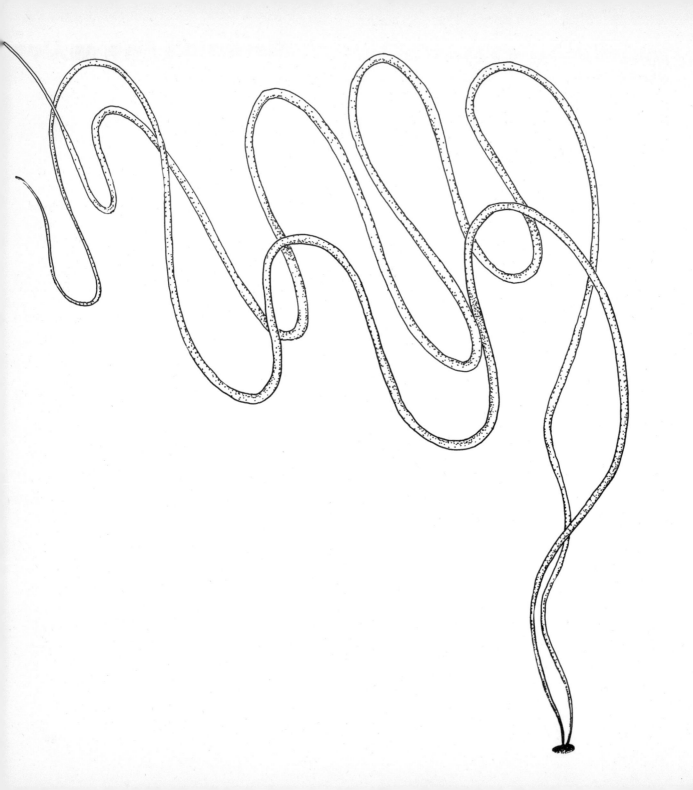

Phylum: Phaeophyta (Brown Algae)

*Chorda filum

Mermaid's Fishing Line

Description: Plants dark caramel colored. Appear to be "all stipe." Smooth, cylindrical, hollow thallus ⅛ to ¼ inch in diameter, usually 1 to 4 yards long. Slightly narrowed at tip and point of attachment but otherwise uniform in width with no branching. Small disc-shaped holdfast.

Habitat: Found growing below the low tide mark in quiet shallow bays with sandy bottoms, in the North Temperate Zone of Baltic and Atlantic coastal waters.

Foraging: An annual. Peak harvest in summer. Plants can be pulled up with grapnels or cut off with sickles or knives.

Preparation: Japan (Sado Island, Sea of Japan)—washed and used fresh.

Use: Japan (Sado Island, Sea of Japan)—fresh clean plants are cut up and eaten as salad.

Nutrients: High iodine, high bromine, high boron, high manganese. Also contains sugar, starch, and trace elements.

Gel: Algin.

Taste: Crisp texture.

Commercial Source: Japan.

FOLK NAMES

Western usage:

mermaid's fishing line

Japan:

tsurumo

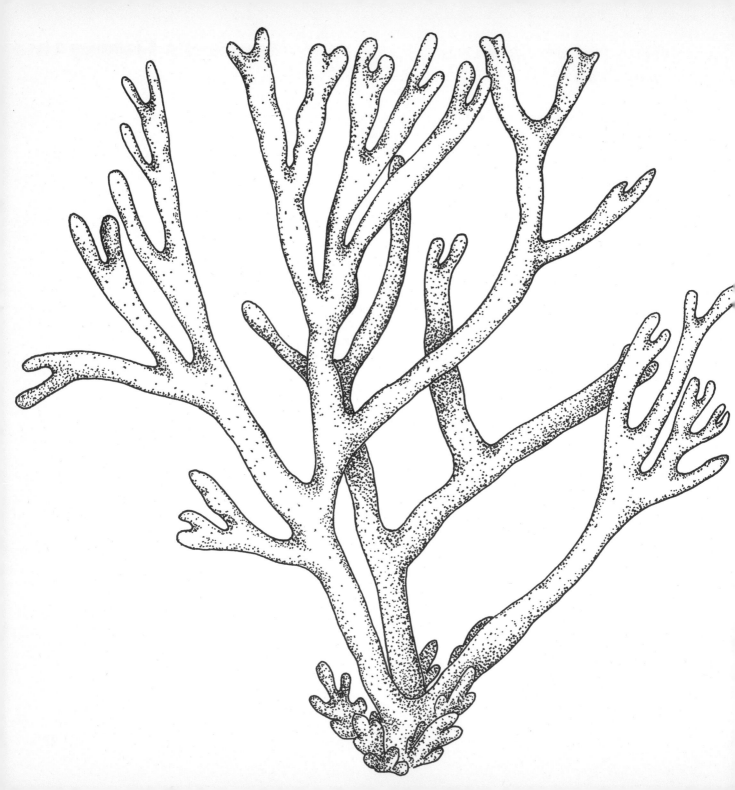

Phylum: Chlorophyta (Green Algae)

Codium fragile

Description: Plants deep green. Usually 8 to 16 inches tall, occasionally growing to 36 inches. Numerous thin branches dividing in twos. Plants form large clusters, feel feltlike and waterlogged to the touch.

Habitat: Found on sandy bottoms near the low tide mark in the Temperate zones of the Atlantic and Pacific coastal waters.

Foraging: A perennial. Peak harvest in spring.

Preparation: Japan—plants washed and used fresh, dried, and sun-bleached or preserved in ash or salt, then rinsed and boiled. Korea—only fresh plants are used as food. Cleaned, chopped, sun-dried plants are used as tea. Plants should be prepared immediately after harvest to avoid decomposition. Clean in lukewarm water. (Hot water softens and disintegrates the plants; cold water does not remove the sand, coral chips, and bits of shell.)

Use: Japan—bleached Codium is soaked, sugared, and eaten as a delicacy. Fresh or boiled cleaned plants are added to soups, mixed with soy sauce and rice vinegar, or used as a garnish for sashime (raw seafood). Korea—fresh plants are blanched and chopped, then added, like garlic, to fruit or vegetable salads. Dried plants are prepared as tea.

Nutrients: Very high iron. Also contains sugar, starch, and trace elements.

Gel: Agaropectin.

Taste: Spongy texture. Piquant taste.

Commercial Source: Chonggak is available dried for use as tea in Korean markets in major cities.

Recipes: Philippine Gulamon Salad (p. 191), Korean Salad with Spice Dressing (p. 187), Korean Spice Tea (p. 239), Hawaiian Codium (p. 250).

FOLK NAMES

North America:

fleece, sponge tang

Japan:

miru

Korea:

chonggak

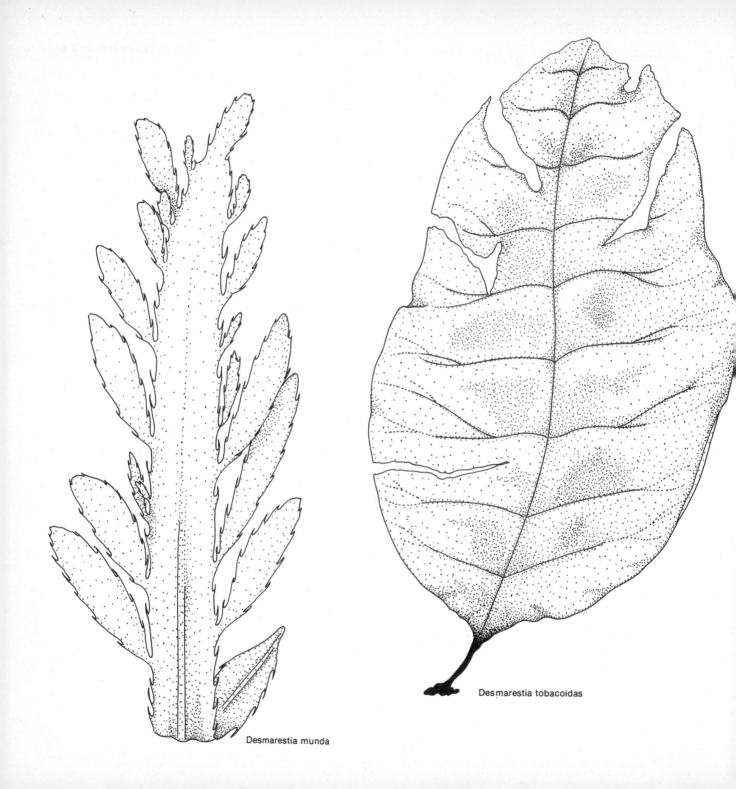

Desmarestia munda

Desmarestia tobacoidas

Phylum: Phaeophyta (Brown Algae)

Desmarestia (various species)

Warning! Plants contain sulfuric acid esters. Severe gastric upset could be expected if plants are ingested.

Description: Plants brownish to olive-brown. Single, erect main axis, cylindrical or compressed. Branching from either side of axis. New blades developing from margin or midrib of old blades. Filamentous protrusions along blade and axis are shed periodically. Some species with evident midrib on blade and axis. Plants of this genus will bleach the color from any alga with which they come in contact.

Habitat: An annual. Found on rocks below the low tide mark in moderately deep waters from the Temperate to the Arctic zones of the Atlantic and Pacific coastal waters. Plants mature in early summer, then disappear or lose their foliage. In northern areas, plants may persist through the winter.

Taste: Sour taste of lemons.

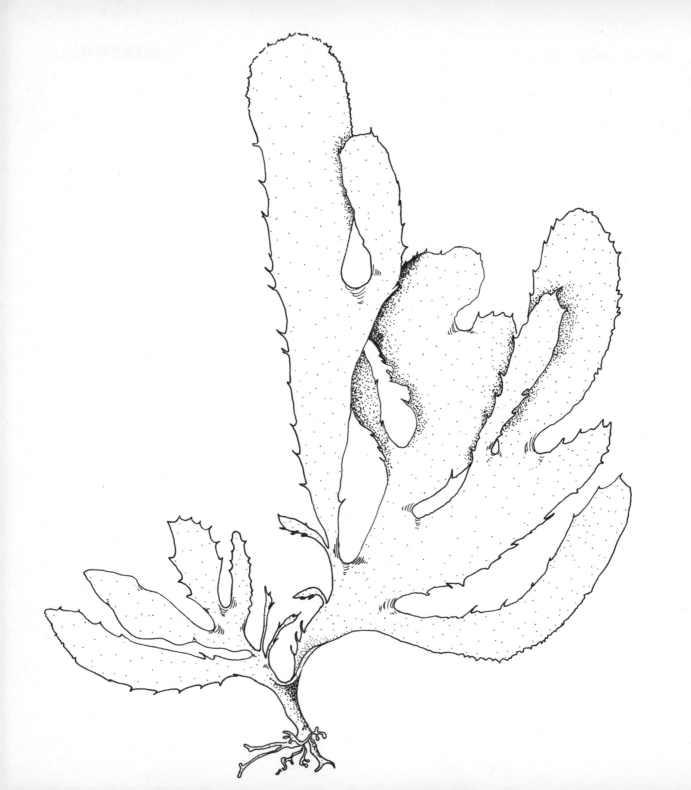

Phylum: Phaeophyta (Brown Algae)

Eisenia bicyclis

Arame

Description: Dark yellow-brown when growing, black when dried. Plant grows in an oval shape and splits in two at one year of age. First-year blades are shed. New blades then flatten, turn up, become wavy, and are increasingly branched and feathery toward tips. Blades 12 inches long and 1½ inches wide have wrinkled surface. Stipe cylindrical and treelike.

Preparation: Japan—sun dried or used fresh.
Use: Japan—added to soups or mixed with soybean sauce.
Nutrients: Protein, starch, sugar, fat, vitamin A, vitamin B_1, vitamin B_2, sodium, potassium, iodine, chloride, calcium, iron, mannitol (sugar alcohol), and trace elements.
Gel: Algin.
Taste: Sweet taste produced by the sugar alcohol in the plant.
Commercial Source: Japan—Produced in south Miyagi and Shizuoka Prefectures.
Recipe: Arame Soup (p. 183).

FOLK NAMES

Japan:

arame, kajimi, sagarame

Phylum: Chlorophyta (Green Algae)

Enteromorpha clathrata

Stone Hair

Description: Plants light green, profusely branched, forming mats of tangled silky, hairlike fronds.

Habitat: Found growing on other algae near the midtide mark, in coastal waters all over the world.

Foraging: Peak harvest from midwinter to early spring. Collected by cutting or plucking. A strainer or colander is useful to contain the slippery plants.

Preparation: America—used fresh. Mainland China and Taiwan—plants are washed in fresh water to remove sand and salt, then sun dried and pulverized with stone implements (mortar and pestle will do) to produce tai tyau feen powder. Powder is stored in a well-sealed vessel. The smell should be very pleasing if the powder has been properly prepared.

Use: America—fresh plants may be added to salads in place of sprouts, then dressed lightly with oil and vinegar or oil and lemon. (Squeeze lemon on when ready to serve to preserve the crisp texture of the algae.)

Botel Tobago Island (Yami tribe)—eaten raw or boiled in salt water.

Taiwan—eaten as a vegetable.

China (Chekiang Province)—important food article in Buddhist diet; often steamed with meat or prepared as tai tyau feen powder and mixed with savory vegetable oil (sesame oil, etc.) to produce an uncooked condiment, or combined with cane sugar as a children's treat or for use in cakes.

Nutrients: Sugar, starch, and trace elements.

Taste: Beanlike taste. Delicate, crisp texture.

Recipes: Shanghai Spring Rolls (p. 166), Mixed Sea Vegetable Salad (p. 188), Tai Tyau Feen (Sea Vegetable Powder) (p. 253), Hawaiian Enteromorpha (p. 250).

FOLK NAMES

Botel Tobago Island:

rupgan

China:

tai tyau, stone hair

Phylum: Chlorophyta (Green Algae)

*Enteromorpha intestinalis

Green Nori

Description: Plants transparent yellowish-green. Compressed, contorted, tubular, and inflated with gas. Most often without lateral branching.

Habitat: Single plants or groups found on rocks or in pools near the upper tide mark in coastal waters all over the world.

Foraging: Peak harvest, early spring. Can be harvested by cutting or plucking from the rocks. A strainer or colander is useful to contain the slippery plants.

Preparation: Japan—sun dried, roasted, and crumbled.
China and Taiwan—used fresh or washed in fresh water, sun dried, pulverized, and stored in airtight containers.
China (Amoy)—plants sun dried (unwashed), pulverized and stored in airtight containers.
China (Chekiang Province)—plants washed in fresh water to remove sand and salt, then sun dried and pulverized with stone implements (mortar and pestle will do) to produce tai tyau feen powder. Powder is then stored in a well-sealed vessel. (The smell should be very pleasing if the powder has been prepared properly.)

Use: Philippines (Llocos Norte Province)—eaten raw as salad combined with sliced tomatoes, onions, vinegar, salt, and black or red pepper to taste.
(La Union and Cagayan Provinces)—eaten.
Malay Peninsula (Chinese community)—eaten.
Japan—dried toasted plants used as a condiment over boiled rice, meat, fish, etc.
China (Amoy)—dried plants used as a substitute filling for spring roll cakes, *Monostroma nitidum* being the preferred alga.
(Chekiang Province)—important in diet of Buddhists; often steamed with meat, prepared as tai tyau feen powder, mixed with savory oil (sesame oil, etc.) to produce an uncooked condiment or combined with cane sugar as a children's treat or for use in cakes.

Nutrients: Sugar, starch, sodium, potassium, magnesium, calcium, sulfur. phosphorus, chloride, iron, silicon, iodine, and trace elements.

Commercial Source: Sold in markets in China (Amoy and Chekiang Province).

Recipes: Shanghai Spring Rolls (p. 166), Mixed Sea Vegetable Salad (p. 188), Tai Tyau Feen (Sea Vegetable Powder) (p. 253), Hawaiian Enteromorpha (p. 250).

FOLK NAMES

Kwakiutl Indians:
ihixlhewis

Philippines:
lumot, ruprupu

Japan:
bo-ao-nori, green nori

China:
tai tyau, stone hair, hu tai (trans. **tiger moss)**

Phylum: Phaeophyta (Brown Algae)

Fucus vesiculosis

Bladderwrack

Description: Plants olive-green, regularly branched, with leathery texture. Branches spiraling. Plants sometimes lacking air bladders but generally with paired bladders. Midrib distinct and stipe unbranched as it comes out of the disc-shaped holdfast.
Habitat: Plants preferring exposed locations on rocks near the low tide mark in the North Temperate Zone of the Atlantic coastal waters.
Foraging: A perennial. Harvest in early fall for very high vitamin C (ascorbic acid) and in summer for high vitamin A.
Preparation: Fresh plants are washed, chopped, and sun dried, then stored in airtight containers for use as tea.

Use: America and Western Europe—dried plants steeped as tea. Plants used fresh to steam and flavor seafood. Though the plants are not themselves eaten, the broth that is produced in the bottom of the pot is sweet, delicious, and healthful!
Bering Sea area—stems eaten fresh.
Nutrients: Very high magnesium, high protein, high vitamin A, high iodine, high bromine, high phosphorus. Also contains sugar, starch, fats, vitamin C, vitamin K, vitamin E, zinc, potassium, calcium, sodium, sulfur, chloride, silicon, iron, manganese, copper, zinc, cobalt, titanium, hydrogen, molybdenum, lead, barium, boron, radium, and trace elements.
Gel: Algin.
Taste: Plants impart a sweet taste to foods with which they are steamed or boiled.
Commercial Source: Chopped dried plants sold as bladderwrack tea in health food stores in North America.
Recipes: Codfish Chowder with Rockweed Flavoring (p. 179), Bladderwrack Tea (p. 240).

FOLK NAMES

Western Europe:

red Fucus, dyers Fucus, swine tang, sea ware, bladder, vraic

America:

rockweed, bladderwrack, popping wrack, wrack

Phylum: Rhodophyta (Red Algae)

Gelidium amansii

Description: Plants dark red when fresh, bleaching to citron yellow. Shape of plant varies with environment. Plant body slightly flat, standing erect and bushy, 4 to 6 inches tall. Upward-turned lateral branches, branching again to pointed tips. Main branches plumelike, subbranches threadlike. Fibrous holdfast.

Preparation: Japan—sun dried and bleached on the beaches. Gelidium species tend to have a rank taste unless the plants are bleached by sun and rain or leached of their reddish color by soaking or boiling in water before use.

Use: China—used with other agar producing species to make commercial gel.

China (Kwangtung Province)—used as gelable food.

Mainland China and Taiwan—dried plant soaked in boiling soup, removed, and dressed with ginger vinegar. Also used to make commercial agar.

Indonesia (Amboina)—used to make homemade agar by soaking a handful of the algae for 2 days in 1 cup of fresh water to which a little vinegar has been added. It is then boiled, filtered through muslin, cooled, and cut into pieces. Pieces are stored by simply keeping them in a dry place and are hydrated for eating by the addition of a little fresh water or by steeping in rose water.

Japan—most important source of commercial agar. Also used for making homemade kanten (dried-frozen agar) and homemade tokoroten (agar jelly).

Taiwan—source of commercial agar.

Nutrients: Very high iodine. Also contains sugar, starch, and trace elements.

Gel: Agar (high quality).

Taste: Prepared plants produce a good-tasting gel.

Commercial Source: Japan (Shizuoka Prefecture). China (Kwangtung Province, Ningpo District).

Recipes: Red Ribbons Jelly from South Africa (p. 231), Tokoroten (Japanese Agar Jelly Dessert) (p. 234), Fluffy Snow Agar (p. 232), Peanut Mousse (p. 227), Shimmery Apple Cider Gel (p. 236), Lime Agar Dessert (p. 234), Kanten Salad (p. 185), Chicken and Kanten Salad (p. 186).

FOLK NAMES

Japan:

tengusa, makusa, genso

China:

niu mau tsai (trans. **cow hair vegetable) stone flower plant**

Indonesia:

Japansche scheleiachtige mos, steen-or klipbloem, hay tsay, olus marinus, sajur laut, tschintschau, tschoo-hoae

Phylum: Rhodophyta (Red Algae)

Gigartina papillata

Grapestone

Description: Plants dull brownish-red, up to 6 inches tall with one or more blades arising from disc-shaped holdfast. Blades dividing into two relatively broad, wedge-shaped segments. Short, blunt, seedlike reproductive structures located on flattened surfaces of blades.

Habitat: Found on rocks near the low tide mark from the North Temperate to Frigid Zone of the Atlantic and Pacific coastal waters.

Foraging: Peak harvest, midspring for high vitamin C (ascorbic acid).

Preparation: Iceland—used fresh or sun dried, then soaked in fresh water before use.

Use: Iceland—prepared plants are chopped and cooked with water and flour or milk and flour, then eaten as a thick pudding served with milk or cream.

Nutrients: Very high vitamin C. Also contains starch, sugar, and trace elements.

Gel: Carrageenan.

Taste: Plants produce a pleasant-tasting gel.

Recipes: Irish Moss Tomato Aspic (p. 188), Beets in Irish Moss Jelly (p. 186), Irish Moss Mousse (p. 228), Irish Moss Blender Pudding (p. 228), Irish Moss Blancmange Pie (p. 230), Skim Milk and Apple Blancmange (p. 233).

FOLK NAME

America:

grapestone

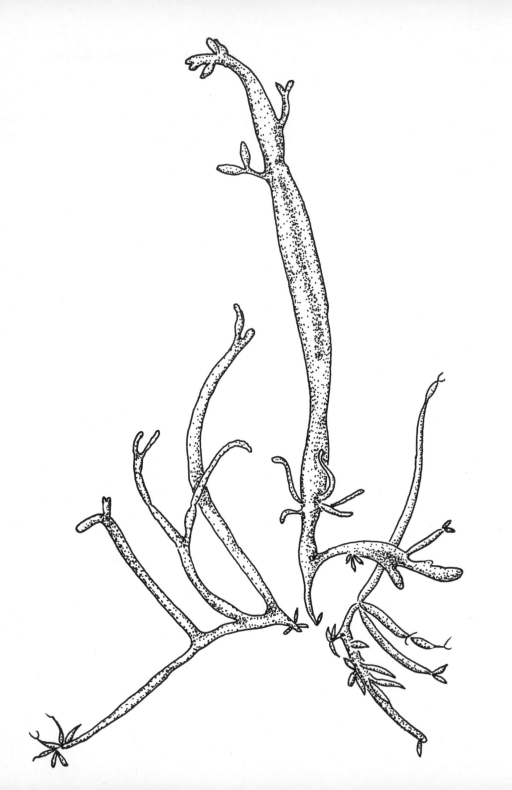

Phylum: Rhodophyta (Red Algae)

Gloiopeltis furcata

Funori

Description: Plants yellowish to maroonish-purple when fresh, pale brown to reddish-brown when dried. Plants 1½ to 6 inches tall, branches $1/10$ to $1/5$ inch wide. Gelatinous, somewhat flattened body. Numerous branches looking like a group of wire rods. Two or three irregular shoots arising from tops of slightly constricted branches. Bottom of plant spread out, as if "sitting" on the rocks. Holdfast a flat membrane.

Habitat: Found on rather clean rocks anywhere from the high tide mark to below the low tide mark from the South Temperate to the Subfrigid zone of the Pacific coastal waters.

Foraging: Highly seasonal. Peak harvest, midspring. Can be scraped from the rocks at low tide with a sharp-edged tool.

Preparation: Japan—sorted, picked clean, spread out on mats, sun dried, then sprinkled with fresh water and redried in strong sunlight (to bleach the plants), then dried again for storage; this product is soaked in a solution of water and rice vinegar to hydrate it for use as food.

Hong Kong—clean plants spread out on oiled circular bamboo trays and sun dried into sheets.

Use: Japan—often used directly as food (fresh), although best grades are most often used as a food-starch thickener. Plants are highly esteemed as an ingredient in soups or mixed with oysters, flour, and water, then fried. Vietnam—used to produce commercial gel.

Mainland China and Taiwan—fresh plants washed and stir fried or boiled quickly with pork. As a sea vegetable, Gloiopeltis is most often used fresh.

Nutrients: Sugar, starch, and trace elements.

Gel: Funoran (nongelling).

Taste: Drying and particularly storing is said to give this alga a disagreeable taste and odor; however, hydration in the vinegar solution not only will counteract this but will render the vegetable especially delicious.

Commercial Source: Japan—raw material produced in Japan (on Hokkaido and in Iwate and Nagasaki Prefectures); processed product available in Hong Kong, China (Amoy), and Japan (Osaka Prefecture). Funori is available in Japanese markets and health food stores of major cities in North America.

Recipe: Oyster Cakes with Funori (p. 197).

FOLK NAMES

Japan:

fukuro, funori

China:

chi tsai (trans. **red vegetable), chiao tsai, kaau tsoi** (trans. **gelatinous vegetable), hung tsoi, hung tsai** (trans. **red vegetable), lu kio tsai** (trans. **vegetable with the horns of a stag, antler plant)**

Western Europe:

gumweed

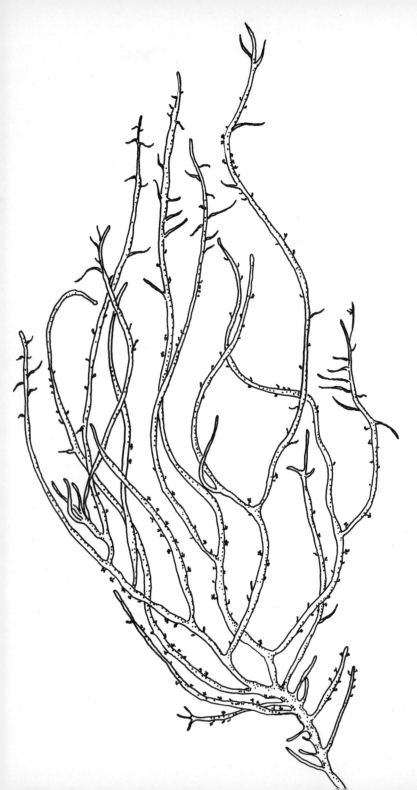

Phylum: Rhodophyta (Red Algae)
Gracilaria verrucosa

Description: Plants dull purplish-red to purple, grayish, brownish, or greenish, translucent. Bushy, usually 8 to 12 inches long. Firm, fleshy, cartilaginous texture, cylindrical throughout. Horny texture when dried. Main branches repeatedly and alternately divided, often almost separating in twos, with numerous side branches. Only uppermost branchlets tapering to the ends.

Habitat: Found in quiet, warm, shallow bays and slightly brackish waters in protected locations. Plants grow on rocks or small stones in sandy beds between the high and low tide marks in nearly all coastal waters.

Foraging: A perennial. Peak harvest, summer for food, and spring for agar. Mature plants tend to break free and float just off the bottom. Plants can be harvested as they wash ashore in late summer or can be collected in shallow water by means of nets.

Preparation: Vietnam—used to make homemade agar. Plants are washed in fresh water, kneaded into "slices," and exposed to the sun. For vegetable dishes, plants are washed and boiled.
Philippines and Southeast Asia—washed well in fresh water and used fresh. Or sun bleached and boiled for gelatin.
Philippine communities in San Francisco—washed well in cold fresh water, then used raw or blanched. Or sun dried, hydrated, and then blanched. Or frozen, then blanched.
Malaysia—sun dried.
Japan—treated with lime water or blanched before eating. Or sun dried for agar.
Plants should be washed well in cool fresh water before use to remove all sand, small animals, and other algae that might be clinging to the branches.
Use: Philippines (Llocos Norte Province)—eaten raw as salad combined with sliced tomatoes, onions, vinegar, salt, and black or red pepper to taste or cooked with other vegetables or prepared as a crude agar dessert with sugar and coconut milk.
(La Union Province)—eaten raw as salad or boiled and mixed with other vegetables.
Philippine communities in San Francisco—eaten fresh or blanched, as salad.
Vietnam—prepared as agar, then boiled and sweetened as xoa xoa or prepared as a vegetable and then eaten with fish as nuoc-mam.

Malaysia—used for both commercial and homemade agar.
North America—eaten.
Australia—used for commercial agar.
Japan—used blanched as a garnish for sashime (raw seafood) or used commercially mixed with *Gelidium amansii* (tengusa) to produce the agar to make kanten (dried-frozen agar) or used alone to make ogo nori kanten.
South Africa—used for agar.
Ceylon—used for commercial agar.
China—used for agar.
Nutrients: Very high manganese. High zinc. Also contains protein, starch, sugar, fat, vitamin A, vitamin B_2, sodium, phosphorus, soluble nitrogen, sulfur, iodine, potassium, calcium, iron, chloride, silicon, and trace elements.
Gel: Agar (high quality).
Taste: Rather stiff texture for eating. Considered inferior unless only young tender plants from sheltered locations are used.
Commercial Source: Australia; Philippines (sold fresh in Manila markets). Blanched ogo is sometimes available in Japanese markets in major cities.
Recipes: Philippine Gulamon Salad (p. 191), Sunomono (p. 190), Glanville Penn's Tortola Iron Jack Cocktail (p. 241), Jarred Limu Oki Oki (p. 243), Ogo Kim Chee (Pickled Ogo) (p. 243), Hawaiian Gracilaria (p. 249).

FOLK NAMES
Japan:

ogo, ogo nori

China:

thin dragon beard plant, hai mien san (trans. **sea noodle**), **fen tsai, hunsai, hai tsai** (trans. **sea vegetable**), **hoi tsoi** (trans. **sea vegetable**)

Philippines:

gulaman, guraman, gulaman dagat, caocaoyan

Ceylon:

Ceylon moss

Vietnam:

nuoc-mam, rau-cau, xoa xoa

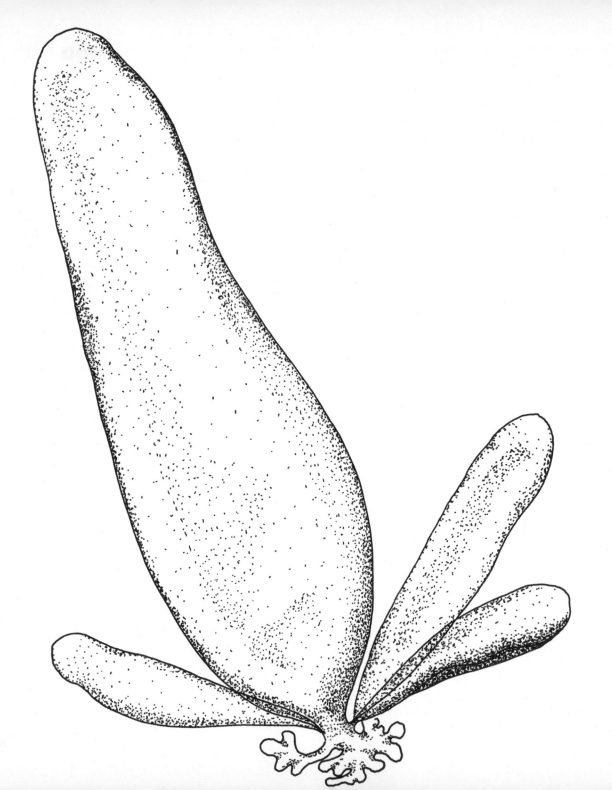

Phylum: Rhodophyta (Red Algae)

Halosaccion glandiforme

Description: Plants yellowish-green to yellowish-brown to olive or reddish-purple. Several oval sacs up to 10 inches tall borne on a single holdfast. Tips are rounded and sacs filled with water. As plants mature, sacs become eroded at the tips and fill with sand.

Habitat: Found near the low tide mark on rocks or in mussel beds from the Arctic to the Subtropic zones of the Pacific coastal waters.

Foraging: Can be gently plucked from the rocks at low tide.

Preparation: Small young plants are used fresh.

Use: USSR (Kamchatka Peninsula)—fresh young plants eaten mixed with various sorts of berries.

Nutrients: Sugar, starch, and trace elements.

Taste: Fresh young plants have crisp texture.

FOLK NAMES

North America:

sea sac

USSR:

kuschutschitsch

Japan:

benifukuronori

Phylum: Phaeophyta (Brown Algae)

Hizikia fusiforme

Hijiki

Description: Plants brown when fresh, black when dried. Plants stand straight in the water. Blades cylindrical. Lateral branches not quite as long as main branches. Most blades are bulbous in the middle and pointed on both ends. Northern variety sometimes with swollen blades, called fukuro hijiki (fukuro meaning bag). Holdfast flat, filamentous with few branches, attaching itself to and seeming to crawl over the rocks.

Preparation: Japan—washed and sun dried or washed, precooked, then sun dried for storage. Fresh, clean plants are used directly in cooking. Dried plants are hydrated first in fresh water and drained before cooking.
China—used fresh or sun dried.
Korea—sun dried, then hydrated for use.

Use: Japan—very important foodstuff. Served boiled, parboiled, or steamed and sautéed or simmered with other vegetables. Often combined with rice. Used with *Ulva lactuca* in soups. China—much used and highly esteemed as a fresh vegetable. Fresh plants used in soup, dried plants prepared as tea.
Korea—boiled, then cooked with garlic and spices as a main dish.

Nutrients: High protein. Also contains starch, sugar, fat, vitamin A, vitamin B_1, vitamin B_2, calcium, phosphorus, iron, and trace elements.

Gel: Algin.

Taste: Unique and delicious nutlike flavor. Crisp texture.

Commercial Source: America—sold dried in Japanese and Korean markets in major cities and through mail-order sources.
China—sold in markets in Hsing Hwa district.

Recipes: Hijiki Salad with Tofu Dressing (p. 185), Maize Shapes with Hijiki and Buttermilk Sauces (p. 202), Hijiki, Pork, Green Pepper, and Chinese Rice Noodles (p. 213), Hijiki Wrapped in Dried Soybean Curd (p. 205), Hijiki al Burro (p. 212), Hijiki and Dried Squid, Korean Style (p. 219), Hijiki with Goma Vinegar Dressing (p. 221), Hijiki Sauté (p. 221).

FOLK NAMES

Japanese:

hijiki

Korea:

nongmichae

China:

hai tso (trans. **seaweed), chiau tsai (**trans. **pig's foot vegetable), hai ti tun, hai toe din, hai tsao, hoi tsou**

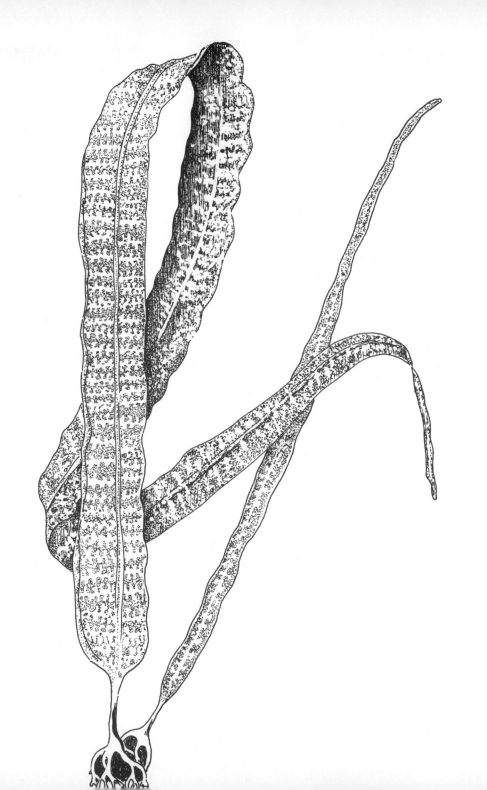

Phylum: Phaeophyta (Brown Algae)

Kjellmaniella gyrata

Tororo Kombu

Description: Plants brownish, blade long, 1½ to 6 yards, and narrow, sometimes tapering at each end. Puckerings on both surfaces of blade. Holdfast filamentous and rootlike.

Preparation: Japan—plants laid out flat on the beaches, partially dried, stipe and holdfasts removed, bundled, tied, then further processed by shaving across the grain as are the thicker Laminarias. For home storage the partially dried blades are tightly braided.

Use: Japan—mucilage-rich pieces of the dried blade are chopped and stirred into hot water, removed, and then the liquid is seasoned with soy sauce to produce a tasty and thickened broth.

Nutrients: Very high sodium. High iodine. Also contains protein, starch, sugar, fat, vitamin B_1, vitamin B_2, chloride, iron, phosphorus, calcium, and trace elements.

Gel: Algin.

Taste: Very rich in taste-producing mucilage.

Commercial Source: Japan—tororo kombu and processed products marketed, but production scarce. Available dried (imported from Japan) in Japanese markets in major cities or from mail-order sources.

Recipes: Kombu Dashi (or Soup Stock) (p. 172), Mackerel Soup (p. 172), Laminaria and Cauliflower Pickle (p. 245), Kombu No Tsukudani (Simmered in Soy Sauce) (p. 246), Laminaria Seasoning (p. 255).

FOLK NAMES

Japan:

tororo kombu (trans.

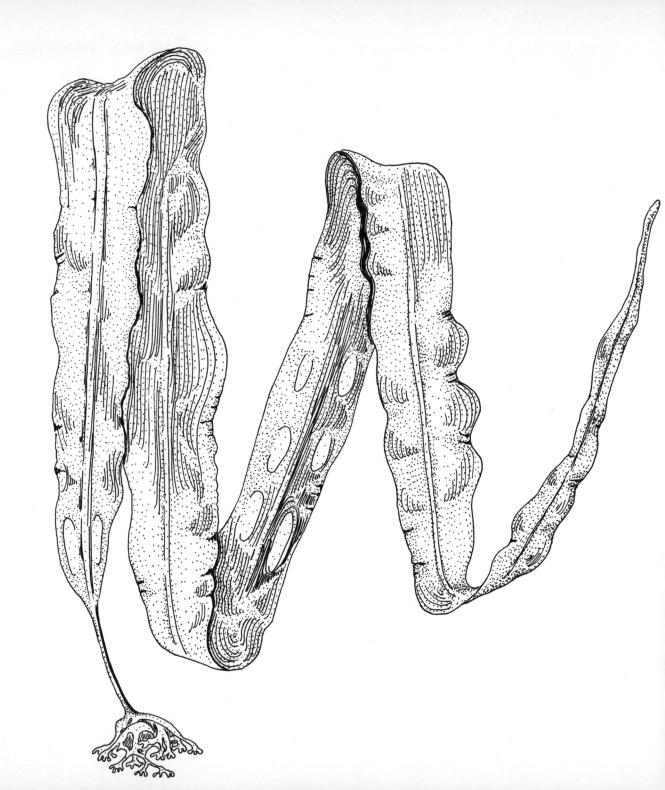

Phylum: Phaeophyta (Brown Algae)

Laminaria angustata

Mitsuishi-kombu

Description: Plants dark brown with leathery texture. Blade 2½ to 10 yards long, 3 to 6 inches wide, with a wedge-shaped midsection and margins slightly ruffled Stipe smooth, solid, cylindrical, 2 inches long, and slightly flattened. Holdfast branching, arising in several whorls. New plants have very narrow blades.

Preparation: Japan—plants are laid out straight and flat, sun dried, stipe and holdfast removed, tied in bundles, and often further processed by shaving with the grain to produce kizami (slivered) kombu.

Use: Japan—most popular boiled and eaten as a vegetable or used to make soup stock, after which the plant is prepared as a vegetable.

Nutrients: Very high iodine, high protein, starch, sugar (according to locality), phosphorus, calcium, and sodium. Also contains fat, vitamin B_1, vitamin B_2, vitamin A, iron, chloride, potassium, sulfur, magnesium, molybdenum, selenium, glutamic acid, and trace elements.

Gel: Algin.

Taste: Rich in taste-producing mucilage. Contains natural, taste-enhancing sodium glutamate. Becomes soft and tasty on boiling.

Commercial Source: Japan—produced in western provinces of Honshu, northern Miyagi Prefecture, and on Hokkaido. Processed products (imported dried from Japan) available in Japanese markets of major cities.

Recipes: Fried Sweet Kelp Chips (p. 166), Kombu Dashi (p. 172), Mackerel Soup (p. 172), Hai Dai Sweep Soup (p. 178), Laminaria Casserole (p. 203), Pork-stuffed Pleurophycus Fronds (p. 214), Laminaria Stew (p. 210), Mixed Sea Vegetable Tempura with Shrimp Cakes (p. 200), Ineh's Matsumae (Vegetables with Tangle) (p. 211), Ham and Laminaria Rolls (p. 165), Kombumaki with Pork Center (p. 220), Laminaria and Cabbage Side Vegetable (p. 219), Laminaria and Cauliflower Pickle (p. 245), Kombu No Tsukundani (Simmered in Soy Sauce) (p. 246).

FOLK NAMES

Japan:

mitsuishi-kombu, sopaushi, shiohoshi-kombu, urakawa-kombu, shamani kombu, tokachi-kombu, dashi-kombu, mizu-kombu

China:

hai dai, hai tai, kunpu

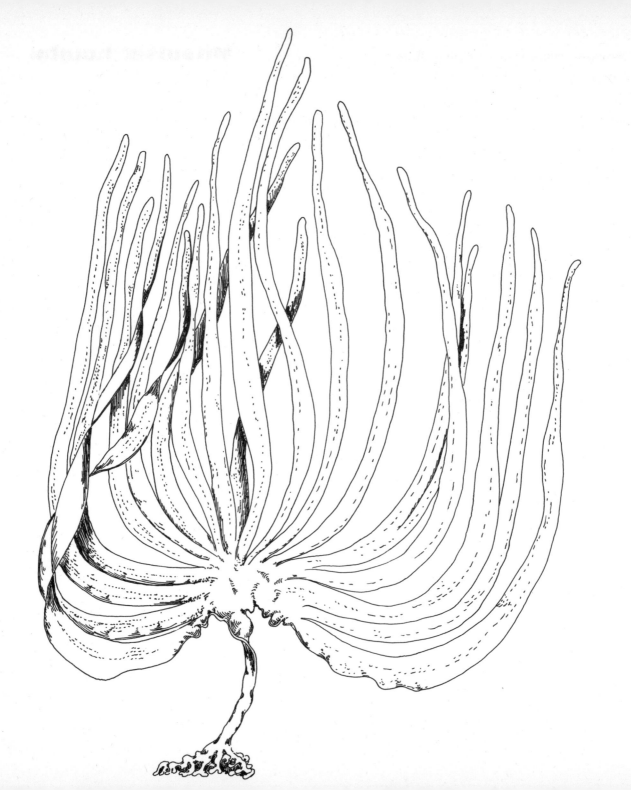

Phylum: Phaeophyta (Brown Algae)

Laminaria digitata

Fingered Tangle

Description: Plants olive-tan to olive-brown, about 12 inches wide and 24 inches tall. Mature blade broad at bottom, becoming heart-shaped and deeply cleft into numerous narrow flat segments of moderately thick texture. Well-developed plants are mucilaginous. Stout stipe, flattened above. Heavy, close, fibrous holdfast.

Habitat: Plants preferring rocky sea bottoms in exposed locations and cold sea currents. Found near and below the low tide mark in the Temperate and more often North Temperate zones of Atlantic coastal waters.

Foraging: An annual blade with a perennial holdfast. Fruiting in winter. Peak harvest spring for high vitamin C (ascorbic acid) but low starch.
North America—harvested at very low spring tides by means of sickles.
Eire—harvested in deep waters from small boats.

Preparation: North America—sun dried or dried over a wood stove (smoke dried) until plants are just pliable, then folded or pressed and, if desired, further prepared by slivering across the grain. Dried plants must be hydrated in water before use. Slivered plants can be dropped into cooking soup.

Use: Iceland—fronds eaten.
North America—prepared plants used as a cooked vegetable and in making soup stock.

Nutrients: Very high iron. High iodine, bromine, phosphorus, boron, and zinc. Also contains protein, sugar, starch, fat, vitamin A, vitamin B_1, vitamin B_{12}, vitamin C, calcium, magnesium, sodium, cobalt, chloride, potassium, sulfur, silicon, vanadium, soluble nitrogen, strontium, aluminum, rubidium, radium, copper, manganese, arsenic, titanium, nickel, and trace elements.

Taste: Contains taste-producing mucilage.

Commercial Source: North America (Massachusetts): Harvested for and retailed by Erewhon Foods, Boston. Laminaria foraged and sold commercially in North America is often labeled kombu.

Recipe: Kombu Dashi (or Soup Stock) (p. 172), Soup with Slivered Kombu (p. 171), Mackerel Soup (p. 172), Laminaria Seasoning (p. 255).

FOLK NAMES

Ireland:

sea tangle

Nova Scotia:

horsetail kelp

America:

kelp

Western Europe:

fingered tangle, tangle

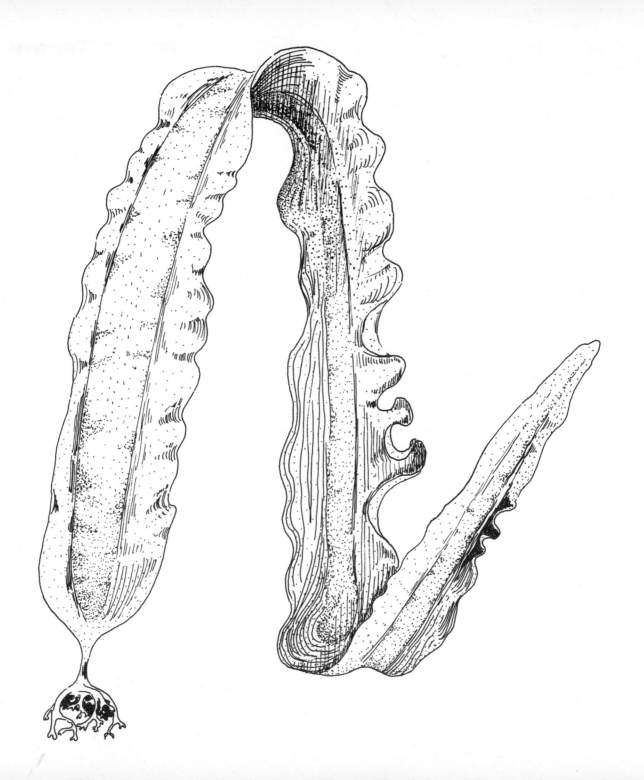

Phylum: Phaeophyta (Brown Algae)

Laminaria japonica

Ma-kombu

Description: Plants green, leathery, but very thin. Wavy blade arising from short, thick, elliptical or compressed stipe. Stipe flattening and broadening above. Blade entire, narrow, and tapering at each end. Margins thin, slightly ruffled, 2½ to 5½ yards long, 8 to 12 inches wide.

Preparation: Japan—plants are laid out flat to sun dry and hydrated before use. Korea—sun dried. Used dried or hydrated before use.

Use: Japan—dried product used to flavor food (soup stock quality rated second to *Laminaria ochotensis*). Pickled or candied as a sweetmeat. Made into a curd with beans. Ground into a powder and made into sweet cakes, tea, or seasoning.

Korea—dried product is hydrated and cooked with meat and other vegetables or fried dry in oil, coated with sugar, and eaten as a snack.

Nutrients: Very high sugar, bromine, and potassium. High protein, mannitol (sugar alcohol), iodine, phosphorus, and calcium. Also contains starch, fat, vitamin B_1, vitamin B_2, vitamin A, vitamin C, sodium, iron, chloride, nickel, arsenic, sulfur, magnesium, selenium, molybdenum, nitrogen, glutamic acid, and trace elements.

Gel: Algin.

Taste: Sweet taste of sugar alcohol (mannitol). Delicate texture. Contains natural, taste-enhancing sodium glutamate.

Commercial Source:

America—available dried (imported from Japan) in Japanese markets of major cities.

China—sold dried in markets.

Japan (Osatsube Village in Kayabe Gun)—dried product of superior quality produced. Also produced on Hokkaido.

Korea—sold dried in markets.

Recipes: West Coast Snack (p. 165), Fried Sweet Kelps Chips (p. 166), Kombu Dashi (or Soup Stock) (p. 172), Mackerel Soup (p. 172), Korean Rib Stew with Tasima (p. 208), Laminaria Seasoning (p. 255).

FOLK NAMES

Japan:

makombu (trans. **true Laminaria), shinori-kombu, hababiro-kombu, oki-kombu, uchi kombu, moto-kombu, minmaya-kombu, ebisume, kombu, hirome, umiyama-kombu**

China:

hai dai, hai tai, kunpu

Korea:

hae tae, tasima

Phylum: Phaeophyta (Brown Algae)

Laminaria longicruris

Description: Plants olive-tan to olive-brown, 3½ to 6 yards long, with elongated blade and broad base. Blade becoming heart-shaped when mature. Fairly thick in midsection, thin and a bit ruffled at edges. Stipe solid, slender below and hollow and inflated above. Large branched holdfast.

Habitat: Found from the shallow waters near the low tide mark to deep waters below the low tide mark, in the Temperate to North Temperate zones of the Atlantic coastal waters.

Foraging: Peak harvest in early spring. Blades harvested by cutting with knife or sickle, at low spring tides.

Preparation: North America—sun dried or dried over a wood stove (smoke dried) until plants are just pliable, then folded or pressed and, if desired, further prepared by slivering across the grain. Dried plants must be hydrated in water before use. Slivered plants can be dropped into cooking soup.

Use: America—prepared plants are cooked as a vegetable or added to soups.

Nutrients: Sugar, starch, iodine, phosphorus, chloride, and trace elements.

Gel: Algin.

Taste: Taste-producing mucilage unknown.

Commercial Source: America (Massachusetts)—harvested for and retailed by Erewhon Foods, Boston; Laminaria foraged and sold commercially in North America is often labeled kombu.

Recipes: Soup with Slivered Kombu (p. 171), Korean Rib Stew with Tasima (p. 208), Laminaria Casserole (p. 203), Laminaria Stew (p. 210), Laminaria and Cabbage Side Vegetable (p. 219), Laminaria and Cauliflower Pickle (p. 245).

FOLK NAMES

America:

kelp, oarweed

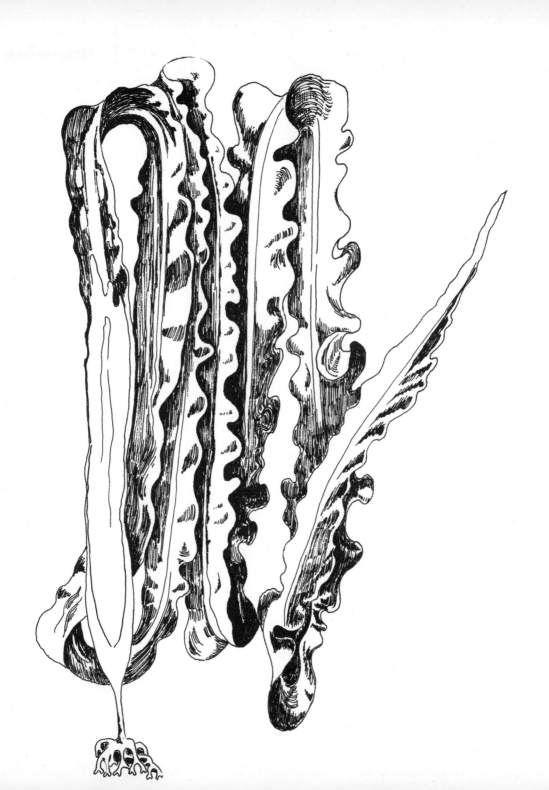

Phylum: Phaeophyta (Brown Algae)

Laminaria longissima

Naga-kombu

Description: Resembling *Laminaria angustata* but slightly thinner and growing to much greater lengths.
Preparation: Japan—see *Laminaria angustata*.
Use: Japan—used as *Laminaria angustata* though slightly less popular.
Nutrients: High protein, fat, sodium, iodine, and phosphorus. Low sugar. Also contains starch, vitamin B_1, vitamin B_2, vitamin A, chloride, glutamic acid, and trace elements.
Gel: Algin.

Taste: Contains natural taste-enhancing sodium glutamate. Rich in taste-producing mucilage and salts.
Commercial Source: Japan—produced in northern Miyagi Prefecture and on Hokkaido. Exported in large quantities to China.
Recipes: Fried Sweet Kelp Chips (p. 166), Kombu Dashi (or Soup Stock) (p. 172), Mackerel Soup (p. 172), Hai Dai Sweet Soup (p. 178), Laminaria Casserole (p. 203), Pork-stuffed Pleurophycus Fronds (p. 214), Laminaria Stew (p. 210), Mixed Sea Vegetable Tempura with Shrimp Cakes (p. 200), Ineh's Matsumae (Vegetables with Tangle) (p. 211), Ham and Laminaria Rolls (p. 165), Kombumaki with Pork Center (p. 220), Laminaria and Cabbage Side Vegetable (p. 219), Laminaria and Cauliflower Pickle (p. 245).

FOLK NAMES

Japan:

naga-kombu (trans. **long lamina Laminaria), ma kombu, nimotsu-kombu, gimberi-kombu, kimberi-kombu, mizu-kombu, shima-kombu, wakaoi**

China:

hai dai, hai tai, kunpu

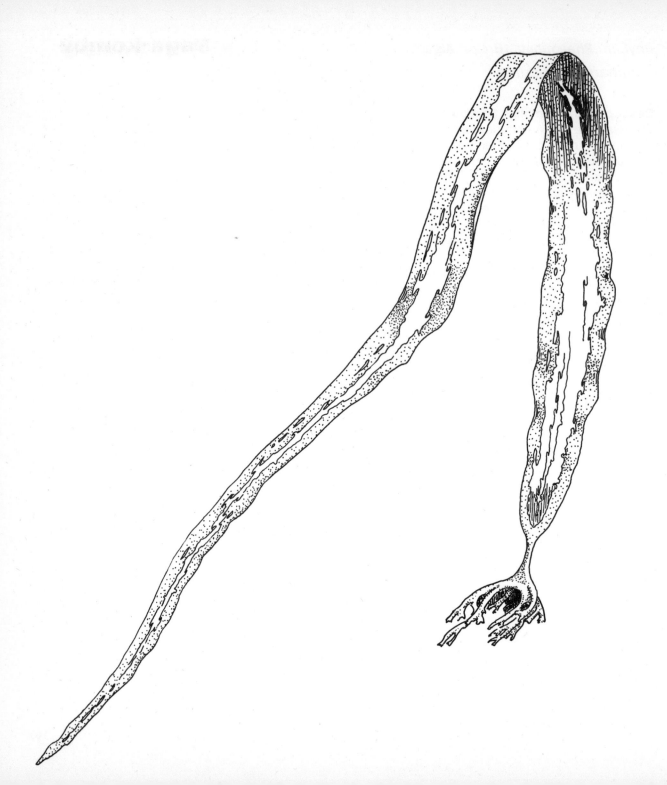

Phylum: Phaeophyta (Brown Algae)

Laminaria ochotensis

Rishiri-kombu

Description: Plants dark green when young, blackish-brown when mature. Blade whole, long, oblong, spindle-shaped or heart-shaped, up to 20 yards long and 3½ to 8 inches wide. Margins thin, slightly ruffled. Stipe short, smooth, elliptical or round, lower end flattened. Hairlike branching holdfast. Plants growing 1 to 20 on one holdfast. Generally resembling *Laminaria japonica* but with tougher texture. Smaller more narrow plants, called hosome, about 1½ to 3 yards long and 1 inch wide crowd up to 90 on a holdfast in some localities. Mucilage in stipes and blades of both types.

Preparation: Japan—plants laid out straight and flat to sun dry.

Use: Japan—best and most popular plant for making soup stock. Used in almost the same way as *Laminaria japonica*.

Nutrients: Very high sugar, high protein, starch, vitamin A, and vitamin C. Also contains fat, vitamin B_1, vitamin B_2, iodine, calcium, phosphorus, chloride, iron, and trace elements.

Gel: Algin.

Taste: Produces a clear soup stock with a highly refined taste.

Commercial Source: Japan—Teshio Prefecture produces best product. U.S.S.R.—produced on western coast of Sakhalin Island

Recipes: Kombu Dashi (or Soup Stock) (p. 172), Mackerel Soup (p. 172), Laminaria Seasoning (p. 255).

FOLK NAMES

Japan:

Rishiri-kombu (trans. Rishiri Island kombu), para-kompo, dashi kombu, Menashi-kombu, Birodo-kombu, Teshio-kombu, kuro-kombu, koteshio, hosome-kombu, shio-kombu

China:

hai tai, kunpu, hai dai

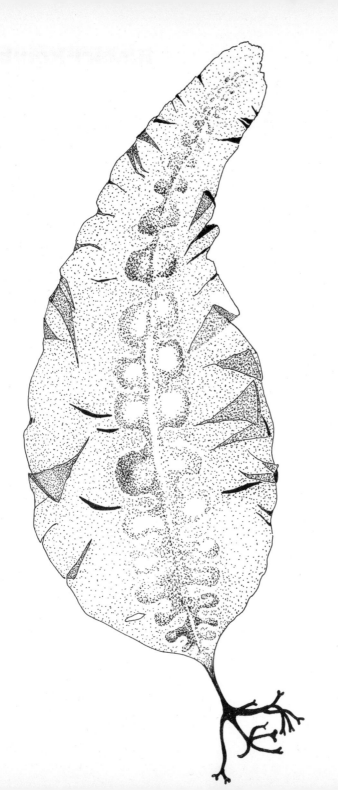

Phylum: Phaeophyta (Brown Algae)

Laminaria saccharina

Sugarwrack

Description: Plants chestnut brown, 3 feet long and 3 inches wide. Blade tapering or rounded at the ends. Old blade in late spring going quickly from wedge-shaped to heart-shaped at base (not ruffled at tip). New summer blades, thin becoming thicker in late spring and summer. Constriction separates new and developing broad ruffled summer blade from old blade. Autumn-winter growth again thick, flat, and mucilaginous. Stipe variable in length greatly exceeding that of blade.

Habitat: Found on rocks below the low tide mark in areas where fresh water enters the sea, from the North Temperate to Subfrigid zones of the Atlantic and Pacific coastal waters.

Foraging: Plants live for 3 years. Sporophytes are produced year-round. Complete regeneration of frond after cutting is possible only when plants are less than one year old. Cast-up plants (those mature individuals, 2 to 3 years old) are gathered for high gel content. Harvest in summer for high sugar alcohol content, late spring for high vitamin C (ascorbic acid).

Preparation: Cast-up plants must be immediately removed from the beaches to a warm, dry area to guard against bacterial decay.
Scotland and China—harvesting done with grapnels. Also harvested with sickles.

Use: Scotland and Ireland—young stipes eaten raw.
Brittany and Normandy Coasts—used with *Chondrus crispus* to prepare a jelly called pain des algues (algae bread).

Nutrients: Very high iodine and bromine. High protein and sugar. Also contains mannitol (sugar alcohol), starch, fat, soluble, nitrogen, vitamin K, vitamin B, vitamin B_{12}, vitamin C, sodium, chloride, rubidium, radium, cadmium, cobalt, boron, manganese, arsenic, nickel, glutamic acid, and trace elements.

Taste: Contains taste-producing mucilage. Dried fronds have sweet sugary taste owing to the deposit of crystals from the sugar alcohol, mannitol. This is enhanced by the taste of sodium and glutamic acid (natural sodium glutamate). Stipes have peanutlike taste.

Commercial Source: China—produced in Tsingtao, Chefoo, and Darien.

Recipes: West Coast Snack (p. 165), Fried Sweet Kelp Chips (p. 166), Laminaria and Cauliflower Pickle (p. 245).

FOLK NAMES

Western usage:

sweet wrack, sugar wrack, sugar tang, oarweed, tangle, kelp, sugar sea belt

Australia:

sweet tangle

China:

hai dai, kouanpon, hai-houan, yan tsai, chai tai, hai tai, kunpu

Japan:

karafuto kombu, karafuto tororo kombu, kan-hoa

Microscopic detail of strand

Lyngbya mats floating at the base of mangrove roots

Phylum: Cyanophyta (Blue-green Algae)

Lyngbya (various species)

Mermaid's Hair

FOLK NAME

North America:

mermaid's hair

Warning! Some species are poisonous. Toxins cause death. Avoid any Blue-green alga with a diameter less than that of a human hair.

Description: Plants dark bluish-green to black. *Lyngbya aestuarii,* known to be lethal to animals. The separate members of the genus *Lyngbya* are too small to classify in the field without aid of a glass. Plants are filamentous, lying loose or forming an irregular or matted layer. Though related to the edible Nostocs, the Lyngbyas are much thinner and easily distinguished.

Phylum: Phaeophyta (Brown Algae)

Macrocystis pyrifera

Giant Kelp

Description: Plants pale yellow-brown, translucent, up to 29 yards long. Last blade of each branch broad and sickle-shaped. Young side blades formed by asymmetrical splitting from top to bottom. Reproductive blades (sporophylls) produced at base of branches usually have floats. Large cone-shaped holdfast, branching, rootlike, and compacted.

Habitat: Growing attached to solid objects, below the low tide mark in the North Temperate Zone of Pacific coastal waters. Found in both Northern and Southern hemispheres.

Foraging: A perennial. Floating or cast-up plants can be gathered if fresh. Growing plants can be harvested by diver using knife.

Preparation: Sun dried or mechanically dried, then pulverized.

Use: America—alga from which most commercial kelp preparations (pills, powder, flakes) are made. Powder and flakes used as a condiment or salt substitute in foods and beverages. Plants are also a source of commercial algin.

Nutrients: Very high vitamin E, vitamin A, high vitamin B, and vitamin D. Also contains starch, sugar, vitamin C, and trace elements.

Gel: Algin.

Taste: Pleasant, slightly salty, vegetablelike taste.

Recipes: Lynn's Bloody Mary with Kelp Seasoning (p. 240), Yogurt Drink (p. 241), Salt Substitute (p. 256).

FOLK NAMES

America:

giant kelp, sea ivy

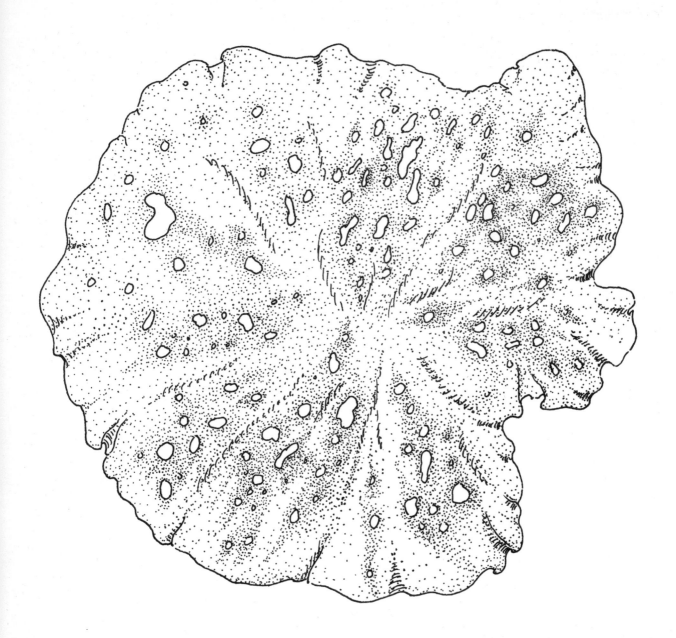

Phylum: Chlorophyta (Green Algae)

Monostroma latissimum

Description: Plants light green, like tissue paper to the touch. Blades large, soft, 5 to 10 inches wide, densely perforated by different-sized holes.

Habitat: Young plants growing on rocks near the high tide mark. Older plants found free floating in calm sheltered places or hanging on mangroves. Plants prefer brackish water to low salinities, and grow well in organic pollution. Found in the Temperate Zone of Atlantic, Pacific, and Mediterranean coastal waters.

Foraging: Peak harvest from early winter to midspring. Harvest only young fronds for tenderness. Floating plants can be collected in quiet shallow waters. Attached plants can be pulled from rocks at low tide.

Preparation: Taiwan—fresh fronds used whole.

Japan—sun dried and processed into sheets, then pulverized. Sun-dried fronds can be pulverized and placed in a shaker for use as seasoning.

Use: Taiwan—cooked with meat, fish, etc., in soups, or prepared as a condiment, with soy sauce, sugar, mushrooms, various species of *Porphyra,* and seasoning.

Japan—processed flakes used as seasoning alone or combined with various other dried ingredients for use on cooked foods such as rice and eggs.

Taste: Fresh young fronds tender and tasty. Dried plants taste rich and nutlike.

Commercial Source: Sold as dried sheets in Japan. Sold as a processed seasoning in Japan and probably in America.

Recipes: Shanghai Spring Rolls (p. 166), Taiwanese Fisherman's Soup (p. 175), Mixed Sea Vegetable Salad (p. 188), Grunting Fish Wrapped in Sea Vegetable, Indian Style (p. 260), Oulachen (Candlefish) in Sea Lettuce, Makah Indian Style (p. 261), Sea Vegetables Taiwan (p. 222), Powdered Green Sea Vegetable Seasoning (Aonoriko) (p. 253), Steamed Sea Lettuce (p. 224).

FOLK NAMES

China:

hai tsai (trans. **sea vegetable)**

Japan:

awo-nori

Phylum: Phaeophyta (Brown Algae)

Nemacystus decipiens

Mozuku

Description: Plants dark brown to olive-brown to green to olive-tan. Slippery, very gelatinous, irregularly cylindrical, thick body. Branches narrower at their tips than at their place of attachment to main stipe.

Preparation: Japan—may be eaten fresh or blanched. May be brined or salted for storage. Brined plants are kept refrigerated in a sealed container and are sometimes but not always rinsed in fresh water and drained before use. Salted plants must be soaked in fresh water before use to remove excess salt.

Use: Japan—eaten fresh, blanched, or otherwise prepared with dressing of soybean sauce or rice vinegar. Blanched plants are often eaten with sashime (raw seafood).

Nutrients: Protein, starch, sugar, vitamin A, vitamin B_1, vitamin B_2, calcium, phosphorus, iron, and trace elements.

Taste: Crisp crunchy fluid texture. Delicate, delicious, and slightly salty taste.

Commercial Source: Fresh brined or salted mozuku sold packaged (imported from Japan) in Japanese markets in major cities.

Recipes: Mozuku in Miso Soup (p. 175), Japanese-style Mozuku Salad (p. 189).

FOLK NAME

Japan:

mozuku

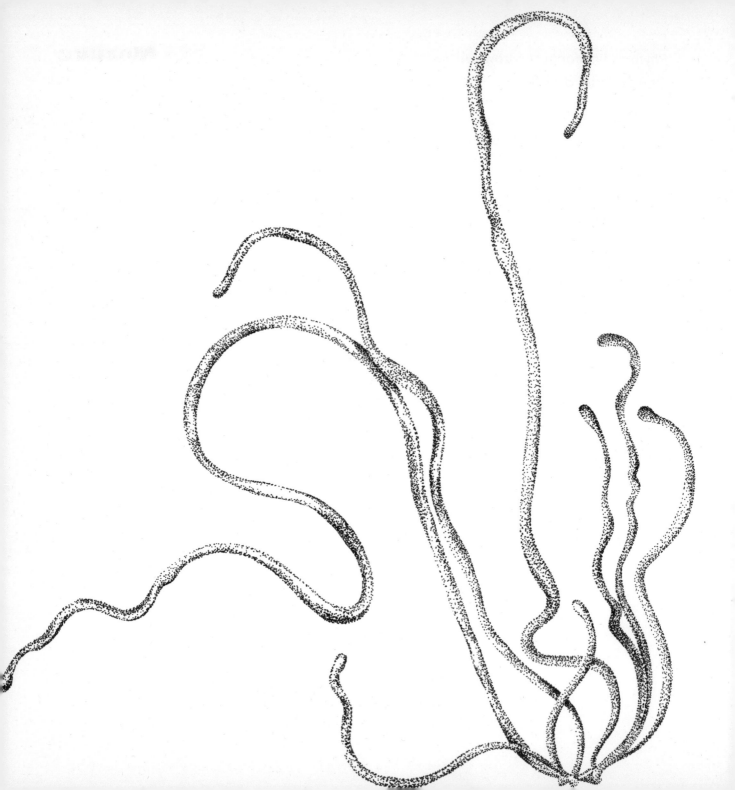

Phylum: Rhodophyta (Red Algae)

Nemalion helminthoides

Sea Noodle

Description: Plants claret red to rusty brown. Small, 4 to 12 inches tall, bushy, stringlike, with firm, cartilaginous slippery texture. Cylindrical stipe seldom branched.

Habitat: Found on rocks, rough surfaces, or profusely filling the insides of empty shells, from the midtide mark to below the low tide mark. Preferring active waters from the Temperate to the Tropical zones of the Atlantic and Pacific coastal waters.

Foraging: Relatively rare plant. Peak harvest from early spring to midsummer. May be pulled from rocks at low tide.

Preparation: Japan—used fresh, sun dried, ash dried, or salted, after which the alga is hydrated for use.

Use: Italy—popularly prepared as a dish known as spaghetti turchi (Turkish spaghetti).

Japan—used fresh or dried, then hydrated, in soups, salads, or dressed with vinegar broth and soy sauce.

Nutrients: Sugar, starch, and trace elements.

Recipes: Mozuku in Miso Soup (p. 175), Japanese-style Mozuku Salad (p. 189).

FOLK NAMES

America:

threadweed

Japan:

umisomen (trans. sea noodle), tsukomo nori

Latin

crop of threads

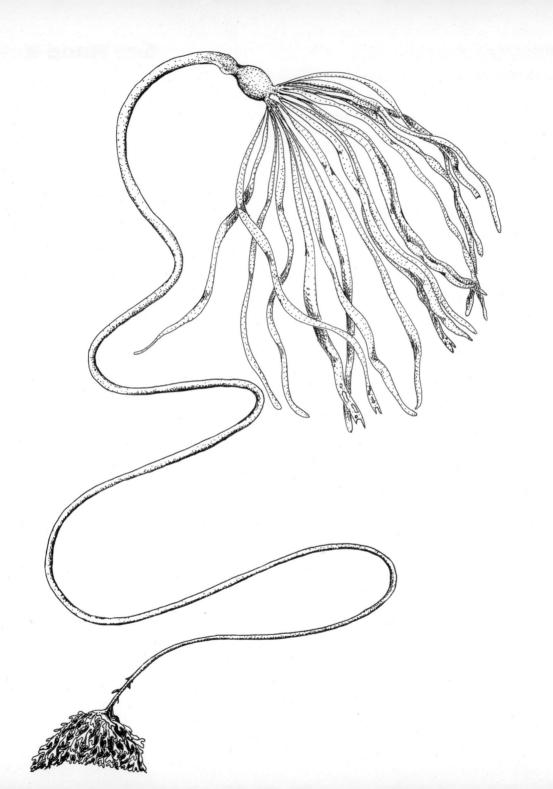

Phylum: Phaeophyta (Brown Algae)

Nereocystis luetkeana

Bull Whip Kelp

Description: Plants olive-green with 32 to 64 long thin blades attached to a bulb at the end of a long thick stipe. Plants grow to 50 yards long. Broad rootlike, branched holdfast.

Habitat: Found growing in extensive beds, on rocks, deep (30 to 50 feet) below the low tide mark with the upper end of stipe growing up to and floating horizontally on the surface of the water. Isolated plants also found in pools between the high and low tide marks. Plants found from the Subfrigid to South Temperate zones of the Pacific coastal waters.

Foraging: Usually an annual. Peak harvest from late summer to early fall (best plants for candying and pickling). Occurring in considerable quantity. Only those plants whose stipes snap crisply in two when bent are fresh and suitable for use as food. Choose only smooth and glistening stipes rather than wrinkled ones. Use stipes no longer than 15 feet and not more than 3 inches in diameter. They may be cut into two-foot lengths at the beach for easy handling. (Kwakiutl and Haida Indians): Blades of the plants weighted down and submerged at mouths of rivers for the herring to spawn on them.

Preparation: Stipes and bulbs desalted by soaking in changes of fresh water for several days, then candied or pickled. Blades can be sun dried. Spawn-laden blades are sun dried then hydrated before use.

(Kwakiutl and Haida Indians)—blades laden with herring spawn were sun dried, bundled in groups of ten and placed in boxes for the winter. Before use, they were soaked overnight, broken into bite-sized pieces, and boiled.

Use: (Kwakiutl and Haida Indians)—prepared blades that were covered with herring spawn were eaten as a delicacy, placed in dishes with oulachen (candlefish) oil poured over them.

America—stipes and bulbs are desalted, candied, and flavored or desalted and pickled. A candied product called seatron was, until recently, available commercially.

America (some Pacific Indian tribes)—dried blades eaten like chipped beef.

Southeast Alaska (Indians)—desalted stipes are prepared as a sweet pickle.

Nutrients: High iodine, high bromine. Also contains sugar, starch, sulfur, phosphorus, potassium, chloride, sodium, magnesium, calcium, iron, silicon, and trace elements.

Gel: Algin.

Taste: Stipe and bulb suitable for eating only after preparation. Narrow end of stipe more tender than that closest to bulb. Blades tasty only after drying. Stipes, bulbs, and spawn-laden blades have crunchy texture. Spawned-on blades can be used as kazunoko kombu. (p. 208).

Recipe: Nereocystis Sweet Pickles (p. 244).

FOLK NAMES

America:

ribbon kelp, giant kelp, bull whip kelp, bull kelp, sea whip, horsetail kelp, bladder kelp, sea otter's cabbage

Quileute Indians:

xopiikis

Quinault Indians:

kotka

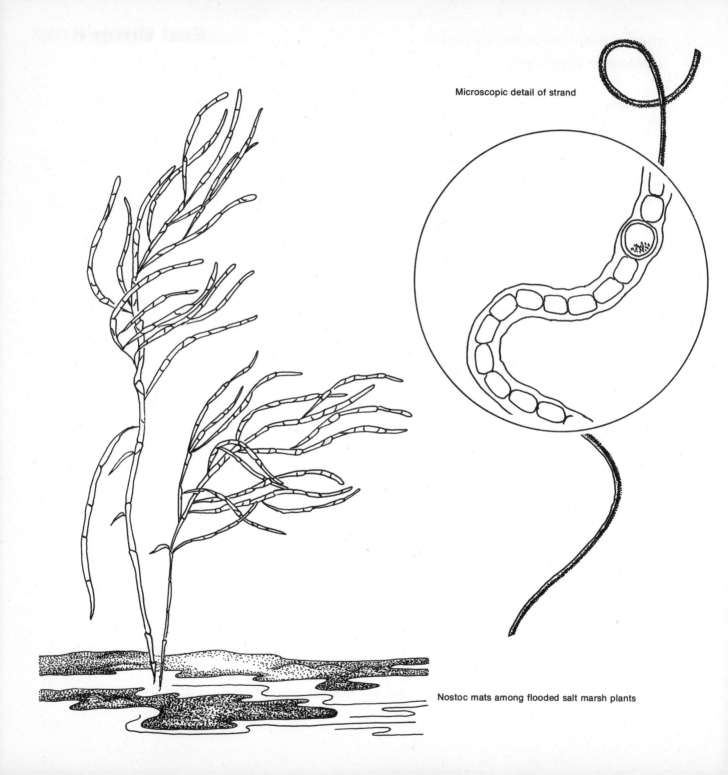

Microscopic detail of strand

Nostoc mats among flooded salt marsh plants

Phylum: Cyanophyta (Blue-green Algae)

Nostoc (various species)

Fairies' Butter

Description: Plants greenish to violet, drying to black. Plant body composed of unbranched, intertwined, contorted filaments. Occurring in large, tangled, gelatinous masses resembling horsehair. In wet weather, forming irregular, leathery gelatinous sheets a few inches broad, gradually drying to form hard, bristly, twisted black patches. Quickly regaining elastic quality when hydrated. Colonies most conspicuous after rain or flooding by the tide.

Habitat: Marine forms found in salt marshes, lagoons, and in the upper reaches of tidal flats from the Temperate to the Tropical Zones all over the world.

Foraging: Masses of plants can be scooped up at the water's edge and deposited in a container.

Preparation: China—fresh or hydrated algae is cleaned by placing it in water to cover and adding a few drops of oil. This method loosens dirt and allows it to fall to the bottom of the pan, leaving the algae clean. The cleaned plants are drained and may then be used fresh or sun dried for storage. Cooked plants should be eaten immediately and not allowed to stand. Standing will cause the plants to shrivel and lose their crispness.

Japan—plants cleaned, mashed, spread on glazed tiles to sun dry, removed and marketed in thin sheets.

Use: Fresh plants may be cleaned and eaten fresh or cleaned and cooked. Dried plants must be hydrated before they are cleaned, then may be eaten fresh or cooked.

South America—boiled with garden vegetables and sea vegetables as a flavoring.

China—cleaned plants (dried or fresh) are added to soups, stir fried or sautéed in oil or fat along with dried, hydrated oysters as a New Year's dish. Prominent in diet of Buddhists. Jelly is made from several species of *Nostoc*. Cleaned algae is blanched with boiling water to form a gelatinous mass, then eaten or used as a thickener for cooked vegetable and shrimp dishes, etc.

Malaysia—eaten in Chinese dishes. Central Asia—eaten.

Nutrients: High protein. Also contains starch, sugar, fatty acids, fats, oils. The marine forms contain trace elements.

Taste: Freshwater species of the plant, whether eaten fresh, stir fried, or sautéed, have crisp, crunchy texture. Marine species tend to be more gelatinous.

Commercial Source: Sold in Chinese markets in major cities (imported from China). Produced in Taiwan (Taipeh), China (Shensi and Kansu), and Japan (Tokyo area).

America—Fah tsoi is sold (imported from China) in Chinese markets in major cities.

Recipes: Fah Tsoi and Dried Oysters (p. 207).

FOLK NAMES

China:

fah tsai, fah tsoi, heaven vegetable, star jelly, hair vegetable, fairies' butter, ke-sien-mi

Japan:

reed falling stars, ajitsaki

American equatorial Indians:

yuyucho

Hong Kong:

black moss, dried moss

Indonesia:

djamur batu

Malaysia:

blue weeds

India:

meat

Palmaria palmata

Description: Plants rose-red to reddish-purple, 8 to 16 inches tall. Tiny disc-shaped holdfast, widening almost immediately into thin elastic fronds. Lobed segments making the plant appear hand-shaped.

Habitat: Found growing on rocks, shells, and other algae from the midtide mark to below the low tide mark in rather deep water from the Temperate to the Frigid Zones of the Atlantic and Pacific coastal waters. Found in both Northern and Southern hemispheres.

Foraging: A perennial. Peak harvest from late spring to midfall. Mid- to late summer for high vitamin A. Early to late fall for high vitamin C (ascorbic acid). Harvested by cutting from rocks at low tide.

Preparation: Western Europe—fresh plants washed in seawater, partially dried, pressed into plugs, refrigerated damp to be used as needed, or washed in seawater and partially dried in the sun and breeze immediately after harvesting to prevent mold. Process takes 6 hours, plants turn black, then return to their dark red color. Fresh plants can be singed on a hot campfire rock, stove, or griddle to produce a toasted flavor.

Iceland—fresh plants washed in fresh water, dried like hay, compressed in barrels or huts where they remain dry for several months.

Dulse

Use: Ireland—young plants chewed raw or eaten after sun drying, as a snack. Sun-dried plants eaten as a relish with potatoes or boiled in milk or oil of citron.

Mediterranean area—young plants eaten raw.

Iceland—eaten as an accompaniment to dried fish with butter and potatoes. Baked into bread. Boiled in milk to which rye flour has been added. Fresh plants fried. Plants cooked in soups, eaten dried as a snack, or as a relish with potatoes.

Alaska (Tlinket Indians and white population of Yakutat Bay)—a linear form of the plant is eaten.

Canadian Maritimes, Iceland, and Alaska—washed, dried, and rolled or pressed into plugs for chewing or eating.

Brittany—used raw.

Alaska (Indians of southeast)—fresh plants panfried or partially dried plants dipped in vinegar and eaten.

Canada—processed into a capsulized vitamin supplement called seadyme. Plants can be dipped in batter and fried as tempura.

USSR (Primorskaya on the Kamchatka Peninsula)—linear form of the plant is fermented into an alcoholic beverage by the Kamchadal inhabitants.

Nutrients: Very high protein, fat, and vitamin A. High iodine and phosphorus. Also contains sugar, starch, vitamin B_6, vitamin B_{12}, vitamin E, vitamin C, soluble nitrogen, yeast, bromine, potassium, magnesium, sulfur, calcium, sodium, radium, boron, rubidium, maganese, titanium, and trace elements.

Gel: Carrageenan.

Taste: Slightly salty, nutlike taste. Exceptionally delicious.

Commercial Source: America—sold dried in seaport markets of Philadelphia, Boston, Seattle, etc. Also sold by health food stores and mail-order houses.

Canada—sold in pubs and markets. Also available from mail-order sources. Produced in Franklin, Maine; Washington State (Puget Sound area); Ireland; Grand Manan Island and Bay of Fundy; New Brunswick and Vancouver, British Columbia.

Recipes: Dulse Miso Soup (p. 176), Chinook-style Chowder with Slivered Dulse (p. 177), Dulse Salad (p. 191), Dulse and Goat's Cheese Salad (p. 194), Baked Dulse Salmon Loaf (p. 203), Dilsea (p. 204), Mixed Sea Vegetable Tempura with Shrimp Cakes (p. 200), Dulse Sauté (p. 225), Yogurt Drink (p. 241), Hot Dulse Lemonade (p. 239), Dulse Condiment (p. 247), Homemade Dulse Plugs (p. 254).

FOLK NAMES

Western usage:

dulse, dulce, red kale, Neptune's girdle.

Iceland:

saccha (trans. vine Fucus), sol

Brittany:

tellesk

Ireland:

dillisk, dillesk, crannogh

Scotland:

water leaf, sheep dulse

Japan:

darusu

Norway:

sou sol

France:

goémon à vache

Tlinket Indians:

raa-ts.

Flower Seaweed

Petalonia fascia

Description: Plants olive-brown to olive-tan. Delicate, long (14 inches), thin, flat, leaflike blades, wedge-shaped at base with pointed tips. Widths of blades in the tuft vary greatly, margins gently ruffled.

Habitat: Found between the high and low tide marks on rocks or in pools in coastal waters all over the world.

Foraging: An annual. Peak harvest from early spring to late fall. Can be plucked or cut from rocks.

Preparation: Japan—sun dried, used fresh or processed as is *Porphyra tenera.*

Use: Japan—young "buds" used as substitute for Undaria. Fresh or dried plants or processed sheets are added to miso soups. Generally used as are species of *Porphyra.*

Nutrients: Sugar, starch, and trace elements.

Commercial Source: Japan—produced on all coasts.

Recipes: Split Pea and Wakame Soup (p. 177), Chinese-style Soup with Wakame (p. 179), Wakame Soup (p. 182), Sea Vegetable Soup with Bean Curd (p. 181), Miyok-Kuk (Korean Sea Vegetable Soup) (p. 181), Wakame and Dried Shrimp with Ginger (p. 223), Wakame in Sweet and Sour Sauce (p. 223), Wakame and Shredded Dried Bonito (p. 225).

FOLK NAMES

Japan:

seiyohabanori (trans. **flower-shaped seaweed)**

Phylum: Phaeophyta (Brown Algae)

Pleurophycus gardneri

Description: Plants light brown to light olive-brown to slightly golden. Broad flat blade, up to 32 inches long and 16 inches wide. Stout stipe up to 20 inches long, flattened near blade and cylindrical near base. Blade smooth, delicately wrinkled and wavy, usually eroded at its tip. Conspicuous, smooth, flat straplike midrib runs up the length of the blade.

Habitat: Found on rocks near the low tide mark and just below, from the Temperate to the Frigid Zone of Atlantic and Pacific coastal waters.

Foraging: Fresh storm-cast plants can be gathered from the beaches. Attached plants can be cut from the rocks at low tide.

Preparation: Fronds are used fresh or sun dried, then hydrated in fresh water before use. Stipes are used fresh.

Use: America—fresh or hydrated blades can be wrapped around various fillings, steamed, then eaten hot or chilled. Fresh stipes can be chopped and added to salad or stuffings.

Nutrients: Sugar, starch, and trace elements.

Gel: Algin.

Taste: Frond has delicate refined taste when steamed or boiled. Stipe has crunchy delicious taste fresh (raw) or cooked.

Recipes: West Coast Snack (p. 165), Fried Sweet Kelp Chips (p. 166), Hai Dai Sweet Soup (p. 178), Stuffed King Salmon Baked in Kelp, Indian Style (p. 260), Korean Rib Stew with Tasima (p. 208), Laminaria Casserole (p. 203), Pork-stuffed Pleurophycus Fronds (p. 214), Laminaria Stew (p. 210), Mixed Sea Vegetable Tempura with Shrimp Cakes (p. 200), Ineh's Matsumae (Vegetables with Tangle) (p. 211), Ham and Laminaria Rolls (p. 165), Kombumaki with Pork Center (p. 220), Laminaria and Cabbage Side Vegetable (p. 219), Laminaria and Cauliflower Pickle (p. 245).

FOLK NAME

America:

kelp

Polyneura latissima

Description: Plants deep pink to rose madder. Blades oblong and tapered at both ends, deeply incised, somewhat lacerated on older plants. Conspicuous veins tying back into one another, covering entire surface of blade, all but the margins.

Habitat: Found on the vertical surfaces of rocks near the low tide mark, somewhat sheltered from full force of waves, from the North Temperate to the South Temperate Zone in the Pacific coastal waters.

Foraging: A perennial. Fresh plants can be gathered by hand at low tide. Grapnels can also be used to wrench plants from their place of attachment.

Preparation: Philippine community in San Francisco—plants are washed quickly and carefully in lukewarm water (hot water will cause the gel in the blades to release; cold water will not remove the sand from the blades), then sun dried in strong sunlight and a good breeze to prevent mold. Individual portions can be washed, drained, sealed in plastic bags, and frozen. Once defrosted, the portions should not be refrozen. Frozen portions can be placed in a colander or strainer and blanched with salted or unsalted boiling water for use. Dried plants are first hydrated for a few minutes in a little cold water then blanched for use.

Use: Philippine community in San Francisco—used fresh (raw) or used fresh and blanched or frozen and blanched. Can be dried, hydrated, then blanched as salad.

Chinese community in San Francisco—sun-dried plants are chopped or sliced and added to soup called expensive soup, containing a whole egg.

Nutrients: High iodine. Also contains sugar, starch, and trace elements.

Taste: Texture of fresh plants is like crepe paper. Strong taste and odor of iodine developing when plants are allowed to stand.

Recipe: Polyneura Salad (p. 194).

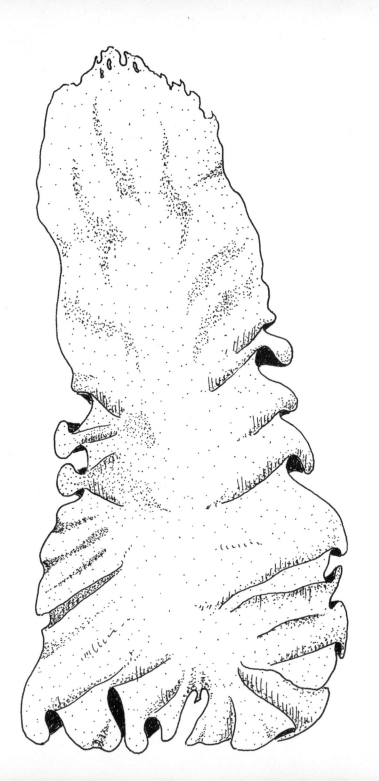

Phylum: Rhodophyta (Red Algae)

Porphyra miniata

Red Laver

Description: Plants reddish-purple, 6 to 20 inches tall. Blade long, narrow, with ruffled margin, tapering at the tip with wedge-shaped base. Disc-shaped holdfast.

Habitat: Found growing on rocks between the high and low tide marks from the Temperate to Tropical zones of the Pacific coastal waters. Found in both Northern and Southern hemispheres.

Foraging: A spring annual. Peak harvest early through midspring (fronds are tough by summer). Harvested by plucking from rocks at low tide. Best-tasting plants are gathered from brackish waters.

Preparation: Washed quickly in cold fresh water, then hung out on a clothesline or spread over close-meshed wire to dry in the sun and breeze. Then stored in sealed plastic bags (the sun-dried plants can be stored in paper bags, but they will readily absorb moisture and should be toasted in the oven or over a flame before use).

Use: Japanese communities in Vancouver, British Columbia, and Puget Sound area of Washington State—prepared plants are sugarcoated and roasted to be used as snacks or are added to soups and various Oriental dishes.

Nutrients: High protein. Also contains sugar, starch, and trace elements.

Taste: Distinctive good taste. Delicate texture.

Recipes: Porphyra Chips (p. 168), Taiwanese Fisherman's Soup (p. 175), Porphyra Soup (p. 174), Pacific Sea Vegetable Soup (p. 176), Grunting Fish Wrapped in Sea Vegetable, Indian Style (p. 260), Oulachen (Candlefish) in Sea Lettuce, Makah Indian Style (p. 261), Stuffed Porphyra Fronds (p. 215), Dilsea (p. 204), Mixed Sea Vegetable Tempura with Shrimp Cakes (p. 200), Laver and Pork Omelet (p. 201), Gluckaston (p. 222), Steamed Sea Lettuce (p. 224), Sea Vegetables Taiwan (p. 222), Nori Okazu (p. 224), Muck a Muck's Porphyra Condiment (p. 248), Homemade Laver Plugs (p. 255), Hawaiian Porphyra (p. 248), High-protein Porphyra Flour (p. 254).

FOLK NAMES

English:

red laver

Japanese:

nori

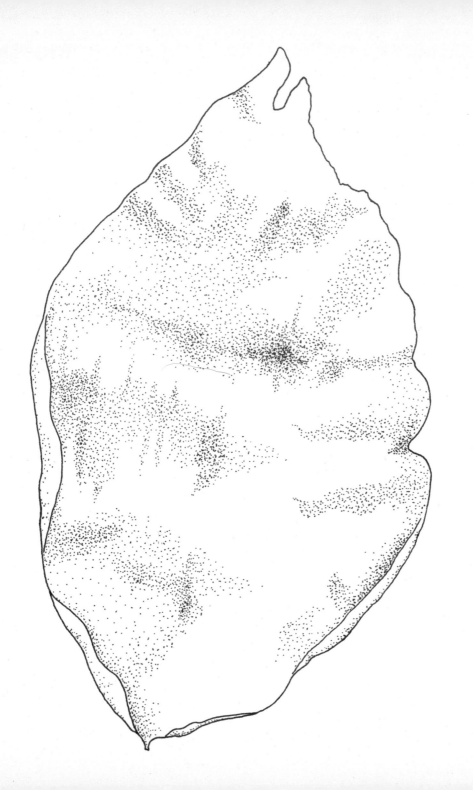

Phylum: Rhodophyta (Red Algae)

Porphyra nereocystis

Chi Choy

Description: Plants deep pink to dull purplish-red, transparent, 10 to 30 inches tall. Blades at first flat, linear to oval. Later becoming concave at bottom. Margins cut into narrow lobes. Disc-shaped holdfast.

Habitat: Growing only on *Nereocystis luetkeana,* the only Porphyra that does this. Found from the North to the South Temperate Zone of Pacific coastal waters.

Foraging: Harvested from late fall to early spring. Plants plucked or cut from the floating stipes of Nereocystis. It is usually necessary to do this from a small boat.

Preparation: Washed quickly in fresh water, to remove sand, then sun dried.

Use: America (Chinese community in Monterey)—stewed with fish and shrimps; (Chinese community in Pacific Grove)—used in soups, etc.

Nutrients: High protein. Also contains sugar, starch, Vitamin B_1, Vitamin C, and trace elements.

Taste: Tender, delicate texture. Thought by the Pacific Coast Chinese to have a flavor superior to those species that grow on the rocks.

Commercial Source: Sold by Chinese purveyors around Monterey.

Recipes: Porphyra Chips (p. 168), Taiwanese Fisherman's Soup (p. 175), Porphyra Soup (p. 174), Pacific Sea Vegetable Soup (p. 176), Grunting Fish Wrapped in Sea Vegetable, Indian Style (p. 260), Oulachen (Candlefish) in Sea Lettuce, Makah Indian Style (p. 261), Stuffed Porphyra Fronds (p. 215), Dilsea (p. 00), Mixed Sea Vegetable Tempura with Shrimp Cakes (p. 200), Laver and Pork Omelet (p. 201), Gluckaston (p. 222), Steamed Sea Lettuce (p. 224), Sea Vegetables Taiwan (p. 222), Muck a Muck's Porphyra Condiment (p. 248), Homemade Laver Plugs (p. 255), Hawaiian Porphyra (p. 248), High-protein Porphyra Flour (p. 254).

FOLK NAMES
English:
red laver, purple laver
Chinese:
chi choy
Japanese:
nori

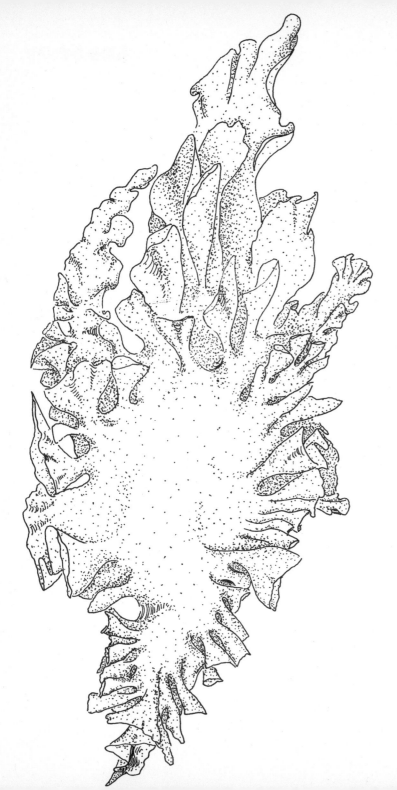

Phylum: Rhodophyta (Red Algae)
Porphyra perforata

Description: Plants steel-gray to brownish-purple, growing to about 5 feet in length. Long, narrow when young, with deeply ruffled edges, usually becoming cut into narrow irregularly shaped lobes with age. Blades have no stipes. Disc-shaped holdfast.

Habitat: Found on rocks or on other algae near the midtide mark from the polar region to the South Temperate Zone of the Pacific coastal waters.

Foraging: A perennial. Peak harvest in late spring when fronds are 3 to 5 inches tall. Also collected later when fronds are 2 to 3 feet in length. Cut from rocks at low tide by means of a long sharp knife or plucked by hand.

Preparation: Kwakiutl and Haida Indians—fresh plants broken into small strips and sun dried or gathered in large baskets, covered and allowed to rot for 4 or 5 days, then pressed into rectangular wooden frames on a large rack and sun dried outdoors in the breeze. Resulting cakes of sea vegetable then placed in a wooden box alternating with layers of chiton juice (chiton was chewed and the juice spit out onto the sea vegetables) and tender young cedar *(Thuja plicata)* boughs. When full, the box was weighted with large rocks, tied down with rope, and allowed to stand for a month. Weights were then removed and the process repeated four times. Cakes were then packed in an empty box (no cedar boughs) and stored for the winter. For use they were torn into strips, chopped with adzes, chewed, placed in a large pot covered with water, and boiled for an extended period until done. Kwakiutl Indians—a sea vegetable powder was made by hanging the freshly collected plants in individual strips on a drying rack suspended over the fire, until they were lightly browned on both sides. The dried strips were then placed in deer hide and beaten with a wedge to a fine powder, stored in boxes, and toasted over hot stones before serving. Prepared *Porphyra perforata* keeps well for one year.

Use: America (Kwakiutl and Haida Indians)—prepared sea vegetable cakes were dressed with oulachen (candlefish) oil and eaten with dried salmon or boiled dog salmon or with squeezed boiled clams. Toasted sea vegetable powder was eaten "as is" or mixed with water and beaten until it frothed and turned white, after which it was served with fresh berries.

(Kwakiutl Indians)—sun-dried pieces of Porphyra were eaten as a snack or boiled with clams or creamed corn to which a large amount of oulachen (candlefish) oil was added.

(Haida Indians)—sun-dried pieces eaten. Also eaten by the Seechelt, Squawmish, Nootka, Bellacoola, Tsimshian, and Tlingit Indians.

(Tsawtainuk Indians and white community of Kingcome Village, British Columbia)—sun-dried pieces of Porphyra cooked in creamed corn and the dish called Gluckaston.

Other Pacific tribes—eaten fresh or baked.

(Indians of southeastern Alaska)— pressed dried "cakes" or "plugs" shaved into warm water and boiled to a thick porridge. Cakes used as an article of barter between coastal and inland peoples. Eaten raw or dried, chopped and added to soups or stews (1 cup to 2 cups liquid).

Commander Islands (Bering Sea)— used for a dish similar to laverbread.

America (Japanese and Chinese communities)—used in soups, over rice, as tempura, etc.

Nutrients: Very high vitamin C, high protein. Also contains sugar, starch, vitamin B, and trace elements.

Taste: Plants prepared Indian-style considered highly superior in terms of tenderness to those prepared by the sun-dried process.

Commercial Source: Pacific Northwest America—collected privately and sold to local health food stores. Also collected by the Kwakiutl Indians and sold locally in British Columbia.

Recipes: Porphyra Chips (p. 168), Taiwanese Fisherman's Soup (p. 175), Porphyra Soup (p. 174), Grunting Fish Wrapped in Sea Vegetable, Indian Style (p. 260), Oulachen (Candlefish) in Sea Lettuce, Makah Indian Style (p. 261), Stuffed Porphyra Fronds (p. 215), Dilsea (p. 204), Mixed Sea Vegetable Tempura with Shrimp Cakes (p. 200), Laver and Pork Omelet (p. 201), Gluckaston (p. 222), Laverbread (p. 119), Steamed Sea Lettuce (p. 224), Nori Okazu (p. 224), Muck a Muck's Porphyra Condiment (p. 248), Homemade Laver Plugs (p. 255), Hawaiian Porphyra (p. 248), High-protein Porphyra Flour (p. 254).

FOLK NAMES

Kwakiutl Indians:

ihekesten, ihekas, atlebal (trans. **cooked Porphyra)**

Haida Indians:

summer seaweed

Alaskan Indians:

sea lettuce

Chinese:

chi choy

English:

purple laver

Japanese:

nori

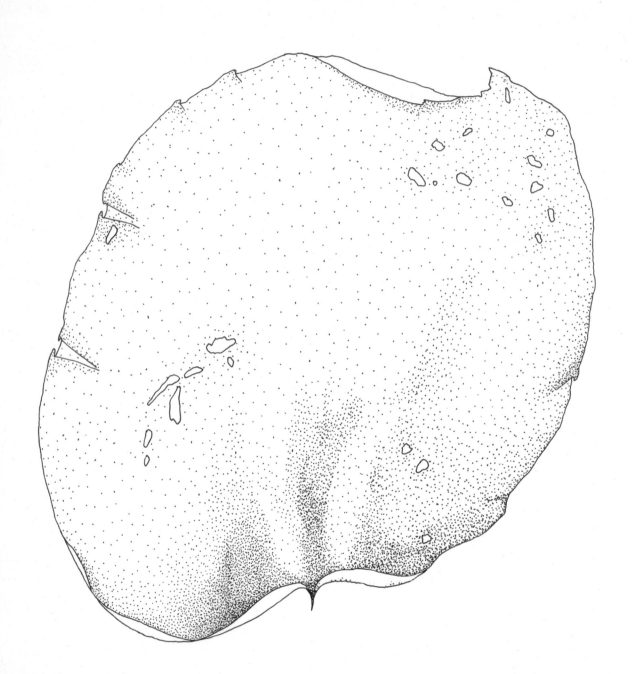

Phylum: Rhodophyta (Red Algae)

Porphyra suborbiculata

Kim

Description: Young plants pinkish, mature plants dark purplish. Circular frond in all stages of development. Young plants with edges entire, older plants with lobed edges. Plants slippery to touch and gelatinous.

Preparation: China—washed and spread on oiled circular sieves, sun dried, and marketed as thin circular sheets.

Japan—see *Porphyra tenera.*

Use: China (Amoy)—dried fronds used in soups.

Japan—prepared plants used in soups, pickles, and sweetmeats. Also manufactured into nori sheets.

Hong Kong—eaten.

Nutrients: High protein. Also contains sugar, starch, and trace elements.

Taste: Rich nutlike taste.

Commercial Source: China (Kwangtung Province, Amoy and Hong Kong)—sold in markets.

North America—imported from Japan and Korea and sold in health food stores, Oriental markets, etc., in major cities.

Recipes: Fillets in Nori Wrappers (p. 169), Toasted Kim (p. 168), Nori Meatball Soup (p. 173), Prophyra Soup (p. 174), Tsu Tsai and Egg Flower Soup from Shanghai (p. 174), Sargasso Sea Soup (p. 181), Scrambled Egg, Pork, and Porphyra Soup from Taiwan (p. 183), Stuffed Porphyra Fronds (p. 215), Sushimaki (p. 198), Mixed Sea Vegetable Tempura with Shrimp Cakes (p. 200), Laver and Pork Omelet (p. 201), Sashime (Raw Seafood) (p. 210), Rice with Beef, Eggs, and Nori Garnish (p. 206), Fish Rice with Nori Garnish (p. 212), Gluckaston (p. 222), Nori Okazu (p. 224), Korean Kim Candy (p. 236), Carrot Cake with Nori Flakes (p. 229), Japanese Sea Vegetable Condiment (Sake Ocha-Zuke Nori) (p. 249), Muck a Muck's Porphyra Condiment (p. 248), Rich Man's Laver (p. 251).

FOLK NAMES

Japan:

mambiama, maruba-amanori

China:

tsz tsai (trans. **purple vegetable), tsu tsoi (**trans. **purple vegetable), tsu tsai (**trans. **purple vegetable), chi tsai (**trans. **red vegetable), hung tsoi, hung tsai (**trans. **red vegetable), chi choy, hai tsai (**trans. **sea vegetable), hai tso (**trans. **seaweed)**

English:

purple laver, red laver

Korea:

kim

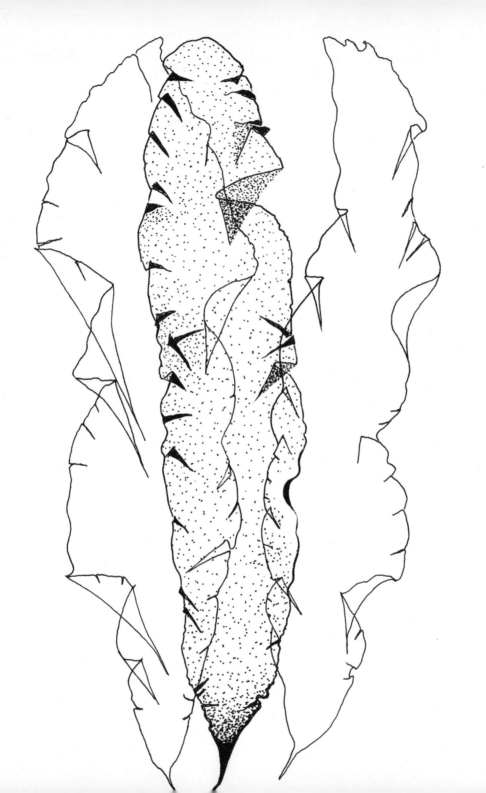

Phylum: Rhodophyta (Red Algae)

Porphyra tenera

Nori

Description: Plants light pink when young, dark purple when older. Plants about 10 inches tall. Long, narrow wavy-edged blade tapering at each end when young, widening or becoming slightly heart-shaped as plants mature. Gelatinous texture. Cushion-shaped holdfast.

Preparation: Japan—used fresh or washed, chopped, soaked in fresh water, spread out on screens, and sun dried into sheets.

China—washed, chopped, and spread on oiled circular sieves, then sun dried into thin circular sheets.

Korea—processing similar to Japan.

Use: China (Kwangtung)—used to produce a gel in cooking. Dried circular sheets used as a dry vegetable in sea vegetable soups or eaten with soy sauce.

Japan—a favorite lunch food in sheet form wrapped around rice. In early spring young blades are eaten fresh.

Korea—uses are similar to those in Japan.

USSR (Kamchatka Peninsula)—eaten.

Nutrients: Very high vitamin A, very high protein. Also contains starch, sugar, fat, niacin, vitamin B_2, vitamin B_1, vitamin C, vitamin D, phosphorus, sodium, calcium, iron, potassium, magnesium, aluminum, sulfur, silicon, chloride, soluble nitrogen, arsenic, iodine, and trace elements.

Taste: Delicious nutlike taste.

Commercial Souce: China—sold in markets of Kwangtung Province. Japan—prepared products produced in most prefectures. Natural Porphyra produced on Hokkaido and in Miyagi, Chiba, Ehime, and Shimane Prefectures. Also produced in Korea and China. Asakusa nori available dried (imported from Japan or Korea) in health food stores and Oriental markets in major cities. Also available, through mail-order sources.

Recipes: Fillets in Nori Wrappers (p. 169), Toasted Kim (p. 168), Nori Meatball Soup (p. 173), Porphyra Soup (p. 174), Tsu Tsai and Egg Flower Soup from Shanghai (p. 174), Sargasso Sea Soup (p. 181), Scrambled Egg, Pork, and Porphyra Soup from Taiwan (p. 183), Stuffed Porphyra Fronds (p. 215), Sushimaki (p. 198), Mixed Sea Vegetable Tempura with Shrimp Cakes (p. 200), Laver and Pork Omelet (p. 201), Sashime (Raw Seafood) (p. 210), Rice with Beef, Eggs, and Nori Garnish (p. 206), Fish Rice with Nori Garnish (p. 212), Gluckaston (p. 222), Nori Okazu (p. 224), Korean Kim Candy (p. 236), Carrot Cake with Nori Flakes (p. 229), Yogurt Drink (p. 241), Japanese Sea Vegetable Condiment (Sake Ocha-Zuke Nori) (p. 249), Muck a Muck's Porphyra Condiment (p. 248), Rich Man's Laver (p. 251).

FOLK NAMES

Japan:

Asakusa nori, amanori, hoshi-nori, kuro nori (trans. **black dried nori), sushi nori, chishima kuro-nori, tisima**

Korea:

kim

China:

tsz tsai (trans. **purple vegetable), tsu tsoi (**trans. **purple vegetable), tsu tsai (**trans. **purple vegetable), chi tsai (**trans. **red vegetable), hung tsoi, hung tsai (**trans. **red vegetable), chi choy, hai tsai (**trans. **sea vegetable), tai tso (**trans. **seaweed)**

English:

purple laver, red laver

USSR:

nuru

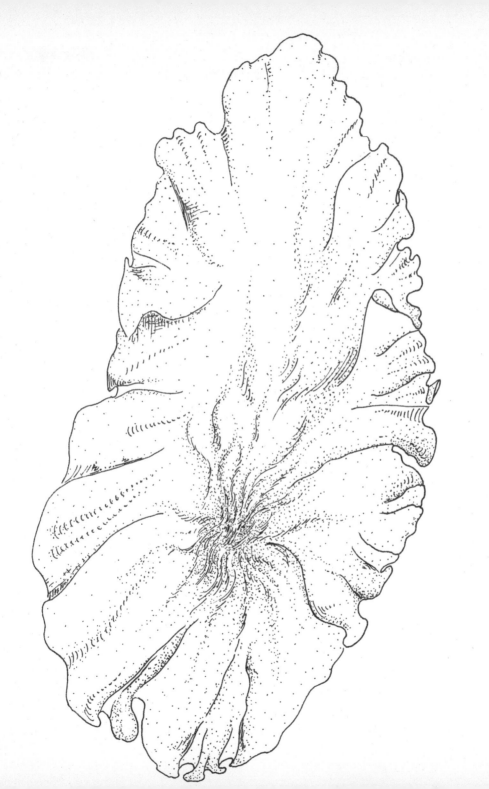

Phylum: Rhodophyta (Red Algae)
Porphyra umbilicalis

Purple Laver

Description: Plants brownish-purple to olive. Narrow when young. Mature plants large, long, broad, bending and wavy about the rounded base. Edges whole or divided into lobes. Thin, soft, but rubbery texture.

Habitat: Found on rocks and on wharfs from the midtide mark to the very low tide mark in the Temperate Zone of Atlantic coastal waters.

Foraging: An annual. Best plants to be found hanging from the undersides of boulders with their free ends in the water.

Preparation: Scotland, Ireland, Wales—prepared jellylike pulp of the boiled plants refrigerated until needed. Cleaned fresh plants can be refrigerated overnight for use the next day.

Use: South Wales, northern England, Scotland, Ireland—fresh cleaned plants sprinkled with oats, then fried in bacon fat (or butter in Ireland) and served as a breakfast dish called laverbread.

Wales, Scotland, Ireland—stewed or boiled with lemon juice or vinegar, oil, and pepper and served as an accompaniment to roast meats, especially mutton (the preparation called sloak, slook, slack, sloke, or marine sauce).

South Wales, England (Devon and Cornwall)—fresh young plants eaten as salad.

Nutrients: High protein. Also contains starch, sugar, fat, vitamin B, vitamin B_2, vitamin A, vitamin D, vitamin C, soluble nitrogen, iodine, and trace elements.

Taste: Good flavor but inferior in texture to the smaller more delicate plants of *Porphyra leucosticta*.

Commercial Source: Fresh product produced in South Wales (Cardiff), northern England, Ireland, and Scotland. Laverbread is served in fish houses in London and throughout the British Isles. Cleaned plants, sprinkled with oats and wrapped in cellophane (ready for cooking) are sold in corner grocery stores in Wales.

Recipes: Porphyra Chips (p. 168), Taiwanese Fisherman's Soup (p. 175), Porphyra Soup (p. 174), Stuffed Porphyra Fronds (p. 215), Dilsea (p. 204), Mixed Sea Vegetable Tempura with Shrimp Cakes (p. 200), Laverbread (p. 199), Gluckaston (p. 222), Steamed Sea Lettuce (p. 224), Muck a Muck's Porphyra Condiment (p. 248), Rich Man's Laver (p. 251), Homemade Laver Plugs (p. 255), Hawaiian Porphyra (p. 248), High-protein Porphyra Flour (p. 254).

FOLK NAMES
English:
purple laver
Scotland:
sloak
British Isles:
slook
Wales:
laver

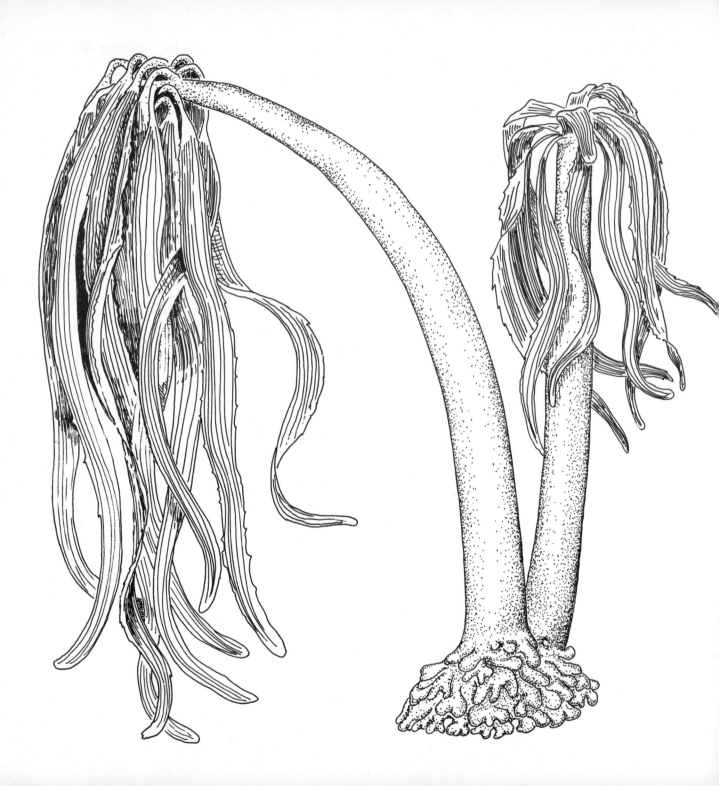

Phylum: Phaeophyta (Brown Algae)

Postelsia palmaeformis

Sea Palm

Description: Plants bright olive to forest green, up to 2 feet tall. Stipes smooth, erect, bending to the tide. Crown of long, thin, corrugated blades hanging down from crest. Conical-shaped holdfast with the appearance of carefully dripped wax.

Habitat: Found on rocks and cliffs exposed to full force of constant, strong surf in the Temperate Zone of eastern Pacific coastal waters.

Foraging: Some readily accessible "groves" do exist and can be seen when plants are periodically exposed by receding waves. But many situations on partially submerged surf-washed rock ledges are difficult to reach. Freshly cast-up plants can be gathered. If plants are fresh, stipes will snap crisply when bent. Peak harvest early spring. Cut or scraped from rocks.

Preparation: America—prepared as Nereocystis (see recipe for Nereocystis Sweet Pickles).
Japanese community in San Francisco—crest of blades is removed from fresh plants. Stipes are then washed in fresh water, cut into bite-sized strips, then boiled or steamed. Washed or unwashed blades can be sun dried.

Use: America—stipes used as a substitute for *Nereocystis luetkeana*, pickled or candied for storage as a preserve. Sun-dried blades can be eaten as snacks.
Japanese community in San Francisco—stipes boiled or steamed and eaten chilled, dressed with lemon juice and soy sauce.

Nutrients: High bromine. Also contains sugar, starch, and trace elements.

Taste: Steamed plants are quite special and delicious.

Recipe: Steamed Sea Palm (p. 193), Nereocystis Sweet Pickles (p. 244).

FOLK NAME

America:

sea palm

Phylum: Phaeophyta (Brown Algae)

Sargassum fulvellum

Mojaban

Description: Plants light brown, soft body, 1½ to 5 yards tall. Stipe twists around, finally fans out slightly to become holdfast on one end, dividing into branches on top. Lower blades spatula- or needle-shaped with toothed edges. Blades thick in texture. Upper blades narrow or needle-shaped. Oval air sacs attached along branches. Sacs round or pointed, sometimes possessing small blades.

Preparation: Japan—used fresh. Korea—used fresh or sun dried for storage.

Use: Japan—fresh young "bud" used in soup or dressed with soybean sauce. Korea—dried plant is first hydrated in fresh water, then cooked with garlic, spices, green onion (scallion), and hot red peppers. Served as a main dish.

Nutrients: High iodine. Also contains sugar, starch, potassium, iron, and trace elements.

Gel: Algin.

Taste: Blades have very tender texture, although they are thick.

Commercial Source: Mojaban is sold dried in Korean markets in major cities.

Recipes: Sargasso Sea Soup (p. 181), Hawaiian Sargassum (p. 248).

FOLK NAMES

Japan:

hondawara

English:

horsetail tangle

Korea:

mojaban

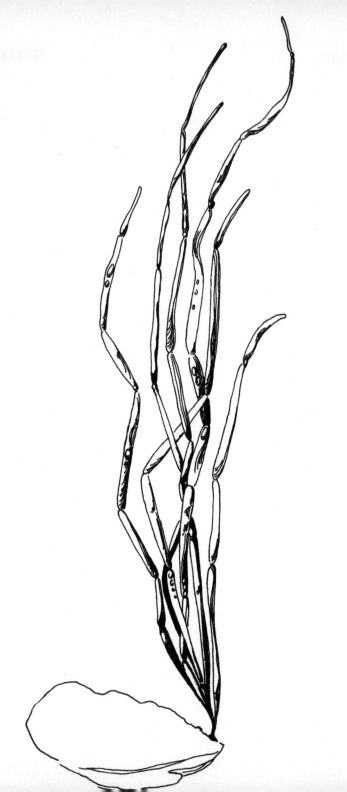

Phylum: Phaeophyta (Brown Algae)

Scytosiphon lomentaria

Sugara

Description: Plants olive-green, 8 to 20 inches tall. Hollow, narrow cordlike body, unbranched, narrow at base, slightly wider at tip. Obvious ringed constrictions along body at varying intervals, like a chain of link sausages.
Habitat: Found growing in groups or clumps on rocks in shallow rock pools near the high tide mark in the Temperate Zones of coastal waters all over the world.

Foraging: Plants can be cut or pulled from rocks at low tide.
Preparation: Japan—washed and sun dried or prepared as sheets like *Porphyra tenera.*
Use: Japan—young "bud" used as a substitute for Undaria, mixed into miso soup or made into dried sheets.
Nutrients: Very high iron. Also contains sugar, starch, and trace elements.
Taste: Beanlike taste. Must be dried before use (drying serves to tenderize fronds and improve taste).
Commercial Source: Japan—produced in all coastal areas.
Recipes: Wakame Soup (p. 182).

FOLK NAMES

Japan:

kayamonori, sugara, mugiwara-nori

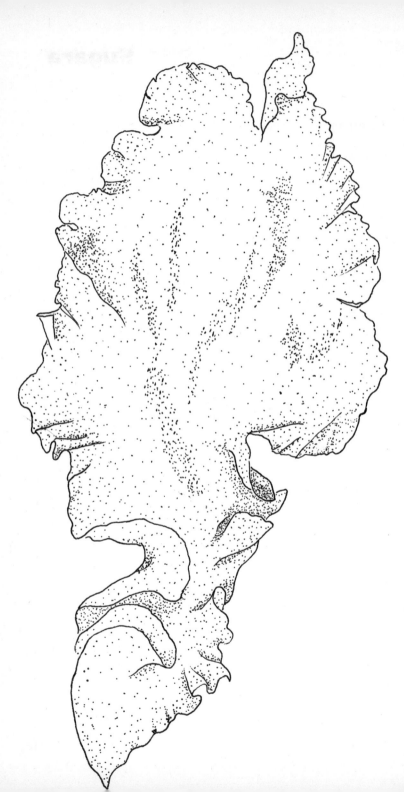

Phylum: Chlorophyta (Green Algae)

Ulva lactuca

Description: Plants bright yellowish-green. Leaflike with undulating wide blades. Blades up to 8 inches tall, heart-shaped, oval, or nondescript, occasionally with some small holes. Like waxed paper to touch.

Habitat: Found in moderately exposed situations on rocks, woodwork, or coarse algae, in pools and quiet shallow waters near the low tide mark. Thrives in brackish water with organic pollution, in coastal waters all over the world.

Foraging: An annual blade, with a perennial holdfast. Harvest young plants in early spring for taste and tenderness. Late spring for high vitamin C (ascorbic acid). Blades are cut or plucked from the rocks at low tide. Drifting plants can be harvested if fresh.

Preparation: Wash well in fresh water, drain, and sun dry. Or use fresh.
Hong Kong—fresh algae is chopped finely and spread on oiled circular bamboo trays and sun dried.
Chile—the Ulva is combined with Porphyra and then partially sun dried for sale.

Use: Scotland—added to soups or salads.
China and Hong Kong—cooked with oysters, meat, and a small amount of noodles or combined with *Hizikia fusiforme* (hoi tsou) in soups.
Eastern Asia—used in soups, as salad, or for garnish.
Philippines (Llocos Norte Province)—used raw in salads combined with sliced tomatoes, onions, vinegar, salt, and black or red pepper, or cooked with vegetables.
Taiwan and Mainland China—added to soups or cooked with meat or fish.
Jamaica and Trinidad—eaten fresh in salads.
Barbados—brewed into a tea.
Chile and Peru—used in soups, as salad, or cooked with other vegetables.
Chile—half-dried balls made up of mixes of *Porphyra columbina* and *Ulva lactuca* are fried and mixed with small pieces of meat.

Nutrients: Very high iron. High protein, iodine, aluminum manganese, and nickel. Also contains starch, sugar, fat, vitamin A, vitamin B_1, vitamin C, sodium, potassium, magnesium, calcium, soluble nitrogen, phosphorus, sulfur, chloride, silicon, rubidium, strontium, barium, radium, cobalt, boron, arsenic, and trace elements.

Taste: Fresh plants are rather coarse and tough in texture unless chopped finely.

Commercial Source: Sold fresh, dried, or in various stages of preparation in markets of Chile, Peru, Iceland, Hong Kong, Malaya (Singapore), Philippines (Llocos Norte Province), China (Kwangtung Province, Hainan, Amoy, Swatow, Pen-Tsao-Kang-Mu, Canton), and Taiwan.

Recipes: Ulva Soup (p. 180), Mixed Sea Vegetable Salad (p. 188), Sea Lettuce Salad (p. 192), Grunting Fish Wrapped in Sea Vegetable, Indian Style (p. 260), Oulachen (Candlefish) in Sea Lettuce, Makah Indian Style (p. 261), Steamed Sea Lettuce (p. 224), Hot Ulva Relish (p. 247), Hawaiian Ulva (p. 246), Powdered Green Sea Vegetable Seasoning (Aonoriko (p. 253).

FOLK NAMES

Western usage:

sea lettuce

Iceland:

lettuce laver, green laver, sea grass

China:

hai tsai (trans. sea vegetable), shih shun, haisai, kun-po, kwanpo

Kwakiutl Indians:

ihixlhewis

Quileute Indians:

klop-tsai-yup (trans. green ocean leaves)

Germany:

meersalat (trans. sea salad)

China:

thin stone brick

Japan:

aosa

Chile:

luche, luchi

Philippines:

gamgamet

Phylum: Phaeophyta (Brown Algae)

Undaria pinnatifida

Wakame

Description: Plants medium to dark brown, 2 to 4 feet long and 12 to 16 inches wide. Blade soft, dividing into winglike protrusions. Thick mucilaginous center vein. Holdfast fibrous and repeatedly divided. Northern variety (nanbu wakame) longer with fruit-bearing blades arising from the lower stipe and blade more deeply divided. Southern variety has shorter stipe with fruit-bearing leaves arising from the upper stipe.

Preparation: Japan—drying techniques differ in each prefecture from south Ibaraki to north Miyagi Prefecture. Sold fresh only in early spring. Desalted product may be ash dried or blanched and dried. The fresh sea vegetable is washed in seawater or fresh water, then sun dried, washed with seawater again, "kneaded" (surface rubbed off), and again sun dried. After washing in fresh water the plant may also be prepared with center vein removed then hung up to dry on ropes and, when half dried, "kneaded," shaved, roasted, or sugarcoated.
Korea—the sun-dried plant is hydrated or blanched before use.

Use: Japan—dried, hydrated plants are added to miso soup, salads, pork, poultry, fish, and especially bean curd dishes. Plants used baked or dried as a snack or garnish for rice dishes. Fresh or hydrated plants prepared as a vegetable side dish or cooked with rice vinegar.
Korea—added to soups, usually meat or egg soups.

Nutrients: High protein, high iron, high calcium, high sodium, high magnesium. Also contains starch, sugar, fat, vitamin A, vitamin B_1, vitamin C, vitamin B_2, phosphorus, potassium, nitrogen, sulfur, selenium, and trace elements.

Gel: Algin.

Taste: Sweet taste, delicate texture. Naruto wakame considered the best product.

Commercial Source: Produced in Japan.
America—sold, dried, in Japanese and Korean markets and health food stores in major cities. Also available from mail-order sources.

Recipes: Split Pea and Wakame Soup (p. 177), Chinese-style Soup with Wakame (p. 179), Wakame Soup (p. 182), Sea Vegetable Soup with Bean Curd (p. 181), Miyok-kuk (Korean Sea Vegetable Soup) (p. 181), Sargasso Sea Soup (p. 181), Cucumber and Wakame Salad (p. 192), Wakame, Cucumber, and Radish Salad (p. 193), Mixed Sea Vegetable Tempura with Shrimp Cakes (p. 200), Wakame and Dried Shrimp with Ginger (p. 223), Wakame in Sweet and Sour Sauce (p. 223), Wakame and Shredded Dried Bonito (p. 225).

FOLK NAMES
Japan:
wakame
Korea:
miyok

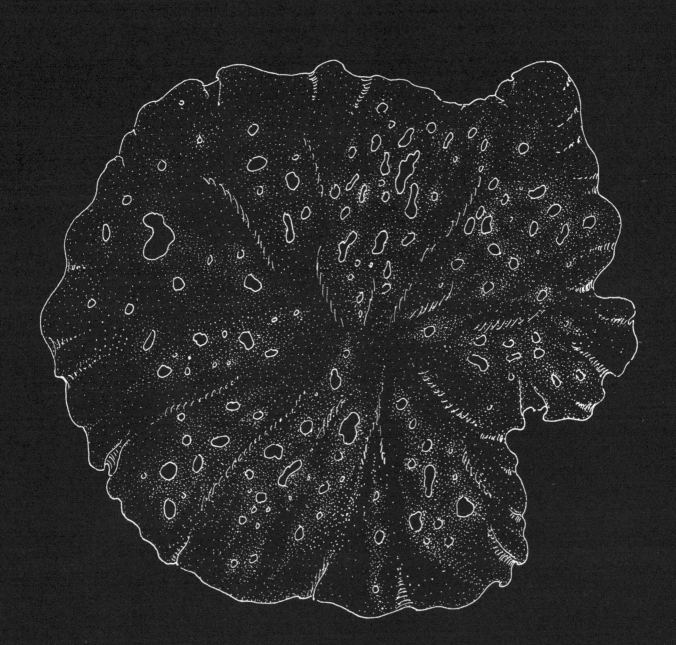

Cooking with sea vegetables

COOKING WITH SEA VEGETABLES

The methods used to cook sea vegetables determine whether and to what extent nutritive values are preserved. When processed or cooked, sea vegetables behave much the same as land vegetables. Just as it is possible to take fresh spinach, beets, or carrots and rob them of their less stable vitamins through improper or prolonged cooking, so it is with algae. One must always follow the common rules for producing healthful cooked dishes.

Blanching vs. boiling   Boiling vegetables is one of the quickest and surest ways of destroying vitamins and other nutritious substances, for cooking water is usually poured down the drain after use and the bulk of soluble nutrients is lost. The time involved in boiling a vegetable to the point of tenderness is also enough to drive off the volatile vitamins. Blanching is a far superior method.

Steaming   The best method, in terms of conserving nutrients, is really steaming. Steaming does not call for immersion of the plant, and it permits very little water to touch the vegetable. In order to steam fresh or hydrated sea vegetables properly, it is necessary to rinse the plants and then shake off the excess water. They should then be placed in a steaming device inside a lidded pot. The steamer will elevate the vegetables above the inch or so of water which is used in the bottom of the pot, while allowing the steam to rise and cook the food. Care must be taken to replace evaporated water so that it does not boil off completely and burn both pan and vegetables. Steaming is at least twice as fast as boiling and the small amount of water used can then be added to gravies, sauces, etc.

Stir frying   Stir frying is another quick and healthful way of preparing vegetables. Most fresh and many hydrated sea vegetables can be cooked this way. *Laminaria, Alaria,* and related genera don't take well to stir frying unless they are first precooked. Parboiling these plants before they are stir fried, sautéed, or prepared as tempura, produces excellent results. For stir frying, sea vegetables should be rinsed, drained, cut into bite-sized uniform pieces, dried on an absorbent towel, then moved around very quickly in a small amount of hot oil. As the vegetables are tossed in the hot cooking oil, they become coated and their nutrients are sealed within.

Herbs and spices   Sea vegetables will lend themselves to a wide variety of herbs and spices, as is evidenced in the diverse algal cuisines around the world. There are no hard and fast rules for the use of these flavoring ingredients except when it comes to salt.

   Salt, when added at the beginning of the cooking, will have time to draw out the natural juices of any food. A sprinkling of salt is best added when food is nearly cooked, moments before it is removed from the heat.

Rules of thumb   As for other rules of thumb regarding sea vegetable cookery, one or two things are worth mentioning. Soups or stews made with algae tend to be best tasting when newly prepared. Sea vegetables should not be left to soak overnight in the liquid.

It is not advisable to leave most prepared foods unrefrigerated for extended periods. Sea vegetable dishes are no exception. Delicate forms of fresh algae will react as does lettuce; they will wilt and become unappetizing. Sea vegetables, properly prepared, are a delight to the senses.

But whether your sea vegetables are foraged or bought, whether they have come halfway across the world or have been gathered from local shores, uncommon pleasures await those willing to try something just a little bit extraordinary.

Selecting recipes It is best, when beginning to use any unfamiliar food, to start out gradually, attempting to prepare only one dish at a time. Try a sea vegetable garnish (Fish Rice with Nori Garnish, p. 211), a soup (Dulse Miso Soup, p. 186), a sea vegetable accompaniment to a main course (Rich Man's Laver, p. 251), or a one or two vegetable tempura dish (Sea Vegetable Tempura with Shrimp Cakes, p. 200). Add more sea vegetable dishes to the meal as your competence grows. In no time at all you will feel comfortable preparing an all-algal meal. Don't be afraid to experiment and create new taste combinations.

Perhaps the simplest way would be to start with those varieties most commonly available sun dried from health food stores. These species with their commercial folk names would include: *Palmaria palmata* = dulse in English; *Chondrus crispus* = Irish moss in English; *Porphyra* (various species) = nori in Japanese, laver in English, kim in Korean, and chi choy in Chinese; *Undaria pinnatifida* = wakame in Japanese or miyok in Korean; *Eisenia bicyclis* = arame in Japanese; and *Laminaria* (various species) = kombu in Japanese, haetae and tasima in Korean, and hai dai in Chinese.

BUYING SEA VEGETABLES

With knowledge of a few of the most used terms, it is easy to make one's way through the aisles of packaged sea vegetables. In Japanese markets subtle distinctions are made among the varieties of sea vegetables and sea vegetable products. These are denoted by the names listed in the Appendix. Other words appearing on the packages usually indicate the manufacturer's name or a brand name.

Basic commercial sea vegetables are as follows:

JAPAN

kombu—sold dried for use as a cooked vegetable or for making soup stock.
hijiki—sold dried for use as a cooked vegetable.
wakame—sold dried or blanched, salted, and vacuum packed for soups, salads, or as vegetable.
arame—sold dried for use as a cooked vegetable.
nori—sold dried for wrapping around rice or for use in soups or as a garnish.
mozuku—sold lightly brined and vacuum packed for use in soups or as a salad.
ogo nori (ogo)—sold blanched for use as salad.
funori—sold dried for use as a cooked vegetable.

The products found in Korean, Chinese, Thai, and West Indian grocery stores are limited to dried sea vegetable plants and don't include the innumerable prepared items sold in Japanese markets. For ease in shopping for these various items, they are listed by folk name according to country or geographical area. Sometimes these names will vary slightly according to the province from which the shopkeeper hails.

KOREA

kim—sold dried for wrapping around rice, etc.
nongmichae—sold dried for use as vegetable.
tasima (haetar) haetae—sold dried for use as a cooked vegetable or for making soup stock.
miyok—sold dried for use in soups.
parae—sold dried for use as a garnish.
chonggak—sold dried for use as a spice or sold dried and powdered for use as tea.
mojaban—sold dried for use as a cooked vegetable.

CHINA

fah tsoi (fah tsai)—sold dried for use as a cooked vegetable.
hai dai—sold dried for use as a cooked vegetable or for making soup stock.
chi choy—sold dried for wrapping around rice and for use in soups or as a garnish.

WEST INDIES

sea moss—sold dried for use in making beverages and gelatins.

CANADA, BRITISH ISLES, UNITED STATES

dulse—sold semidried for use as a snack, condiment, or vegetable.
Irish moss—sold dried for making gelatin and for use as a vegetable.
bladderwrack—sold chopped and dried for use as tea.
powdered kelp—used as a seasoning.
edible kelp (Alaria)—sold dried for use as a cooked vegetable.

THAILAND

sa-lai-thalee—various sea vegetables, sold dried.

Consumer advice on buying   Checking on the product quality of commercial algae is not so difficult as one might think. The foreign companies dealing with various aspects of the sea vegetable industry are governed by health laws in their respective countries. Japan as the major exporter of algal products enforces strict sanitary laws regulating food products.

It is not necessary to deal only with major companies to ensure product quality. Checking the sources of algae gathered by individuals and purveyed to health food stores, etc., can be done with a little effort. Ask your local shop owner where the sea vegetable comes from, what the genus and species names are, and how it is processed for sale. He should know this. If he doesn't, ask him to find out for you. These kinds of inquiries on the part of the consumer will quickly raise the level of consciousness of both the store owner and the harvester. It will avoid mislabeling of products owing to ignorance of the genus and species to which they belong, and halt the confusion arising from the flagrant coining of arbitrary folk names. The consumer should no more have to open up a bag labeled Pacific dulse, purchased in a local store, and find *Porphyra nereocystis* instead of *Palmaria palmata,* than he should have to ask for mushrooms and be sold black-eyed peas!

Standards   There are a few recognized standards that may be applied when purchasing commercially produced nori *(Porphyra)*. Plants, harvested when young and tender, have rich color and a shiny surface. This indicates that they are from the "first picking" and have been carefully sun dried without coming in contact with fresh water of any kind, including rain. This is the best product available in terms of nutrition, taste and tenderness.

The prepared sheets of nori are rated on the basis of the number of tiny pieces of chopped *Porphyra* per square inch and on the closeness of these pieces on the sheet. That is, sheets of nori which are filled with holes are considered of inferior quality and are used mostly in soups. Sheets whose surfaces are entire are of the best quality and are used to wrap around sushi rice. Prices vary according to quality.

Occasionally sea vegetables are sold which still contain bits of sand. However, these instances are rare, and a quick swish in a pan of tepid water will do the job.

Quality is very high for the majority of sea vegetables available commercially. The different grades are most often clearly marked on the packages.

Product adulteration   Some companies use ingredients like refined sugar and synthetic monosodium glutamate (MSG) in their algal products; this is a problem for those who consider these ingredients detrimental to health. It is possible to find exceptions by checking labels carefully. The combination of sodium salts and glutamic acid occurs naturally, as a taste-producing entity in many sea vegetables. The substance is largely accountable for the refined taste quality of the classic soup stock made from certain species of kombu and basic to all Japanese cooking.

The dyeing of some sea vegetables with malachite green and certain red dyes is done by some companies. Unnatural tone and uniformity in the color of the product make it obvious when this has been done. Many producers are now giving up on this artificiality and returning to all-natural processing. I would hope that the use of artificial ingredients in sea vegetables is on the wane. Public opinion can quickly convince the largest of companies that adulteration of their food products will deter sales.

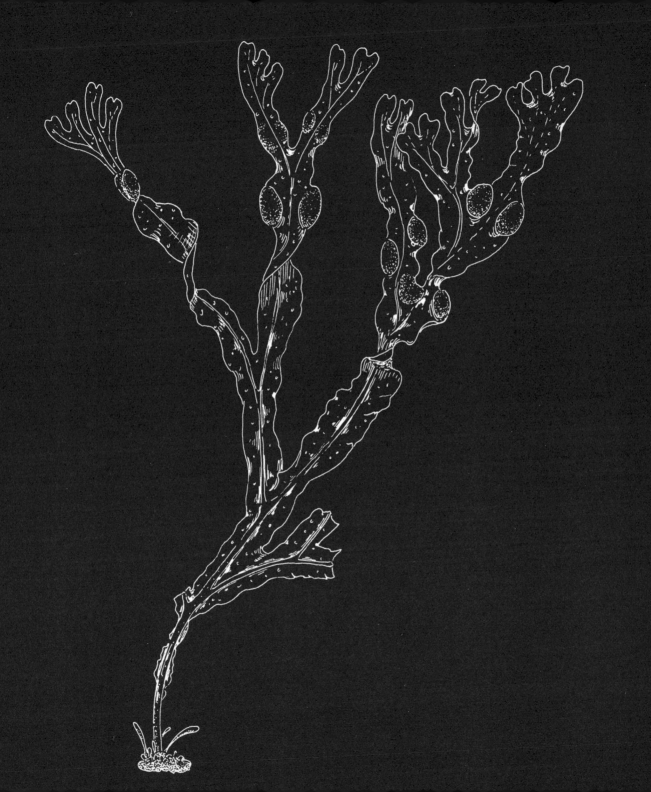

Sea vegetable recipes

Appetizers and snacks

Ham and Laminaria rolls
West Coast snack
Fried sweet kelp chips
Shanghai spring rolls
Porphyra chips
Toasted kim
Fillets in nori wrappers

Laminaria angustata

Ham and Laminaria rolls

Quick and easy party snacks don't have to be fattening or nonnutritious.

10 pieces dried Laminaria
10 slices smoked ham
water
¼ cup soy sauce
3 tablespoons honey
string or toothpicks

Substitutes

Laminaria longissima
Pleurophycus gardneri

- Soak the Laminaria for 1 hour in enough cold water to cover. Drain. Cut it into large rectangles and cut ham to same size.
- Place a slice of ham on top of each piece of sea vegetable and roll up from one end. Tie with a piece of string or pin with toothpicks.
- Place in a saucepan. Pour in water to cover. Add soy sauce and honey.
- Cook over medium heat uncovered until the liquid is almost evaporated and the Laminaria is soft (about 30 minutes).

Laminaria saccharina

West coast snack

Makes a healthful snack for the children!

- Rinse sea vegetable in cold water to remove any sand. Spread out in strong sun and wind until completely dry. Store in plastic bags.
- When ready to use, snip into 2- to 3-inch pieces or squares and bake at 200 degrees for 15 to 20 minutes.
- Prepare marinade, mixing well. Place partially toasted strips in the marinade and toss to coat.
- Place coated strips on a foil-lined baking sheet and bake at 200 degrees for about 20 to 30 minutes, turning at intervals until crisp.

MARINADE
½ cup soy sauce
½ cup honey

Substitutes

Pleurophycus gardneri
Laminaria japonica

Laminaria (various species)

Fried sweet kelp chips

Laminaria, gathered and sold commercially in North America, is often labeled kombu. The thinner, more delicate species are delicious prepared this way.

16 cups fresh kelp fronds

- Dried Laminaria may be fried in oil as is, without soaking in water. Just cut the large fronds into squares or rectangles of about 1 inch by 2 inches and fry in peanut oil, a few at a time. Remove to an absorbent paper towel.
- Sprinkle with raw sugar. Serve.

Substitutes

Pleurophycus gardneri
Laminaria saccharina

Monostroma (various species)

Shanghai spring rolls

ABOUT 18 SPRING ROLLS

For an even more delicious flavor, the Thais heat the hot chili oil with some ground peanuts. Guests then turn the 1-inch rounds on edge and fill each with a teaspoon of hot peanut sauce.

Spring roll skins are also known as Shanghai-type spring roll skins and are available in some Oriental markets in 1-pound packages. Substitutes: Lumpia skins, available in Philippine markets, may be substituted. Egg roll skins may also be substituted, but they are much thicker.

Substitutes

Enteromorpha (various species)

SPRING ROLL SKINS

1 cup unbleached white flour
½ teaspoon sea salt
2 eggs, beaten
about 2 cups water
vegetable oil

SPRING ROLL FILLING

peanut oil
omelet slivers (2 eggs)
½ cup fresh Monostroma fronds
2 celery ribs, sliced thinly on diagonal
1 pound mung bean sprouts
¾ cup matchstick-cut bamboo shoots
¼ cup matchstick-cut water chestnuts
2 teaspoons light soy sauce
½ teaspoon honey
½ pound flaked crab meat
½ teaspoon sesame oil
2 tablespoons minced scallion
2 tablespoons cornstarch
coriander sprigs (cilantro)
Chinese mustard
Chinese hot chili oil

- Sift flour and salt into mixing bowl. Add eggs and enough water to make a smooth, thin batter similar to crepe batter. Always beat batter in one direction to gain elasticity. Let stand 20 minutes.
- Lightly oil a 6-inch skillet or crepe pan and heat over low heat. Beat batter in same direction and pour 2 tablespoons into pan, tilting pan to cover entire surface with batter.
- Cook until set. Pancake should be sheer and pliable. When it shrinks away slightly from the edges, turn over and cook just to set. Remove to flat dish and cover with slightly dampened tea towel.
- Repeat process with remaining batter, oiling pan as necessary, remembering to stir batter in one direction each time.

- Prepare an omelet by beating the eggs thoroughly and pouring quickly into a hot, oiled skillet. Tilt the pan quickly to ensure a thin, even coat. Cook. Allow to cool and cut into slivers.
- Wash the sea vegetable fronds quickly in cold water. Do not soak! Drain. Chop finely.
- Heat peanut oil and stir fry celery, bean sprouts, bamboo shoots, chopped sea vegetable, and chestnuts with 2 teaspoons soy sauce, and ½ teaspoon honey for 2 minutes. Stir in crab and remove from heat.
- Pour off any juices and add sesame oil, scallion, cornstarch, and omelet slivers.
- Cool and place 3 tablespoons of mixture on edge of spring roll skin. Place a coriander sprig on top and fold skin over twice. Then fold in sides and roll like a jelly roll. Deep fry, seam side down, in peanut oil until crisp and golden. Drain, cut into 1-inch slices.
- Serve immediately with separate dips of mustard, Chinese chili oil, and soy sauce.

Porphyra miniata

Porphyra chips

This is best prepared just before using, as Porphyra read-ily absorbs moisture from the air and is tastiest when crisp. When these tasty chips are ready they are placed in stacks and fastened with toothpicks. Otherwise the slightest breeze would float them off the plate.

● Wash fresh Porphyra quickly in cold water to remove any sand. Do not soak! Spread out in strong sun and breeze until completely dry. Store in plastic bags.
● When ready to use, snip into 2- to 3-inch strips and bake at 200 degrees for 20 to 30 minutes until crisp. Eat like potato chips, with tea or cocktails.

Substitutes

Porphyra (various species)

Porphyra suborbiculata

Toasted kim

6 SERVINGS

● Mix the salt and oil together. Rub a thin coat of this mixture on one side of each dried sea vegetable sheet. Lay the sheets one atop another. Roll them up and allow them to stand for 5 minutes.
● Unroll, separate, and broil each sheet directly over a low flame in a hot pan until it is crisp. Cut each sheet into 4 pieces and serve with hot rice or with cocktails.

Substitutes

Porphyra (various species)

Porphyra tenera

Fillets in nori wrappers

As a testimonial to the instant and overwhelming success of this dish, I prepared some 65 pieces and saw them devoured as an appetizer by my 8 dinner guests, leaving me without a main course!

2 pounds fish fillets (tight fleshed fish)
10 sheets dried nori
½ cup whole wheat flour
½ cup wheat germ
1 teaspoon Japanese chili powder
2 to 3 eggs, beaten
peanut oil

- Wash fish and pat dry with a clean towel. Cut fillets to about 2 inches by 4 inches.
- Cut nori sheets in fours. Wrap the nori around the fillets.
- Combine the flour, wheat germ, and chili powder. Paint each wrapper with beaten egg and roll in the flour mixture. Coat about 6 to 8 at a time and fry in hot peanut oil until they become a rich golden brown. Then turn and fry the other side.
- Serve hot.

Substitute

Porphyra suborbiculata

Porphyra (various species)

Soups

Soup with slivered kombu
Alaria vegetable soup
Mackerel soup
Dashi kombu (or soup stock)
Nori meatball soup
Tsu tsai and egg flower soup from Shanghai
Porphyra soup
Taiwanese fisherman's soup
Mozuku in miso soup
Pacific sea vegetable soup
Dulse miso soup
Chinook-style chowder with slivered dulse
Split pea and wakame soup
Codfish chowder with rockweed flavoring
Hai dai sweet soup
Chinese-style soup with wakame
Ulva soup
Miyok-kuk (Korean sea vegetable soup)
Sargasso Sea soup
Sea vegetable soup with bean curd
Irish moss soup
Wakame soup
Arame soup
Scrambled egg, pork, and Porphyra soup from Taiwan

*Alaria esculenta, Laminaria
longipedalis and L. diabolica*

Soup with slivered kombu

4 SERVINGS

*Dried slivered kombu is available commercially as
kizami kombu. Alaria foraged and sold commercially in
North America is often labeled wakame. This is a very
basic soup to which a number of foods, especially leftover fish, might be added.*

**1 quart water
1 tablespoon dehydrated vegetable powder
½ cup slivered kombu (page 256)**

● Place water, vegetable powder, and slivered Alaria
in a saucepan. Cover and simmer for about 2 hours or
until sea vegetable is tender. Serve.

Substitutes

*Laminaria digitata
L. longicruris*

Alaria esculenta

Alaria vegetable soup

6 TO 8 SERVINGS

**¼ cup dried Alaria
2 quarts water
oil for sautéing
4 carrots, cut into chunks
2 onions, cut into chunks
2 tablespoons miso
sea salt
cracked pepper**

● Soak the Alaria overnight in 2 quarts of water. Drain.
Cut the frond across the midrib into ½-inch pieces.
Sauté the sea vegetable in a small amount of oil until it
becomes bright green and sweetly aromatic. Place it in a
deep pot and add the soaking water. Boil uncovered for a
half hour. Add more water if necessary to cover the
Alaria. Cover and boil for an hour and a quarter.
● Add the carrots and onions. Cover. Boil another 45
minutes.
● Remove from heat. Add miso. Season. Serve.

Substitutes

Alaria (various species)

Laminaria ochotensis

Mackerel soup

4 SERVINGS

This soup makes a particularly attractive first course with the beautiful markings on the fish skin glistening through the clear broth.

¼ pound mackerel, split (skin on)
salt
2 radishes, cut lengthwise into ¼-inch pieces
1½ pints water
one 5-inch piece of dashi kombu
2 tablespoons rice wine
1 teaspoon rice vinegar
1 tablespoon scallion, sliced into ⅛-inch pieces

● Cut each mackerel fillet into 4 pieces. Sprinkle with salt. Let stand for 1 to 2 hours.
● Wash the mackerel, pour boiling water over the pieces, then wash again with cold water. Place mackerel in a pan with the radishes cut lengthwise, dashi kombu, water, and wine. Bring the liquid to the boiling point, then remove the sea vegetable for use in another recipe. Reduce heat and simmer for 20 minutes, removing any froth.
● Add vinegar and salt to taste. Pour into a tureen and sprinkle with scallion. Serve.

Substitutes

*Laminaria japonica, L. angustata,
L. longissima, L. digitata, Kjellmaniella gyrata*

Laminaria ochotensis

Kombu dashi (or soup stock)

ABOUT 3 CUPS

Kombu dashi is the basic soup stock of Japanese cuisine. Its uncomplicated yet refined taste suits the Japanese palate.

● Use a length of dried kombu about 4 inches wide by 6 inches long. Place it in a pot with about 3 cups of water. Bring the water just to the boiling point. Do not allow the water to boil because this will produce a less than subtle stock.

● The spent kombu can then be steamed or boiled again in fresh water and eaten as a vegetable.

Laminaria japonica, L. angustata,
L. longissima, L. digitata, Kjellmaniella gyrata

Porphyra tenera

Nori meatball soup

4 TO 6 SERVINGS

This hearty soup is a meal in itself. Porphyra substantially increases the protein value without increasing the caloric value.

MEATBALLS

1 pound ground beef
1 egg
1 tablespoon cornstarch
2 tablespoons soy sauce
2 teaspoons salt
1 teaspoon crushed red pepper
2 tablespoons water
½ teaspoon honey

SOUP

1 bouillon cube
4 cups water
2 sheets dried nori
salt and pepper
½ teaspoon sesame oil
2 stalks chopped scallions

Substitutes

Porphyra (various species)

● Prepare meatball mixture, blending well. Shape into teaspoon-sized balls.
● Dissolve bouillon cube in boiling water.
● Cut the nori into strips about 1 inch by 3 inches. Add the nori and stir with a fork. When the nori is soft, drop the meatballs into the boiling soup. Add salt and pepper to taste.
● When ready to serve, pour the soup into bowls, float a little sesame oil on top of each and sprinkle with chopped scallions.

Porphyra (various species)

Shanghai
Tsu tsai and egg flower soup

4 SERVINGS

Soups made with whole eggs are called expensive soups in China.

3 sheets dried Porphyra or ¾ cup dried fronds
2 eggs
1 or 2 stalks scallion (green part only)
6 cups chicken broth
white pepper
1 tablespoon sesame oil

- Tear the laver into 1-inch pieces.
- Beat the eggs thoroughly.
- Cut ¼-cup scallion greens into ¼-inch pieces.
- Bring broth to a boil and add salt to taste. Add scallion and Porphyra. Stir.
- Pour in egg mixture. Allow soup to come to a boil. Remove from heat. Stir. Sprinkle with white pepper.
- Pour into a soup tureen. Float the sesame oil on top. Serve.

Porphyra (various species)

Porphyra soup

3 TO 4 SERVINGS

Porphyra consists of about 20 percent protein while possessing very few calories.

1 tablespoon salad oil
1 small onion, thinly sliced
½ cup thinly sliced celery
¼-inch fresh ginger, minced
1 tablespoon soy sauce
1 14-ounce can beef broth
1 cup water
½ cup dried crumbled Porphyra
½ cup slivered Porphyra from homemade plugs,
   (page 255)

- Heat oil in a saucepan over a medium flame and sauté the onion and celery until the onion is translucent, 5 to 7 minutes.
- Stir in the ginger, soy sauce, beef broth, water, and sea vegetable. Bring to a boil. Reduce heat and simmer covered for 5 minutes.

Monostroma (various species)

Taiwanese fisherman's soup

4 TO 6 SERVINGS

In rural coastal areas, fishermen cook with a great variety of sea vegetables. Seasonally available algae is popped into the cooking pot and boiled up with the day's catch of fish.

1 cup fresh young sea vegetable fronds
2 quarts cold water
1 pound fresh fish, split
¼ teaspoon crushed red peppers
¼ cup dry white wine

Substitutes

Porphyra (various species)

- Wash fresh sea vegetables well in cold water. Cut into bite-sized strips or squares. Cut fish into chunks, leaving skin on.
- Combine water, fish, sea vegetables, and seasonings. Simmer gently for 5 minutes. Add wine.
- Remove from heat. Let stand for 10 minutes. Serve.

Nemacystus decipiens

Mozuku in miso soup

4 SERVINGS

Fresh mozuku is available lightly brined and vacuum packed (imported from Japan) in Japanese markets. Futo (thick) mozuku is sometimes available in stores. Though a different species (Tinocladia crassa), *it is just as tasty as mozuku.*

2 cups fresh mozuku
4 raw egg yolks
2 tablespoons rice wine
2 tablespoons soy sauce
4 tablespoons miso
4 cups boiling water

Substitute

Nemalion helminthoides

- Open the package over a strainer or colander and drain the brined mozuku.
- Divide the mozuku evenly among 4 soup bowls. Carefully place a raw egg yolk on each mound of sea vegetable.
- Add the rice wine, soy sauce, and miso to 4 cups boiling water. Pour over the sea vegetables.

Porphyra nereocystis

Pacific sea vegetable soup

4 SERVINGS

A well-flavored fish stock is the secret to this tasty soup. Fish stock can often be purchased in dehydrated form as bullion cubes. However, it is simple to make and can be stored in the refrigerator or frozen. Simply boil the head and bones of the fish in enough water to cover, adding salt and a little white wine. Then boil uncovered until the liquid is reduced by half and then strain through cheesecloth.

sesame oil
1 small onion, thinly sliced
4 2-inch by 5-inch strips dried Porphyra fronds
1 cup snow pea pods
¼-inch slice fresh ginger root, minced
1 tablespoon soy sauce
2 cups fish stock, heated

Substitutes

Porphyra (various species)

- Heat a little oil and sauté the onion until it becomes translucent.
- Stir in remaining ingredients and bring to a boil. Reduce heat. Simmer for 5 minutes, covered. Serve.

Palmaria palmata

Dulse miso soup

4 SERVINGS

These light and low-calorie ingredients produce a very rich-tasting soup.

¼ cup dried dulse
1 cup parsnips or 1 cup carrots, diced
1 quart water
1 teaspoon miso

- Chop the dried dulse coarsely. Boil the carrots or parsnips in the water until tender. Add the chopped dulse.
- Boil 10 minutes. Remove from heat. Add the miso. Serve.

Palmaria palmata

Chinook-style chowder with slivered dulse

4 TO 6 SERVINGS

The nutty flavor and rich red color of dulse complement this sumptuous chowder.

3 tablespoons butter
1⅓ cup diced raw potatoes
1 cup diced onions
freshly ground black pepper
1 cup clam juice
3 cups boiling water
¼ pound of smoked salmon, thinly sliced and cut into bite-sized pieces
1 cup tightly packed fresh spinach leaves (or sorrel leaves)
¼ cup slivered dulse (page 254)
2 tablespoons light cream (optional)

- Melt the butter in a heavy saucepan over a low heat. Add the potatoes and onions. Season generously with pepper; use no salt. Sauté, stirring constantly for about 5 minutes or until the onions are translucent but not brown.
- Add the clam juice and the boiling water. Cook until the potatoes are completely tender.
- Add the salmon, spinach (or sorrel), and the dulse. Cook over low heat for 2 to 3 minutes or until the spinach is wilted. Season again with pepper if desired.
- When ready to serve, remove from heat and stir in the heavy cream.

Undaria pinnatifida

Split pea and wakame soup

6 TO 8 SERVINGS

This soup makes a nourishing pickup for frosty days.

1 cup dried split peas
1½ quarts water
¼ cup dried wakame, crumbled
1 carrot, sliced in rounds
1 medium onion, sliced in rounds
2 tablespoons sesame seed paste
sea salt

Substitute

Petalonia fascia

- Simmer the split peas in the water until tender, about 1 hour.
- Add the crumbled wakame, carrot, and onion. Cover and simmer to a creamy consistency, about 40 minutes longer.
- Remove from heat. Stir in sesame seed paste. Add salt to taste. Serve.

Fucus vesiculosis

Codfish chowder
with rockweed flavoring

Fucus imparts a sweet, delicious flavor to any food with which it is boiled or steamed.

2 cups fresh rockweed
2 quarts water
2 large potatoes, diced
1 pound fresh cod fillets, cut into chunks
1 cup dry white wine
1 tablespoon celery salt
½ teaspoon sage
½ teaspoon thyme
1 teaspoon crushed hot red pepper
1 teaspoon sea salt
2 tablespoons olive oil
1 tablespoon whole wheat flour

Substitutes

Fucus (various species)

● Wash the rockweed thoroughly in cold water to remove all sand. Place it in a cheesecloth bag and suspend the bag in a large soup pot containing the water and potatoes. Boil until the potatoes are almost cooked. Remove the spent sea vegetable bag and discard.
● Add all other ingredients except flour. Simmer gently for 15 minutes.
● Dissolve flour in a little cold water and add to the chowder, stirring constantly. Simmer 5 minutes more. Serve.

Laminaria angustata

Hai dai sweet soup

6 TO 8 SERVINGS

Sweet soup is a traditional favorite among older Chinese. The special taste produced by the rock sugar can be approximated by using honey.

1 cup fresh or ½ cup dried Laminaria fronds
2 quarts water
1 cup dried mung beans or mung bean sprouts
¼ cup rock sugar

● If dried sea vegetable is used, soak it for 30 minutes in enough cold water to cover. Drain, reserving water. If fresh Laminaria is used, simply rinse it well in cold water.
● Cut the Laminaria into 1-inch squares. Measure the

soaking water, adding more water if necessary to bring the volume to 2 quarts, and bring to a boil.
● Add sea vegetable, mung beans, and rock sugar. Boil over medium heat for 1 hour. The rock sugar should be completely dissolved before removing from the heat.
● If mung bean sprouts are used, add them to the last 10 minutes of the cooking. Serve.

Substitutes

Laminaria longissima
Pleurophycus gardneri

Undaria pinnatifida

Chinese-style soup with wakame

2 SERVINGS

Petalonia, growing in profusion on the American coasts, is much appreciated in Japan. The plants are an excellent substitute for Undaria which grows only in Japanese waters.

1 piece wakame 2 inches by 2 inches
2 dried Chinese mushrooms
4 string beans, stringed
2 scallions
2 tablespoons boiled bamboo shoots (fresh or canned)
1 small piece of fresh ginger root, peeled
1 teaspoon sake
cracked pepper
2 cups soup stock
1 egg, well beaten
1 teaspoon soy sauce
1 teaspoon sesame oil

● Soak the wakame and the mushrooms in cold water for 10 minutes. Drain. Cut the wakame into bite-sized strips or squares.
● Remove the hard core from the mushrooms and cut the remainder into pieces. Cut the string beans, scallions, and bamboo shoots into matchlike slivers.
● Add the mushrooms, ginger, bamboo shoots, sake, and pepper to the soup stock. Bring to a rapid boil.
● Gradually drip in the egg as the stock boils. Add the wakame, string beans, scallions, soy sauce, and sesame oil. Serve hot.

Substitute

Petalonia fascia

Ulva lactuca

Ulva soup

Ulva creates a very nice soup base and background flavor for most clear soups.

½ cup fresh Ulva fronds
2 quarts water
½ cup carrots, chopped
½ cup leftover cooked chicken, diced
2 tablespoons soy sauce
½ teaspoon cracked black pepper

Substitutes

Ulva (various species)

- Wash and clean the Ulva thoroughly in lukewarm fresh water. Remove any small snails that may be feeding on the blades.
- Boil the carrots in the water until they are tender. Cut the Ulva into 1-inch squares and drop into the boiling soup. Add the diced chicken.
- Simmer gently 5 minutes more. Season. Serve.

Undaria pinnatifida

Korean sea vegetable soup

Miyok-kuk

4 TO 6 SERVINGS

Miyok-kuk is a traditional Korean soup, though in Korea only the wealthy would use meat.

½ ounce dried Undaria
¼ pound raw lean beef, thinly sliced
3 cloves garlic, finely chopped
1 teaspoon sesame salt
3 tablespoons soy sauce
2 teaspoons sesame oil
½ teaspoon black pepper
6 cups water

Substitute

Petalonia fascia

- Place the Undaria in a colander or strainer and blanch by pouring boiling water over it. Drain. Cut into 2-inch pieces.
- Sauté the beef quickly in a little sesame oil, adding garlic, sesame salt, soy sauce, and black pepper. Sauté until the meat is brown.
- Add the sea vegetable and the water. Simmer 30 minutes or until Undaria is tender. Check seasoning. Bring to a boil. Serve.

Sargassum fulvellum
Porphyra tenera
Undaria pinnatifida

Sargasso sea soup

The Sargasso Sea, once thought to be as thick as this hearty soup, is actually an area sparsely populated by floating Sargassum plants.

½ cup fresh or dried Sargassum
   (use blades of uppermost fronds only)
8 cups chicken broth
½ cup dried nori sheets
½ cup dried wakame fronds
½ cup small dried shrimp
½ cup dried sardines
½ cup soy sauce
2 tablespoons sesame oil

Substitutes

Sargassum (various species)
Porphyra (various species)

- If fresh Sargassum is being used, rinse it in cold water to free it of sand.
- Boil the broth and blanch the sea vegetables in it to make them pliable. Remove the leaflike blades from the Sargassum.
- Chop the nori and wakame and add to the boiling broth.
- Add the dried shrimp and sardines.
- Add soy sauce and sesame oil.
- Boil gently for about 2 hours or until all is tender.

Undaria pinnatifida

Sea vegetable soup with bean curd

¼ ounce dried Undaria
4 cups beef broth
⅛ teaspoon dried crushed hot red peppers
1 cake bean curd cut into bite-sized pieces
2 tablespoons peanut oil
10 small scallions, chopped
4 tablespoons miso

Substitute

Petalonia fascia

- Place the Undaria in a colander or strainer and blanch by pouring boiling water over it. Drain and cut into bite-sized squares or rectangles.
- Bring the beef broth to a boil.
- Add the sea vegetable and crushed red peppers. Simmer 10 minutes. Remove from heat.
- Add the bean curd, peanut oil, scallions, and miso. Serve.

Chondrus crispus

Irish moss soup

⅛ cup dried Irish moss
4 quarts cold water
1 stalk celery with leaves, cut up
6 carrots, cut up
3 to 4 pounds stewing beef, cut up
2 cups tomatoes (optional)
1 tablespoon sea salt
2 tablespoons soy sauce
1 teaspoon cracked black pepper
¼ teaspoon crushed red pepper
2 bay leaves
pinch of sage
pinch of thyme
1 cup dry white wine

In the year 1842, the Domestic Dictionary and House-keepers' Manual referred to Irish moss as "exceedingly nutritious and by no means disagreeable when made into soup with meat and other vegetables; it is, in fact, quite equal to the famed birds' nest soup of the Chinese."

- Soak the Irish moss for 30 minutes in cold water to cover. Wash. Drain. Remove any foreign matter. Chop into flowerets about the size of thumbnails.
- Place all of the soup ingredients, including the sea vegetable, in a deep pot. Simmer until tender (several hours). Serve.

Undaria pinnatifida

Wakame soup

4 SERVINGS

Properly fermented miso contains the full complement of enzymes necessary to complete the digestive process.

1 ounce dried wakame
5 cups boiling water
⅓ cup cooked bonito (flaked)
1 tablespoon miso

Substitutes

Petalonia fascia
Scytosiphon lomentaria

- Soak wakame for 10 minutes in enough cold water to cover. Wash well. Drain. Cut into pieces 1-inch square, removing center vein. Add to the boiling water.
- Add bonito flakes. Cover. Cook 10 minutes.
- Add miso. Stir well. Serve.

Eisenia bicyclis

Arame soup

½ ounce dried arame
3 ounces raw pork
1 tablespoon cornstarch
1 tablespoon bacon fat
3½ cups dashi stock (page 00)
2 eggs
sea salt

- The commercial arame will come cut in slender noodle-like strips. Soak the arame for 5 minutes in cold water. Drain. Cut the strips into lengths of about 3 inches.
- Cut the pork into thin strips about ¼ inch by 2 inches.
- Dissolve the cornstarch in a little water.
- Heat the bacon fat in a frying pan.
- Heat the soup stock.
- Add the arame and pork and sauté until tender.
- Beat the eggs and make an omelet, cutting it into thin strips about ¼ inch by 2 inches. Add the omelet pieces and cornstarch liquid to the stock.
- Arrange a few pieces of pork and sea vegetable in the bottom of each soup bowl and pour the hot liquid over it. Season. Serve immediately.

Porphyra (various species)

Taiwan scrambled egg, pork, and Porphyra soup

Cornstarch keeps the attractively shaped pieces of meat and sea vegetable floating on the top of the soup.

6 cups chicken stock
2 sheets or ½ cup dried Porphyra fronds, crumbled
1 teaspoon cornstarch
½ cup cooked pork, sliced into matchlike slivers
2 eggs, beaten with a little water

- Boil the stock and cut the sea vegetable into bite-sized squares.
- Dissolve the cornstarch in a few tablespoons of cold water. Add to the stock.
- Add the Porphyra and pork. Bring the stock to a rolling boil.
- Drip the beaten egg mixture into the boiling stock. Serve.

Salads

Hijiki salad with tofu dressing
Kanten salad
Chicken and kanten salad
Beets in Irish moss jelly
Korean salad with spice dressing
Irish moss tomato aspic
Mixed sea vegetable salad
Japanese-style mozuku salad
Sunomono
Philippine gulamon salad
Sea lettuce salad
Dulse salad
Cucumber and wakame salad
Wakame, cucumber, and radish salad
Steamed sea palm
Dulse and goat's cheese salad
Polyneura salad
Sea grape salad

Hizikia fusiforme

Hijiki salad with tofu dressing

Bean curd (tofu), a beautifully versatile and easy-to-use food, adds an esoteric note to any dish, and is a common commodity in most supermarkets.

½ cup dried hijiki
1 bean curd cake
4 tablespoons olive oil
1 tablespoon rice vinegar or rice wine
1 tablespoon sesame paste or ground walnuts
¼ cup scallion tops, chopped finely
1 ripe tomato, peeled and chopped (optional)

- Soak the hijiki for 30 minutes in enough cold water to cover. Drain well. Chop into bite-sized clumps.
- Blend the bean curd, olive oil, rice vinegar or rice wine, and sesame paste until it is almost smooth. Mash in chopped scallion tops and mashed tomatoes if desired.
- Mix with the hijiki. Serve.

Gelidium (various species)
Gracilaria (various species)

Kanten salad

2 TO 4 SERVINGS

Kanten is a dried-frozen agar, a sea vegetable extract (gel). The Japanese translation for kanten is "cold sky." It was invented in 1665, the era of Mei-reki, when an unwitting servant threw leftover agar dessert out into the snow. The subsequent thaw produced the first "dried-frozen" gel.

4 ounces of strand kanten
1 tablespoon dashi powder
1 teaspoon sesame oil
1 tablespoon rice vinegar
1 teaspoon honey
2 scallions cut in 2-inch-long slivers
2 carrots cut in 2-inch-long slivers
1 cucumber, peeled, seeded, and cut in
  2-inch-long slivers
2 tablespoons toasted sesame seeds

- Soak kanten in cold water for 2 minutes. Drain. Wash in cold water. Drain again.
- Combine dashi powder, sesame oil, rice, vinegar, and honey. Toss with vegetables and sprinkle with sesame seeds.
- Serve at room temperature or serve chilled.

Gelidium (various species)
Gracilaria (various species)

Chicken and kanten salad

2 TO 4 SERVINGS

Kanten (dried-frozen agar) is the perfect addition to a diet or health salad, for it supplies minerals and provides bulk but adds few calories.

½ **ounce (1 stick) of kanten** *
4 cups of water
1 whole chicken breast
1 egg
sea salt
vegetable oil
10 scallions, green parts only
1 teaspoon sesame seeds

- Soak kanten in 2 cups of cold water for 10 minutes. Drain. Cut into 1½-inch pieces.
- Boil 2 cups of water and add the chicken breast. Bring to a second boil. Turn flame to low, cover, and cook for 15 minutes. Allow the chicken to cool in the broth.
- Beat egg thoroughly. Add salt. Beat again.
- Heat a little vegetable oil in a 12-inch skillet. Remove from heat. Pour in egg, tipping the pan quickly to coat entire surface. When the egg has set and is cool enough to handle, slice it into thin strips. Set aside.
- When the chicken can be handled, drain. Discard skin and bones. Cut breast into thin strips. Set aside.
- Cut the green parts of the scallions into ¼-inch pieces.
- Combine sauce ingredients. Set aside.
- Mix kanten pieces with chicken, egg, and scallion. Then toss this with the sauce. Top with sesame seeds. Serve.

SAUCE
1 tablespoon light soy sauce
2 tablespoons sesame oil
½ **teaspoon honey**

Chondrus crispus

Beets in Irish moss jelly

2 SERVINGS

Irish moss will soon be grown as a cash crop on undersea farms, as hand raking gives way to vacuum compressor harvesting.

Substitutes

Gigartina (various species)

¼ ounce dried Irish moss
2 medium-sized fresh beets
2 cups water
1 tablespoon lemon juice
1 bay leaf
4 peppercorns

- Soak Irish moss for 30 minutes in enough cold water to cover. Wash well. Drain. Pick it over to remove any foreign matter.
- Scrub beets and cut them into thin rounds. Place the beets in a steaming device and steam for 10 minutes or until tender, reserving the juice. Put cooked beets aside.
- Pour the water and beet juice into the top of a double boiler.
- Place the sea vegetable, bay leaf, and peppercorns in a square of cheesecloth (a piece about 8 inches square). Tie up the ends and suspend the bag in the liquid. Bring the mixture to a boil. Reduce heat and cook for 30 minutes. Press the bag against the side of the pan occasionally to release the gel. Stir continually.
- Remove from heat. Discard the bag. Add lemon juice and stir well.
- Arrange beet slices in the bottom of two small molds that have been dipped in cold water. Pour the liquid into the molds. Cover tightly and refrigerate for several hours before serving.
- Unmold onto lettuce leaves.

Codium fragile

Korean salad with spice dressing

6 TO 8 SERVINGS

In Korean cooking, Codium is used much as we would use garlic.

1 teaspoon fresh Codium, chopped
lettuce leaves
¼ cup olive oil
¼ cup fresh lemon juice

- Wash the Codium thoroughly in lukewarm water. Remove all sand and bits of clinging coral chips or rock. Cut off the holdfast and any hardened portions.
- Prepare a large salad bowl full of lettuce leaves. Toss thoroughly with about ¼ cup olive oil.
- Toss again with a mixture of lemon juice and chopped Codium. Serve.

Chondrus crispus

Irish moss tomato aspic

6 SERVINGS

Irish moss is still collected in great quantities along the Massachusetts coast. Men rake the plants from the rocky bottom and haul them aboard dories. A good mosser is able to harvest more than 2,000 pounds in a day.

1¼ cup dried Irish moss
1 quart cold water
juice of 1½ lemons
3 tablespoons parsley, finely chopped
2 tablespoons celery leaves, finely chopped
⅛ teaspoon sage
⅛ teaspoon powdered ginger
2 tablespoons carrot juice
2 tablespoons horseradish
pinch of white pepper
pinch of sea salt
¾ cup tomato juice
¾ cup clam juice

- Soak the Irish moss for 30 minutes in enough cold water to cover. Wash well. Drain. Pick it over to remove any foreign matter.
- Pour the water into the top of a double boiler.
- Place the sea vegetable in a square of cheesecloth (a piece about 12 inches square). Tie up the ends and suspend the bag in the water. Simmer for 30 minutes. Press the bag against the side of the pan occasionally to release the gel. Stir continually.
- Remove from heat. Discard the spent bag. Allow the liquid to cool for 5 minutes. Add all other ingredients. Pour the mixture into a mold that has just been dipped in cold water. Cover tightly and refrigerate for several hours before serving.

Substitutes

Gigartina (various species)

Ulva lactuca
Enteromorpha intestinalis
Monostroma latissimum

Mixed sea vegetable salad

2 TO 4 SERVINGS

A famous French algologist was the creator of this salad.

- Wash the fresh sea vegetables quickly in lukewarm water. Pat the fronds dry with a clean towel. Chop the

Substitutes

Ulva (various species),
Enteromorpha (various species),
Monostroma (various species)

½ cup fresh young Monostroma fronds
1 cup fresh Enteromorpha fronds
1 cup fresh Ulva fronds

CREAM DRESSING
4 tablespoons heavy cream
1 tablespoon wine vinegar or fresh lemon juice
pinch of cayenne pepper
sea salt

Monostroma into inch-square pieces. Chop the Enteromorpha coarsely. Chop the Ulva finely.
● Mix the cream dressing and pour over salad. Toss gently.

Nemacystus decipiens

Japanese-style mozuku salad

4 SERVINGS

Mozuku is one of the most naturally delicate and delectable sea vegetables. As salad it makes a refreshing change for a summertime menu.

1 cup mozuku (prepared or fresh)
4 lemon wedges

● Using commercially prepared mozuku, packed in brine, simply empty the chilled contents of the vacuum-sealed container into a dish.
● To blanch the fresh vegetable, place it in a strainer or colander and pour boiling water over it. Drain and chill.
● Place the prepared sea vegetable in a dish.
● Serve mozuku dressed and garnished with lemon wedges.

DRESSING
2 tablespoons rice vinegar
2 tablespoons honey

Substitute

Nemalion helminthoides.

Graciolaria verrucosa

Sunomono

Ogo is commonly sold fresh but already blanched. In Northwestern cities it is often flown in from Hawaii, though comparable plants grow profusely along the coast.

1 cup fresh ogo
boiling water

- Clean and wash the ogo carefully, removing sand, crustaceans, and other clinging algae.
- Blanch it by placing it in a colander or strainer and pouring boiling water over it. The color will change from a brownish-red to a brownish-green. Drain.
- Chill and serve with one of these dressings.

DRESSING I
½ cup rice or cider vinegar
1 tablespoon honey
½ teaspoon sea salt

DRESSING II
¼ cup fresh lemon or lime juice
2 tablespoons honey
½ teaspoon sea salt

DRESSING III
¼ cup rice or cider vinegar
1 teaspoon soy sauce
1 tablespoon honey
½ teaspoon sea salt

DRESSING IV
¼ cup miso
2 tablespoons rice or cider vinegar
2 tablespoons honey

Substitutes

Gracilaria (various species),

Codium fragile
Graciiaria verrucosa

Philippine gulamon salad

1 pound (3 cups) fresh Codium or Graciiaria, tightly packed
4 large tomatoes
1 teaspoon sea salt
½ cup chopped scallions
¼ cup chopped fresh ginger root
2 tablespoons soy sauce

- Wash and clean the sea vegetable in cold water. Cut off the hard ends of the Codium plants, if used. Blanch by placing the sea vegetable in a strainer or colander and pouring boiling water over it. The Graciiaria will change from a brownish-red color to a brownish-green. Let stand a few minutes. Drain well.
- Chop or mash the tomatoes and combine with the blanched sea vegetable.
- Add the remaining ingredients. Mix gently. Serve cold.

Substitutes

Graciiaria (various species)

Palmaria palmata

Dulse salad

8 SERVINGS

Dulse is a highly digestible, protein-rich sea vegetable whose nutlike taste will enrich almost any dish.

3 ounces dried dulse
2 apples, sliced
3 large carrots, grated
1 cup alfalfa sprouts
½ ripe avocado, cut up
¼ cup currants

DRESSING
⅔ cup safflower oil
juice of 1 lemon
4 tablespoons soy sauce

- Chop the dried dulse finely. Mix all salad ingredients together.
- Mix the dressing and pour it over the salad. Toss well.

Ulva lactuca

Sea lettuce salad

2 TO 4 SERVINGS

5 cups fresh Ulva fronds
½ cup onions, sliced into thin rounds

CREAM DRESSING
8 tablespoons fresh cream
½ tablespoon fresh lemon juice
½ tablespoon cider vinegar
1 tablespoon olive oil
pinch of cayenne pepper

Substitutes

Ulva (various species)

- Wash the fresh sea vegetable quickly in lukewarm water. Pat the fronds dry with a clean towel. Chop finely.
- Prepare the cream dressing. Pour over salad and toss with the onion rounds.

Undaria pinnatifida

Cucumber and wakame salad

2 TO 4 SERVINGS

3½ ounces vacuum-packed fresh wakame
1 cucumber

DRESSING
4 tablespoons cider vinegar
3 tablespoons dark soy sauce
2 tablespoons honey

- Cut cucumber into thin slices, salt lightly, and let stand for 30 minutes.
- Rinse the wakame quickly in cold water to remove the salt in which it is packed. Do not soak! Drain. Cut into 1½-inch lengths, removing center vein.
- Pat the cucumber dry with a clean cloth. Combine cucumber and wakame in a salad bowl.
- Prepare the dressing and pour it over the salad. Toss gently and serve.

Undaria pinnatifida

Wakame, cucumber, and radish salad

½ **ounce dried wakame**
1½–2-**ounces white radish, grated**
2 **ounches cooked fish flakes (leftovers can be used)**
1 **cucumber, peeled and cut into thin strips**

DRESSING
1 **tablespoon honey**
2 **tablespoons rice vinegar**
1 **teaspoon soy sauce**

- Place the wakame for 10 minutes in enough cold water to cover. Do not soak! Drain. Cut into bite-sized pieces.
- Prepare the dressing.
- Place the fish flakes, grated radish, sea vegetable pieces, and cucumber strips in a bowl.
- Mix the dressing well and pour it over the salad. Toss gently. Serve.

Postelsia palmaeformis

Steamed sea palm

4 TO 6 SERVINGS

Though the sea palm looks like a tiny palm tree, all parts of it are tender and delicious, when prepared. The Chinese community in San Francisco considers this sea vegetable a special treat!

4 **cups fresh sea palm (stipe only), about 4 to 6 plants**

DRESSING
½ **cup rice or cider vinegar**
4 **tablespoons honey**
salt and white pepper to taste

- Collect only fresh sea palms. (Stipes should snap crisply when bent.) Dry the blades for tasty snacks. Rinse the stipes in cold water. Cut into 2-inch lengths. Steam them, then cut again down the center. Chill well.
- Mix the dressing and pour over the sea vegetable. Serve.

Palmaria palmata

Dulse and goat's cheese salad

2 SERVINGS

The rich nutlike taste of dulse blends especially well with a bland food, like goat's cheese.

2 cups watercress
½ cup goat's cheese
1 teaspoon dulse condiment (page 247)

- Wash and drain the watercress. Use it raw or steam it lightly.
- Prepare two beds of watercress.
- Spread flakes of goat's cheese on top of each serving. Sprinkle each serving with ½ teaspoon of dulse condiment.

Polyneura latissima

Polyneura salad

4 TO 6 SERVINGS

This dish is prepared by the Philippine community in San Francisco.

1 cup dried Polyneura
2 cups fresh tomatoes, chopped coarsely
½ cup Bermuda onion, chopped coarsely

DRESSING
¼ cup cider vinegar
1 tablespoon honey
pinch cayenne pepper

- Wash the Polyneura well in lukewarm water. Dry quickly to prevent mold. Store in sealed plastic bag.
- When ready to use, hydrate in a little cold water. Drain. Place in a colander or strainer and blanch with salted or unsalted boiling water. Drain. Chop coarsely.
- Combine with tomato and onion.
- Mix dressing and toss.

Caulerpa racemosa uar. racemosa

Sea grape salad

Caulerpa (sea grapes) is considered such a delicacy in the Philippines that even when other fresh vegetables are available in the markets, it is always sold out first. Species of caulerpa are even cultivated and transported into Manila and Quezon City. The succulent sea vegetables arrive in the afternoon and are unloaded from the bancas as local housewives stand by, anxious to purchase the day's salad fixings. The five-gallon cans go quickly and even regular customers often are forced to go home empty-handed.

Caulerpa remains fresh for only a few hours after picking and plants should be refrigerated during this period.

½ cup fresh sea grapes
vinegar for dipping.
2 servings

- Wash the fresh sea grapes, in cool water to remove all sand. Drain carefully so as not to bruise the nodes.
- Dip each portion in vinegar before eating.

Main dishes

Oyster cakes with funori
Sushi rice
Sushimaki)
Laverbread
Mixed sea vegetable tempura with shrimp cakes
Laver and pork omelet
Maize shapes with hijiki and buttermilk sauces
Laminaria casserole
Baked dulse salmon loaf
Alaria vegetable stew
Dilsea
Hijiki wrapped in dried soybean curd
Rice with beef, eggs, and nori garnish
Buddha's delight
Fah tsoi and dried oysters
Korean rib stew with tasima
Kazunoko kombu (or herring roe on tangle)
Fillet of sole, Ningpo style
Laminaria stew
Sashime (raw seafood)
Ineh's matsumae (vegetables with tangle)
Hijiki al burro
Fish rice with nori garnish
Hijiki, pork, green pepper, and Chinese rice noodles
Pork-stuffed Pleurophycus fronds
Stuffed Porphyra fronds

Gloiopeltis furcata

Oyster cakes with funori

The distinctive, strong taste of fresh Gloiopeltis can be toned down, if desired, by soaking the sun-dried fronds in a mild vinegar and water solution or steeping them in rose water.

¼ cup fresh funori
1 cup fresh oysters
water
½ an egg
¾ cup unbleached white flour
peanut oil for frying

- Wash the fresh funori in cold water to remove all sand, etc. Drain. Chop coarsely.
- Shuck the oysters, reserving their juice. Measure out ¾ cup of juice and strain. Add water if necessary to bring liquid up to 1 cup. Chop the oysters coarsely.
- Beat the egg and combine with the liquid. Add the flour. Mix quickly.
- Add the chopped oysters and sea vegetable to the batter. Mix.
- Heat about 2 inches of oil in a large skillet. Spoon out small patties of the mixture into the hot oil, a few at a time. Cook until each side is a rich golden brown. Serve hot.

Sushi rice

YIELDS ENOUGH TO FILL 10 NORI SHEETS

¼ cup dried shrimp
¼ cup rice vinegar
¼ cup honey
2 teaspoons sea salt
2 teaspoons dashi stock
4 cups steamed brown rice

- Soak the shrimp in the vinegar, dashi stock, honey, and salt until they are tender, about 1 hour. Drain, reserving the liquid.
- Reserve ½ cup of this vinegar liquid for sprinkling on the nori sheets while preparing sushimaki. Pour the remainder over the cooled rice and toss lightly. This will prevent the rice from becoming gummy.

Porphyra tenera

Sushimaki

2-ounce package kanpyo
dashi stock (page 172)
honey
soy sauce
sea salt
10 sheets dried nori
2-ounce package shiitake mushrooms
2 medium carrots
10 stalks watercress
4 ounces raw tuna fish, cubed
small bamboo mat on which to roll sushi
vinegar liquid
sushi rice (page 197)

● KANPYO: Wash and cook in water until it is soft. Add enough dashi stock to cover and cook until tender. Add 4 tablespoons honey, 3 teaspoons soy sauce, and 2 teaspoons salt, and continue cooking for 10 minutes. Cut to the length of the nori sheets.

● SHIITAKE MUSHROOMS: Wash and cook in enough water to cover until it is soft. Continue cooking until the mushrooms are very tender. Add 3 tablespoons honey and 4 tablespoons soy sauce, and cook until the sauce is absorbed. Cut into 1½-inch-long strips.

● CARROTS: Cut them lengthwise into ¼-inch strips. Cook in 1 cup of water for 7 to 10 minutes. Add 2 tablespoons honey and 1 teaspoon salt and cook for 5 minutes more.

● WATERCRESS: Clean and steam for 1 minute until it is slightly wilted. Drain. Gently squeeze out the remaining water.

● RAW TUNA: Cook in a saucepan with 3 tablespoons honey and 4 tablespoons soy sauce until the fish changes color slightly.

● Place a sheet of nori on a lightly oiled square bamboo mat. Sprinkle some vinegar liquid on the nori sheet and spread sushi rice on ⅔ of the nori to a thickness of about ½ inch. Arrange 5 strands of kanpyo and 1 row each of mushrooms, carrots, watercress, and tuna lengthwise on the rice about ⅓ from the farthest edge of the nori.

● Roll away from you taking care to keep the ingredients in place with your fingers. When the edge of the mat touches the rice, lift the mat slightly and apply a gentle pressure to tighten the roll. To serve as hors d'oeuvres, cut into ½-inch rounds. To serve as a main course, cut in half and then in fours. Arrange on plates, cut side up.

Variation

● Line the rice with grated vegetables like carrots or radishes, chopped scallions, and sautéed cabbage leaves.

Substitutes

Porphyra (various species)

Porphyra umbilicalis

Laverbread

4 SERVINGS

A traditional Welsh and Scottish breakfast food, this dish is now served in most London fish houses. In Scotland, Porphyra umbilicalis is hawked to unsuspecting tourists in place of the smaller, more delicate P. leucosticta.

1½ cups dried or 3 cups fresh laver
bacon fat
1 cup rolled oats
sea salt
cracked pepper

● Soak the dried laver for a minute in enough cold water to cover. Drain well.
● Place the laver in the hot bacon fat. Sprinkle the oats on top. Fry on both sides until done (about 10 minutes).
● Season to taste and serve.
● If fresh fronds are used, simply wash quickly in cold water and drain.
● For overnight storage, spread a piece of waxed paper and sprinkle the oats evenly on top. Place the moist laver over the oats and fold the edges of the paper up to form a package. The oats will adhere to the laver. Refrigerate.
● When ready to use, heat a little bacon fat in a frying pan. Drop in the laver bread and fry on both sides.

Substitutes

Porphyra (various species)

Laminaria (various species)
Undaria pinnatifida
Palmaria palmata
Porphyra (various species)
Chondrus crispus

Mixed sea vegetable tempura with shrimp cakes

* *Laminaria angustata.*
† *Chondrus crispus.*
‡ *Porphyra* (various species).
§ *Palmaria palmata.*
‖ *Undaria pinnatifida.*

1 cup shrimp
¼ teaspoon crushed red peppers
½ cup dried kombu* fronds
½ cup dried Irish moss†
½ cup dried nori ‡ sheets or fronds
2 tablespoons dashi powder
2 tablespoons unbleached white flour
½ cup dried dulse§ fronds

SHRIMP CAKES
¼ cup dried wakame‖
½ egg, beaten
¾ cup water
¾ cup unbleached white flour
1 cup shrimp, cooked, cleaned, and chopped
** coarsely**
1 scallion, chopped finely
peanut oil

6 TO 8 SERVINGS

Comments on the different sea vegetables will supply animated dinner conversation.

● Wash and clean the shrimp. Put them in a pot with water to cover. Add the crushed red peppers. Bring to a boil over a moderate heat. Remove from heat and allow to cool in the liquid. When they are cool enough to handle, drain and chop coarsely.
● Soak the kombu and the Irish moss in cold water for 30 minutes. Drain.
● Boil the kombu in water to cover until it is tender (about 15 minutes). Remove and drain. Cut into 2 two-inch strips.
● Blanch the Irish moss in boiling water for about 60 seconds. Cut into manageable-sized flowerets.
● If dried nori fronds are used, also blanch for a few seconds. Drain. Chop to 4-inch lengths.
● Sprinkle the kombu, moss, and nori fronds (if used) with dashi powder and then dust with flour. The dulse and nori sheets need no preparation. Prepare the shrimp cakes.
● Soak the dried wakame in cold water for about 5 minutes. Drain. Chop coarsely. Sprinkle with dashi powder and dust with flour.
● Combine the beaten egg with the water. Add additional water to bring the liquid up to 1 cup. Add ¾ cup flour. Mix quickly.
● Add chopped shrimp, scallion, and wakame to the batter.

TOSHI'S LIGHT TEMPURA BATTER

pinch of baking soda
3 heaping tablespoons unbleached white flour
1 egg
½ cup water

GINGER TEMPURA SAUCE

½ cup water
3 tablespoons soy sauce
1 tablespoon dashi powder
1 ounce grated fresh ginger

Substitutes

* *Laminaria longissima*
* *Pleurophycus gardneri*

- Heat about 2 inches of peanut oil in a heavy skillet. Scoop up the shrimp cake mixture a tablespoon at a time and deposit it in the hot oil. Alternate with batter-covered sea vegetables. Cook on each side until the coatings turn a light golden color.
- Serve with tempura sauce for dipping.
- Sift the baking soda into the flour.
- Beat the egg with the water. Place the liquid in a low, wide bowl.
- Sprinkle the flour and baking soda mixture over the top. Gently fold the flour into the liquid so that a very lumpy batter results.
- Roll the sea vegetables in and out of the batter with one motion of the hand. Try not to homogenize the batter in the process, and don't attempt to cover every speck of vegetable with batter. Make batter in several small batches rather than one large one.
- Boil the water, soy sauce, and dashi powder for one minute. Add grated ginger. Let stand until it reaches room temperature. Serve.

Porphyra (various species)

Laver and pork omelet

4 SERVINGS

All over Southeast Asia, species of Porphyra *are eaten cooked with eggs. This delicate sea vegetable, though high in protein, is low in calories.*

8 large eggs
4 tablespoons milk
vegetable oil
4 sheets dried laver or 1 cup dried fronds cut into small pieces
1 cup finely shredded, cooked pork

- Beat eggs with the milk.
- Heat the oil slowly in an omelet pan. Stir in the laver. Add pork pieces. Stir.
- Pour in egg mixture. Cover and cook over low heat until done. Serve.

Hizikia fusiforme

Maize shapes with hijiki and buttermilk sauces

1 ounce dried hijiki
1 cup tortillina powder or corn flour
1¾ cups water
1 small clove garlic, crushed
1 sliver garlic, crushed
4 tablespoons soy sauce
½ teaspoon sea salt
4 teaspoons peanut oil
½ cup buttermilk
1 small slice fresh ginger root

- Rinse hijiki thoroughly under cold running water. Soak for 1 hour in enough cold water to cover. Drain or shake dry. Chop fine.
- Mix together: tortillina powder, ¾ cup water, garlic clove, 1 tablespoon soy sauce, and sea salt. Blend to a soft sticky dough. Form into 3 large balls. Let stand for 5 minutes, then cut into small shapes about an inch wide.
- Heat 1 tablespoon peanut oil in a large heavy pan. Add 1 tablespoon soy sauce. As it begins to sputter, pour in ½ cup water. Reduce heat.
- Put in the maize shapes a few at a time. Shake pan to prevent sticking. Cover. Simmer 5 minutes. Turn shapes over with a spatula and separate if necessary.
- Add buttermilk and ¼ cup water. Shake pan again. Cover. Simmer 12 to 15 minutes, stirring frequently. Then empty pan contents into a bowl and keep them warm.
- Blend the crushed garlic to a smooth paste. Add ginger and 2 tablespoons soy sauce. Blend.
- Heat a clean pan with a sprinkling of peanut oil (1 teaspoon), just enough to make an oil film. Drop in the sea vegetable. Stir. Add the soy sauce and ginger mixture and ¼ cup water. Stir. Allow it to simmer for a second or two.
- Add half the quantity of maize shapes to the pan with about 3 tablespoons of the buttermilk sauce. Shake the pan. Cover. Cook gently for 15 minutes more. Stir from time to time to prevent sticking.
- Serve maize shapes with sea vegetable and buttermilk sauces over dry-cooked brown rice.

Laminaria angustata

Laminaria casserole

6 TO 8 SERVINGS

½ cup dried Laminaria
1 cup onion, chopped
1 cup carrot, chopped
1 cup turnip, chopped
1 cup rutabaga, chopped
1 cup parsnip, chopped
peanut oil
sea salt and cracked pepper

- Soak the Laminaria for 1 hour in enough cold water to cover. Drain, reserving soaking water. Cut sea vegetable into 1-inch squares. Return it to the soaking water and boil covered for 2 hours or pressure-cook for 1 hour. Replace water as necessary to keep the Laminaria covered. Drain.
- Sauté the other vegetables in a little peanut oil for about 10 minutes.
- Line a casserole dish with the sea vegetable squares. Then layer the other vegetables. Sprinkle each layer with salt and pepper.
- Bake in a 250-degree oven for several hours until the vegetables are tender.

Substitutes

Laminaria longissima, L. longicruris, Pleurophycus gardneri

Palmaria palmata

Baked dulse salmon loaf

4 SERVINGS

This pale salmon fleked with deep red dulse is an attractive and impressive dish, also quick and easy to prepare.

1 ounce dried dulse
½ cup whole milk
¾ cup cracker crumbs
3 eggs, unbeaten
juice of ½ lemon
1 tablespoon parsley, chopped
1 teaspoon sea salt
1 16-ounce can salmon

- Chop dried dulse finely.
- Warm the milk and mix in the cracker crumbs. Mix in all other ingredients.
- Preheat oven to 350 degrees. Lightly grease the inside of a mold. (A flavorless oil like corn oil is best.)
- Fill the mold with the salmon mixture. Bake for 1 hour. Unmold. Serve hot or cold with lemon wedges.

Alaria esculenta

Alaria vegetable stew

1 cup dried Alaria
corn oil for sautéing
1 cup carrots, cubed
1 cup turnips, cubed
1 cup radish, cubed
1 cup parsnips, cubed
1 cup rutabagas, cubed
2 teaspoons powdered ginger
1 cup dry white wine
sea salt
cracked pepper

- Soak the Alaria overnight in enough cold water to cover. Drain.
- Cut fronds across the midrib into ½-inch strips.
- Sauté them in a little oil until they are bright green and sweetly aromatic. Add water to cover. Boil uncovered for a half hour. Add water if necessary to cover the Alaria. Cover pot. Boil 2 hours or pressure cook 1 hour.
- Add the other vegetables, powdered ginger, white wine, salt, and pepper. Simmer until all vegetables are thoroughly cooked.

Substitutes

Alaria (various species)

Palmaria palmata
Porphyra (various species)

Dilsea

4 TO 6 SERVINGS

This is a traditional Irish dish; though dilsea was made with the red alga, Dilsea carnosa, *dulse approximates the taste.*

1 cup fresh dulse
1 cup dried laver
1 cup oat or sweet rice dumplings
4 quarts periwinkles

- Soak the fresh dulse for 3 hours in cold water to cover. Then add the laver and simmer for 3 hours. Replace water to keep the sea vegetable covered.
- Simmer periwinkles in seawater for 10 minutes. Drain the periwinkles and cut off the hard brown portion that seals the shell. Remove them from their shells with the aid of a straight pin or sewing needle.

OAT DUMPLINGS

¾ cup fine-cut oatmeal
¼ cup whole wheat flour
3 teaspoons baking powder
1 teaspoon sea salt
½ teaspoon baking soda
1 egg, beaten
2 tablespoons sour cream
¼ cup milk
additional milk

- Add water to the cooking vegetables to bring the liquid up to 1½ quarts.
- Prepare the dumpling mixture. Sift the dry ingredients together. Beat the egg and add the sour cream and milk. Add the liquid to the dry ingredients. Add additional milk to make a stiff dough.
- Add the dumpling mixture by spoonfuls to the boiling soup.
- Cover and cook for 12 to 15 minutes. Remove from heat. Add periwinkles. Serve.

Hizikia fusiforme

Hijiki wrapped in dried soybean curd

2 TO 4 SERVINGS

Hijiki, besides being extremely nutritious with more than 20 percent protein, adds few calories to the diet.

1 cup dried hijiki
1 carrot
1 dried bean curd skin
4 string beans, stringed
1 egg, beaten
1 cup chicken stock
1 tablespoon soy sauce
1 tablespoon sake
1 teaspoon honey

- Place the dried hijiki in a colander and wash it under cold running water. Put it in a deep pot with the carrot and dried bean curd and water to cover. Bring to a boil. Boil for 15 minutes. Remove from heat. Drain, reserving 1 cup of stock.
- Remove bean curd.
- Chop hijiki, carrot, and string beans. Add beaten egg. Mix well.
- Stuff this mixture into the bean curd. Place the stuffed curd in a saucepan.
- Combine the chicken and sea vegetable stocks. Add the soy sauce, sake, and honey to the stock. Pour over the stuffed bean curd. Simmer until liquid is almost evaporated.
- Remove to a shallow dish. Pour in the remaining stock. Serve.

Porphyra tenera

Rice with beef, eggs, and nori garnish

4 SERVINGS

¾ cup beef stock
4 tablespoons sake
4 tablespoons soy sauce
2 tablespoons honey
1 small onion, sliced thinly
½ pound thinly sliced beef
4 eggs
8 ounces cooked brown rice
4 scallions, chopped finely
1 sheet dried nori or ¼ cup dried fronds

Substitutes

Porphyra (various species)

- Put the stock, sake, soy sauce, honey, and onion in a frying pan and slowly bring to the boiling point.
- Add meat and cook until the meat changes color and is tender.
- Add the beaten eggs and tilt the pan to cover the entire surface with egg. Cover. Cook for 2 to 3 minutes, until the eggs are just set.
- Place the rice in 4 serving bowls and put ¼ of the egg and meat mixture in each. Sprinkle with scallion.
- Hold the nori sheet or nori fronds over a flame (candle or stove) for a few seconds to make them crisp. Do not let them burn.
- Cut the nori sheets into strips ¼ inch by 3 inches or crumble the fronds and sprinkle over the beef and egg mixture. Serve.

Bangia fuscopurpurea

Buddha's delight

8 SERVINGS

This is a famous Buddhist vegetarian dish usually combining 10 to 12 different kinds of vegetables, fresh and dried.

16 dried tiger lily buds
4 medium-sized dried Chinese mushrooms
4 lotus roots
¼ cup dried tree ears
1 tablespoon dried hair sea vegetable
20 ginkgo nuts
14 snow pea pods
¼ cup vegetable steaks

- Soak the following ingredients in separate bowls of water for about 20 minutes: tiger lily buds, mushrooms, lotus roots, tree ears, and hair sea vegetable. Wash and drain.
- Crack ginkgo nuts and shell them. Pour boiling water over nuts and let stand for 5 minutes. Remove their pinkish inner skin.
- Parboil the snow peas and let them float in cold water.

¼ cup taro or 1 small potato
1 teaspoon sea salt
1 teaspoon honey
1 teaspoon soy sauce
6 water chestnuts
¼ cup cooked carrots, sliced
¼ cup bamboo shoots, sliced
½ teaspoon sesame oil

- Slice the water chestnuts. Cut the vegetable steak into 1-inch pieces. Cut lotus roots and mushrooms into pieces of similar size. Halve the taro. If using Irish potato, cut into thin slices.
- Bring 1 cup water to boil. Add mushrooms, tree ears, tiger lily buds, lotus root, and ginkgo nuts, and continue to boil for 5 minutes. Add salt, honey, and soy sauce. Mix well.
- Add water chestnuts, carrots, bamboo shoots, and vegetable steak. Mix a few times.
- Cover and cook over medium heat for 5 to 7 minutes. Add taro or sliced potato. Mix and cook for 2 more minutes. Add snow peas. Mix thoroughly and cook for 1 minute more.
- Just before serving add ½ teaspoon sesame oil and sprinkle on the dried sea vegetable. Serve hot or cold.

Nostoc (various species)

Fah tsoi and dried oysters

4 TO 6 SERVINGS

A traditional New Year's dish in China. This has a delightful crunchy consistency. Cook just before you are ready to eat.

2 to 3 dozen dried oysters
½ pound dried fah tsoi
sesame oil, peanut oil, or chicken fat for
    sautéing

- Soak the oysters in water overnight. Drain.
- Soak the fah tsoi for about 15 minutes in warm or cold water to cover. Add several drops of oil to facilitate cleaning. (The fah tsoi is packaged uncleaned. Adding oil to the soaking water will free it of clinging impurities.) Drain the sea vegetable well.
- Sauté the fah tsoi and the drained oysters in the fat or oil over a low heat for about one minute. Serve immediately.

Laminaria (various species)

Korean rib stew with tasima

6 SERVINGS

½ ounce dried Laminaria
2 pounds short ribs of beef
2 tablespoons honey
2 tablespoons sesame oil
½ cup soy sauce
3 medium scallions, chopped
1 head (all cloves) garlic, finely chopped
3 tablespoons sesame salt
¼ teaspoon cracked black pepper
1 tablespoon flour
1 carrot
6 mushrooms, sliced
1½ cups water
1 egg
2 tablespoons sake
2 tablespoons pine nuts

• Soak the Laminaria for 30 minutes in warm water. Drain. Cut into bite-sized squares or rectangles.
• Score each piece of meat deeply several times with a sharp knife. Place meat in a heavy lidded pot. Marinate the meat for 1 hour in a mixture of honey and sesame oil. Turn ribs occasionally in the marinade. Add the soy sauce, scallions, garlic, sesame salt, pepper, and flour to the meat and marinade. Mix well.
• Cut the carrot diagonally into oval slices ¼-inch thick and add them to the meat. Add mushrooms, sea vegetable, and water. Cook rather gently for about 1 hour.
• Separate the egg and fry yolk and white separately, forming thin sheets. Slice into slivers or small wedges.
• When meat and sea vegetable are tender, add the sake and bring the stew to a simmer. Just before serving, sprinkle with pine nuts and decorate with pieces of egg.

Substitute

Pleurophycus gardneri

Laminaria (various species)

Kazunoko kombu

Komachi wakame, herring roe on wakame (Undaria), *is prepared in the same way. These products are available in Japanese markets. The herring also deposit their spawn on dulse* (Palmaria palmata). *This nameless treat is prized by experienced American foragers.*

• Kazunoko kombu is a seasonal delicacy. In the spring the herring lay their eggs on the growing tangle, covering most of the frond. These egg-laden sea vegetables are harvested, then salted and dried or steeped in brine for preservation. The dried product is washed in fresh water before using.

● Either dried or fresh may then be drained, cut into small pieces, and eaten as a salad, dressed with fresh ginger and soy sauce, or batter-dipped and cooked in hot oil as tempura (the author's favorite). The consistency in either case is crunchy and the taste quite special.

Fillet of sole, Ningpo style

4 TO 8 SERVINGS

DIP

¼ cup sour cream
2 teaspoons hoisen sauce
2 teaspoons hot red chili sauce
2 teaspoons tomato catsup
⅛ teaspoon crushed garlic
1 red or green bell pepper

TEMPURA BATTER

1 cup unbleached white flour
1 pinch baking soda
4 teaspoons tai tyau feen (sea vegetable powder, page 253)
1 cup club soda

THE FISH

1 pound sole fillets
2 tablespoons unbleached white flour
2 cups peanut oil for frying

● Prepare the dip well ahead of serving time. Combine all ingredients except pepper. Blend to a smooth consistency. Cover and refrigerate.

● Cut the pepper in half and remove seeds. Use the pepper halves as containers for the dip.

● Combine flour, baking soda, and sea vegetable powder, then mix with the club soda.

● Wash, drain, and cut each fillet into rectangles, 1 inch by 2 inches. Wipe dry. Dust each side with flour.

● Heat peanut oil to 350 degrees. Dip the sole into the tempura batter. Deep fry, a few fillets at a time, for about 5 seconds on each side.

● Place the dip in the center of a large platter and arrange the fish around it.

Laminaria angustata

Laminaria stew

The short cooking time indicated in this recipe requires that the more delicate species of Laminaria *be used.*

2 ounces dried Laminaria
1 pound lean pork, sliced into ½-inch by 1-inch
  pieces
¼ cup soy sauce
2 tablespoons sea salt
5 cups water

Substitutes

Laminaria longissima, L. longicruris,
Pleurophycus gardneri

- Soak the Laminaria for 20 minutes in enough cold water to cover. Cut the Laminaria frond into pieces ½ inch by 1 inch. Bring the water to a boil.
- Add pork pieces, soy sauce, and salt. Boil for 15 minutes.
- Add Laminaria sections and simmer 10 minutes more. Serve.

Porphyra tenera

Sashimi

4 TO 6 SERVINGS

Red clam, octopus (parboiled), abalone, sea bass, bream, sea urchin, cuttlefish, mackerel (marinated in vinegar), and conch are also popular additions to the fare.

½ cucumber
4 to 6 radishes
4 ounces raw tuna
1 fresh squid (medium-sized)
½ sheet dried nori
1 raw egg yolk
4 fresh large shrimp
3 lettuce leaves
1 tablespoon Japanese powdered green
  horseradish
soy sauce
3 to 4 ounces smoked salmon in ⅛-inch slices
1 slice lemon

- Cut the cucumber and radishes into thin strips.
- Cut tuna into ½-inch cubes.
- Cut squid lengthwise at the back and open the body. Remove legs and wash skin. Cut in half. Make cuts on the outside at ¼-inch intervals.
- Hold the sea vegetable over a flame (candle or stove) for a few seconds until crisp. Be very careful not to let it burn. Place this on the side of the squid that is not cut. Roll up from the end. Cut into ¼-inch slices.
- Cut the remaining half of the squid into thin strips.

Arrange them in a mound and top with raw egg yolk.
- Peel the raw shrimp. Remove veins. Cut into ¼-inch pieces. Place in a strainer. Rinse with cold water. Drain. Place on lettuce leaves.
- Mix dried green horseradish powder with equal parts of water.
- Place all the elements on a platter.
- Horseradish and soy sauce are mixed together by each guest and the seafood is dipped before eating.

Substitutes

Porphyra (various species)

Laminaria angustata

Ineh's matsumae

This delicious "home" recipe is served only to very special customers at Japanese sushi bars.

3 dried squid
1 long frond dried or fresh tangle
1 tablespoon dashi powder
2 cups sake
½ cup mirin
1 cup soy sauce
4½ cups water
pinch of cayenne pepper
1 carrot, shredded
2 tablespoons honey

- Soak the squid overnight in enough warm water to cover.
- Wash the fresh sea vegetable frond in cold water to remove all sand, or soak the dried frond for about 30 minutes in cold water to cover. Reserve the soaking water.
- Slice the tangle across the frond into very fine strips.
- Drain the squid. Cut the squid into matchlike slivers.
- From sea vegetable soaking water, measure out the 4½ cups needed for the recipe. Place this water in a pot with all seasonings. Bring to a boil. Boil 5 minutes.
- Add the squid and sea vegetable. Mix well. Remove to a container and cover tightly. Refrigerate and allow the preparation to marinate for at least 3 days. Mix it well about 3 times per day.
- This appetizer is best tasting after 7 days.

Substitutes

Laminaria longissima
Pleurophycus gardneri

Hizikia fusiforme

Hijiki al burro

1 cup dried hijiki
½ pound butter, softened
½ cup heavy cream
¾ cup parmesan cheese, freshly grated
sea salt
cracked pepper

- Soak the hijiki for 30 minutes in enough water to cover. Wash well. Drain, squeezing gently to release the water. Separate the hijiki into bite-sized clumps. Set aside.
- Beat the butter by hand until it becomes fluffy. Beat in the cream, a few tablespoons at a time. Beat in ½ pound of the cheese. Cover the bowl and set it in the refrigerator.
- Warm a serving plate in the oven at 250 degrees.
- Sauté the hijiki in a little melted butter until tender (about 15 minutes). Transfer to the hot serving plate.
- Add the cream, butter, and cheese mixture. Toss until all strands are coated. Season generously with salt and pepper. Serve immediately with grated parmesan cheese.

Porphyra tenera

Fish rice with nori garnish

4 SERVINGS

This easy-to-prepare dish, using nori as a garnish, is a good confidence builder for the beginner.

1 pound brown rice
1½ pints water
4 tablespoons sake
sea salt
3½ tablespoons soy sauce
½ pound loose-fleshed nonoily fish, for
    example, bass, turbot
1 sheet dried nori or ¼ cup dried fronds

- *Prepare rice:* wash the rice and place it in a heavy pan. Place the flat of your hand on top of the rice. Then pour in enough water to cover your hand. This method produces a perfect dry rice.
- Add the sake, ¼ tablespoon salt, and 1½ tablespoons soy sauce. Bring to a rolling boil. Reduce heat to low. Cover. Cook until done (about 35 to 45 minutes).
- Remove from heat. Fluff. Transfer to a bowl.
- While the rice is cooling, cook the fish in boiling,

lightly salted water. Drain, remove skin and bones, wrap in cloth, and rub the flesh lightly until it flakes.

● Place the fish in a heavy skillet with the honey, 2 tablespoons sake, 2 tablespoons soy sauce, and a pinch of salt. Cook, stirring briskly to prevent sticking, until the fish becomes dry in texture.

● Put the fish over the rice.

● If using foraged dried fronds, hold them over a flame for a few seconds and allow them to toast. Take care not to let them burn! Then either cut the commercial sheets in thin strips or crumble the foraged fronds over the fish and rice as a garnish.

Substitutes

Porphyra (various species)

Hizikia fusiforme

Hijiki, pork, green pepper, and Chinese rice noodles

2 TO 4 SERVINGS

Hijiki is the most popular sea vegetable both in Japan and in America. A light sauté brings out its unique flavor.

¼ pound pork, sliced into matchlike slivers
sake
¼ cup Chinese rice noodles
2 tablespoons vegetable oil
⅛ cup dried hijiki
1 green pepper, cut into very thin pieces
2 medium carrots, shredded
¼ pound bean sprouts
½ cup water
soy sauce
cracked pepper

● Sprinkle the pork slices with sake and let stand for a few minutes.

● Put the rice noodles in a pan and pour boiling water over them. Let stand 5 minutes. Drain and cut into 4-inch lengths.

● Add oil to skillet and sauté the pork pieces.

● Add hijiki and all other ingredients.

● Pour in ½ cup water. Season with soy sauce and ground pepper to taste. Sauté until liquid is evaporated. Serve.

Pleurophycus gardneri # **Pork-stuffed Pleurophycus fronds**

Stuffed fronds are an excellent choice of fare to be served at buffet dinners. Large numbers can be made up and refrigerated until needed.

5 Pleurophycus fronds (fresh or dried)
1¼ pounds ground lean pork
2½ cups cooked brown rice
10 fresh mushrooms, chopped
6 sprigs parsley, chopped
2 tablespoons wine vinegar
½ teaspoon paprika
sea salt and cracked pepper
3 tablespoons chopped almonds
½ teaspoon ground mace
4 dashes Tabasco
3 teaspoons powdered ginger
4 teaspoons horseradish
6 tablespoons soy sauce
toothpicks
¼ pound cheddar cheese (optional)

- If the fronds are fresh, merely rinse them for a few minutes under cold running water and cut them into lengths of about 5 inches. Cut off their stems. These stems can be chopped and added to the stuffing mixture or used in another recipe.
- If the fronds are dried, soak them for 20 minutes in enough cold water to cover. Wash well. Drain.
- Sauté the pork slowly until it releases its fat, about 5 minutes. Then add rice and other ingredients. Continue to sauté until all ingredients are blended, about 10 minutes. Remove from heat. Let cool a bit.
- Make little patties of stuffing mixture. Lay each frond down on a flat surface. Place the stuffing at one end and roll the mixture up in the frond, pinning it tightly with two toothpicks.
- Stack these rolls in a steaming device and steam for 45 minutes. Serve hot.
- Cheese is optional, or it can be added to only half the stuffing mixture, leaving the other half plain.

Substitutes

Laminaria angustata
L. longissima

Porphyra (various species)

Stuffed Porphyra fronds

4 TO 6 SERVINGS

This mouth-watering dish is a good choice for a large dinner party since most of the preparation can be done ahead of time.

1 cup pearl barley
3 cups beef broth
1 cup onions, chopped
2 cloves garlic, chopped
3 tablespoons butter or margarine
1 teaspoon sea salt
1 teaspoon cracked black pepper
6 large Porphyra fronds (fresh or dried)
corn oil

- Place the barley in a heavy skillet and dry roast for a few minutes until it turns a light yellow color and begins to smell nutlike. Place in a deep, covered pot.
- Add broth, onions, garlic, butter or margarine, salt, and pepper. Simmer gently, stirring occasionally, for 1 hour.
- Dip the dried sea vegetable fronds in boiling water for 1 second to make them pliable. Drain. Spread them out on waxed paper.
- Place a suitable amount (depending upon the size of the frond) of the barley stuffing in each frond and roll up the edges to cover the filling with several layers of frond.
- Sauté the stuffed rolls in a little corn oil for about 5 minutes until the Porphyra is tender.

Variation

- Sauté 2 to 3 teaspoons ground cumin for a minute or two in a frypan.
- Add ¼ pound ground beef. Sauté until meat is cooked. Add 2 to 3 teaspoons tumeric. Add cooked barley mixture. Stir well. Use this as an alternate filling.

Side dishes

Boiled Alaria
Sautéed Ascophyllum
Alaria with spring greens
Kizami kombu
Hijiki and dried squid, Korean style
Laminaria and cabbage side vegetable
Kombumaki with pork center
Stir-fried Irish moss
Hijiki with goma vinegar dressing
Hijiki sauté
Gluckaston
Sea vegetables Taiwan
Wakame and dried shrimp with ginger
Wakame in sweet and sour sauce
Nori okazu
Steamed sea lettuce
Wakame and shredded dried bonito
Dulse sauté

Alaria esculenta

Boiled Alaria

2 TO 4 SERVINGS

1 cup dried Alaria
2 cups water
4 tablespoons melted butter
juice of ½ lemon
1 tablespoon fresh parsley, finely chopped
cracked black pepper

- Soak the Alaria overnight in enough cold water to cover. Drain.
- Cut the frond across the midrib into ½-inch pieces. Sauté in a small amount of oil until bright green and aromatic.
- Add water to cover. Boil uncovered for a half hour. Add water if necessary to cover the Alaria. Cover pot. Boil 2 hours or pressure cook for 1 hour. Remove and drain.
- Squeeze the lemon juice into the butter. Mix. Pour over the vegetable. Top with chopped parsley. Sprinkle with salt and cracked pepper. Serve.

Substitutes

Alaria (various species)

Ascophyllum mackaii

Sautéed Ascophyllum

2 TO 4 SERVINGS

This dish is relished by people along the Massachusetts shore.

2 cups fresh young Ascophyllum
peanut oil
4 tablespoons soy sauce

- Collect this species only in very early spring before the fruiting bodies appear, that is, when plants are immature and delicate. Wash well in cold fresh water to remove sand, etc.
- Chop plants into bite-sized lengths. Steam until tender. Stir fry quickly in a little oil and soy sauce. Season to taste. Serve hot.

Alaria esculenta

Alaria with spring greens

Like Japanese wakame, Alaria has a sweet, tender midrib.

½ cup dried Alaria
corn oil
½ cup young dandelion greens
2 cups burdock greens
½ cup kale
½ cup chickweed
½ cup sorrel
½ cup mallows
½ cup watercress
½ cup parsley
½ cup mustard greens
½ cup celery leaves
white or cider vinegar
butter
sea salt and cracked pepper

- Soak the Alaria overnight in enough cold water to cover. Drain.
- Cut the frond across the midrib into ½-inch pieces. Sauté in a small amount of oil until bright green and sweetly aromatic.
- Add water to cover. Boil uncovered for a half hour. Add water if necessary to cover the Alaria. Cover pot. Boil 2 hours or pressure-cook for 1 hour. Remove. Drain.
- Steam the other greens until they are tender. Toss them with the Alaria. Serve with white or cider vinegar, butter, salt, and pepper.

Laminaria (various species)
Kjellmaniella gyrata

Kizami kombu

Dried slivered kombu, made from the Laminarias and related genera like Kjellmaniella, *is available commercially as kizami kombu.*

1 cup kizami kombu
2 cups water
4 tablespoons butter
sea salt and cracked pepper

Substitute

Homemade slivered Alaria (page 257)

- Boil the kombu in the water for 10 minutes. It should become tender and take up almost all the water. Drain off remaining water.
- Season with the butter, cracked black pepper, and salt. Serve.

Hizikia fusiforme

Hijiki and dried squid, Korean style

2 TO 4 SERVINGS

1 dried squid
1 ounce dried hijiki
1 fresh red pepper
1 teaspoon ginger root
1 teaspoon sesame seeds
sesame oil
1 cup water
3 tablespoons soy sauce
2 tablespoons sake

- Soak the squid in cold water overnight. Drain. Cut into bite-sized pieces.
- Soak the hijiki in cold water for 20 minutes. Rinse well. Drain. Separate into bite-sized clumps.
- Cut the fresh red pepper and the ginger into fine slivers.
- Roast the sesame seeds in a heavy frying pan.
- Sauté the squid and hijiki in a little sesame oil for about 5 minutes.
- Add the water, soy sauce, sake, ginger, and fresh red pepper. Cook uncovered over a low heat until the liquid evaporates. Serve.

Laminaria angustata

Laminaria and cabbage side vegetable

4 SERVINGS

Laminaria foraged and sold commercially in North America is often labeled kombu.

1 cup dried Laminaria
1 cup cabbage, slivered into thin strips or 1 cup carrots, coarsely slivered
2 tablespoons sesame oil

Substitutes

Laminaria longissima, L. longicruris, Pleurophycus gardneri

- Soak the Laminaria for 1 hour in enough cold water to cover. Drain. Reserve the soaking water.
- Cut into 1-inch squares.
- Boil uncovered in the soaking water for 1 hour. Cover and boil for 2 hours or pressure-cook for 1 hour. Drain.
- Sauté the cabbage or the carrots quickly in sesame oil. When they are slightly wilted, remove and toss lightly with the Laminaria. Serve.

Laminaria angustata

Kombumaki with pork center

Kombumaki (rolled kombu) is available commercially with a variety of fillings.

8 ounces dried kombu or 4 ounces fresh fronds
1 pound ground lean pork
4 tablespoons fresh ginger root, peeled and minced
⅓ cup soy sauce
1 teaspoon sea salt
3 tablespoons honey
1 teaspoon cracked pepper

Substitutes

Laminaria longissima
Pleurophycus gardneri

● Soak the dried kombu for 1 hour in cold water to cover. If fresh kombu is used, simply wash the fronds in cold water to remove all sand and drain well.
● Cut into lengths 5 inches by 2½ inches. Place a tablespoon or 2 of pork in each piece of frond. Add a pea-sized portion of minced ginger. Roll the frond up from one end and tie with a piece of string.
● Put the kombumaki in a saucepan, add water to cover, and cook gently until tender (1½ to 3 hours, depending upon the thickness of the species of Laminaria used). Add the remaining seasoning and cook 20 minutes more.
● Remove the kombumaki from the saucepan and serve.

Chondrus crispus

Stir-fried Irish moss

Seacoast residents of Massachusetts enjoy this healthful and good-tasting dish.

1 cup fresh or ½ cup dried Irish moss
4 tablespoons peanut oil
4 tablespoons sesame oil

● Wash the fresh Irish moss thoroughly in cold water. Drain. Soak the dried sea vegetable for about 30 minutes in enough cold water to cover. Drain. Pick over to remove any foreign matter. Chop into bite-sized flowerets.
● Heat the oil in a wok or skillet. Stir fry the vegetables quickly in a mixture of the two oils until tender. Serve.

Hizikia fusiforme

Hijiki with goma vinegar dressing

⅓ cup dried hijiki
1 carrot
1 dried bean curd skin
2 teaspoons vinegar
1 teaspoon soy sauce
2 teaspoons honey
2 tablespoons white sesame seeds

- Place the hijiki in a colander and wash it under cold running water.
- Place the carrot, hijiki, and bean curd in a pot with enough cold water to cover. Bring to a boil. Boil 15 minutes. Remove from heat. Drain.
- Remove the bean curd and cut it into bite-sized pieces. Chop the carrot and hijiki into a coarse mixture. Put all in a frying pan and sauté with 1 teaspoon vinegar, 1 teaspoon soy sauce, and 1 teaspoon honey.
- Pan roast the sesame seeds, then grind them with mortar and pestle, adding more vinegar and honey to form a paste.
- Combine the chopped hijiki and carrot with the bean curd and coat the mixture with sesame/vinegar paste. Serve.

Hizikia fusiforme

Hijiki sauté

6 TO 8 SERVINGS

This popular dish has made many a convert.

½ cup dried hijiki
2 cups carrots, sliced into rounds
2 cups onions, sliced into rounds
¼ cup peanut oil
1 tablespoon sesame oil
sea salt and cracked pepper to taste

- Soak the hijiki for about 30 minutes in enough cold water to cover. Drain well. Chop into bite-sized clumps.
- Sauté the carrots in a little hot oil until they are almost cooked.
- Add the onions and sauté until they are wilted. Add a little more oil if needed.
- Add the hijiki. Sauté for 5 to 7 minutes. Season to taste. Serve hot.

Porphyra perforata

Gluckaston

6 TO 8 SERVINGS

Gluckaston was a popular dish prepared by both the Tsawatainuk Indian Tribe and the colonial population of Kingcome Village, British Columbia. It was made with Royal City Canned Cream Corn, a favored brand in the old days.

1 cup dried laver
4 cups corn, removed from husk
2 cups milk
1 cup fresh heavy cream
3 tablespoons corn oil

- Crumble the dried laver into small bits. Measure out 1 cup. Place the corn, sea vegetable, and milk in the top of a double boiler and boil gently for 30 minutes. Add cream and oil. Reheat, but do not boil. Serve.

Substitutes

Porphyra (various species)

Porphyra (various species)
Monostroma (various species)

Sea vegetables Taiwan

2 TO 4 SERVINGS

A great variety of seasoned sea vegetables are enjoyed by the Taiwanese.

1 cup fresh Porphyra fronds
1 cup fresh Monostroma fronds
½ cup sliced fresh mushrooms
1 teaspoon honey
2 tablespoons soy sauce
cracked pepper to taste
4 tablespoons peanut oil

- Wash fresh sea vegetables quickly under cold running water. Do not soak! Pat dry with a clean towel.
- Combine soy sauce, honey, and spices.
- Heat oil in frying pan. Gently sauté mushrooms until soft.
- Add sea vegetables and sauté for 2 minutes more.
- Pour in spice-liquid mixture. Bring to a quick boil. Serve hot.

Undaria pinnatifida

Wakame and dried shrimp with ginger

2 TO 4 SERVINGS

1 ounce dried wakame
½ cup water
½ teaspoon honey
1 tablespoon soy sauce
½ pound dried shrimp
½ ounce fresh ginger cut in matchlike slivers

- Soak the dried sea vegetable in cold water for 5 minutes. Remove. Drain. Cut into strips or squares.
- Boil the ½ cup of water. Add the honey, soy sauce, and dried shrimp. Cook for 10 minutes.
- Add the wakame and ginger. Continue to cook until the liquid evaporates. Serve alone or over brown rice.

Substitute

Petalonia fascia

Undaria pinnatifida

Wakame in sweet and sour sauce

2 SERVINGS

2 ounces dried wakame
2 scallions
2 slices fresh ginger root
1 tablespoon cornstarch
½ cup cold water
2 tablespoons soy sauce
3 tablespoons cider vinegar
2 tablespoons honey

- Soak the wakame for 10 minutes in enough cold water to cover. Wash well. Drain. Cut wakame into 1-inch by 4-inch pieces, removing center vein.
- Cut scallions into matchlike slivers 4 inches long. Mince the ginger root.
- Dissolve the cornstarch in cold water. Add the soy sauce, vinegar, and honey.
- Stir fry the ginger and scallions in the sesame oil until they become wilted.
- Add the liquid mixture and bring to a boil.
- Add the wakame. Turn heat down, stir, and simmer gently for 10 minutes. Serve piping hot.

Substitute

Petalonia fascia

Porphyra (various species)

Nori okazu

This spicy side dish according to Japanese custom is meant to accompany a bland food such as rice.

3 tablespoons peanut oil
1 clove garlic, chopped coarsely
1 teaspoon fresh ginger root, chopped coarsely
2 cups fresh or 1 cup dried nori
2 tablespoons soy sauce
2 tablespoons dashi stock

- Heat the peanut oil in a frying pan. Add the garlic and ginger. Sauté these until they are golden brown, then remove them from the oil.
- If dried nori is used, first dip in cold water, drain immediately, and pat dry. Chop the nori and add it to the hot oil.
- Cover the pan tightly and sauté gently until very soft (about 25 minutes).
- Add the soy sauce and dashi stock. Stir. Serve over rice.

Ulva lactuca

Steamed sea lettuce

2 TO 4 SERVINGS

Depending upon the season, Monostroma and Porphyra, sometimes referred to as sea lettuce, may be more tender than Ulva.

1 cup fresh young sea lettuce fronds
2 tablespoons butter
pinch dashi powder or 2 tablespoons cider
  vinegar

- Wash the fresh foraged fronds in cold water. Do not soak! Drain. Steam the fronds until they are tender (about 10 minutes). Place in individual bowls. Sprinkle with dashi powder or vinegar. Top with a pat of butter. Serve.

Substitutes

Ulva (various species), *Monostroma*
(various species), *Porphyra* (various species)

Undaria pinnatifida

Wakame and shredded dried bonito

2 TO 4 SERVINGS

1 ounce dried wakame
1 tablespoon white sesame seeds
1½ ounces dried bonito flakes
2 tablespoons honey
2 tablespoons sake

- Soak the sea vegetable in cold water for 5 minutes. Drain. Cut into small pieces.
- Dry roast the sesame seeds in a heavy frying pan.
- Simmer the wakame and bonito flakes with 2 tablespoons honey and 2 tablespoons sake until the liquid evaporates.
- Sprinkle with toasted sesame seeds. Serve immediately.

Substitute

Petalonia fascia

Palmaria palmata

Dulse sauté

2 TO 4 SERVINGS

Dulse is particularly delicious in combination with fresh vegetables.

¼ cup turnips, sliced into thin rounds
¼ cup carrots, sliced into thin rounds
¼ cup celery, coarsely chopped
¼ cup corn or peanut oil
1 cup soft cooked oats
1 ounce dried dulse, chopped

- Sauté the vegetables quickly in the oil.
- Add the oats, which have been cooked to a mushy consistency in a generous amount of water for several hours.
- Add the chopped dulse. Simmer for 1 hour or more.

Desserts

Peanut mousse
European apricot candy
Irish moss blender pudding
Irish moss mousse
Carrot cake with nori flakes
Irish moss blancmange pie
Red ribbons jelly from South Africa
Fluffy snow agar
Homemade yokan
Skim milk and apple blancmange
Lime agar dessert
Tokoroten (Japanese agar jelly dessert)
Shimmery apple cider gel
Korean kim candy

Gelidium (various species)
Gracilaria (various species)

Peanut mousse

8 SERVINGS

The combination of peanut butter and lemon juice transforms the common ingredients in this favorite dessert of the Congo.

2 tablespoons agar powder
2 cups boiling water
1 cup fresh lemon juice
4 tablespoons honey
½ cup peanut butter
6 egg whites, stiffly beaten
1½ cups whipping cream, whipped
8 teaspoons chocolate shavings

● Dissolve the agar powder in the boiling water. Let cool for 5 minutes.
● Add the lemon juice, honey, and peanut butter. Mix to a homogeneous liquid.
● Fold in the beaten egg whites and about two-thirds of the whipped cream.
● Pour into stemmed glasses. Chill. Top with extra whipped cream. Sprinkle with chocolate shavings. Serve.

Gelidium (various species)
Gracilaria (various species)

European apricot candy

YIELDS ABOUT 2½ POUNDS

2 cups pureed apricots
3 cups honey
4 teaspoons agar powder
¼ cup butter
³/₅ cup cornstarch

● Dried apricots can be used. Just soak overnight in warm water to cover, then puree the fruit with its soaking water.
● Heat the pureed apricots, honey, and agar powder together in a heavy skillet. Boil carefully until the mixture registers 225 degrees on a candy thermometer.
● Add butter and cornstarch.
● Pour onto a shallow wooden frame or into a low pan or dish. Allow the mixture to coagulate. Cut into squares.

Chondrus crispus

Irish moss blender pudding

This quick and easy dessert is a child-pleaser and can be made up and stored in the refrigerator for days.

¾ cup dried Irish moss
1 quart whole milk
2 cups fresh strawberries, pureed
½ cup honey
pinch of sea salt

- Soak the Irish moss for 30 minutes in enough cold water to cover. Wash well. Drain. Pick it over to remove any foreign matter.
- Pour the milk into the top of a double boiler.
- Place the sea vegetable in a square of cheesecloth (a piece about 8 inches square). Tie up the ends and suspend the bag in the milk. Simmer for 30 minutes. Press the bag against the side of the pan occasionally to release the gel. Stir continually.
- Remove from heat. Discard the spent bag.
- Pour the milk mixture into the blender. Add the pureed strawberries, honey, and salt. Blend at a high speed.
- Pour into dessert dishes. Cover tightly and refrigerate for several hours before serving.

Substitutes

Gigartina (various species)

Chondrus crispus

Irish moss mousse

4 SERVINGS

½ cup Irish moss
1 pint milk
½ teaspoon vanilla extract
¼ cup honey
1 egg yolk, beaten
1 egg white, stiffly beaten
½ pint whipping cream

- Soak the Irish moss for 15 minutes in enough cold water to cover. Drain. Remove any foreign matter.
- Place the Irish moss in a cheesecloth square (about 8 inches square). Tie up the ends.
- Place the milk and flavoring in the top of a double boiler. Suspend the cheesecloth bag in the milk. Slowly bring liquid to a boil. Reduce heat and simmer very

gently for not more than 20 minutes. Press the bag against the side of the pan occasionally to release the gel. Stir constantly. Remove from heat. Discard the spent bag.

- Allow mixture to cool a bit. Add the honey.
- Pour the mixture into a bowl, and while it is still warm, stir in the freshly beaten egg yolk. Finally fold in the stiffly beaten egg white.
- Spoon into stemmed glasses. Cover tightly and refrigerate. Top with whipped cream just before serving.

Substitutes

Gigartina (various species)

Porphyra tenera

Carrot cake with nori flakes

6 SERVINGS

Varying amounts of nori can be used in this recipe. Doubling the sea vegetable will produce an extra-nutty, rich taste.

½ cup melted butter
1 sheet dried nori
1 cup finely grated raw carrot
1¼ cups whole wheat flour
2 eggs
½ cup honey
2 teaspoons baking powder
½ cup fresh lemon juice

- Preheat oven to 350 degrees.
- Melt the butter in a saucepan.
- Tear the nori into pieces about the size of peas, and add to the melted butter to hydrate (about 5 minutes).
- Combine all ingredients. Mix well.
- Pour into well-buttered 5-cup mold or bread pan. Bake 1 hour.
- Let cool 10 minutes before removing from pan. Cool completely before serving.

Substitute

Porphyra suborbiculata

Chondrus crispus

Irish moss blancmange pie

8 SERVINGS

Chartreuse pistachio nuts against the shimmery mauve background of the pie produce a beautiful effect guests will long remember.

GRAHAM CRACKER PIECRUST
1¼ cup graham cracker crumbs
¼ cup raw sugar
½ teaspoon cinnamon
⅓ cup very soft butter or margarine

1½ cups dried Irish moss
1 quart whole milk
1 cup strawberry preserve
1 tablespoon frozen orange juice concentrate
pinch of sea salt
½ cup pistachio nuts, shelled and chopped

● Prepare graham crust and refrigerate it uncovered for 1 hour. Combine crumbs, sugar, and cinnamon in a bowl. Add the butter and blend with a fork. Press crumb mixture evenly over bottom and sides of a 9-inch pie plate. Chill.
● Soak Irish moss for 30 minutes in enough cold water to cover. Wash well. Drain. Pick it over to remove any foreign matter.
● Pour the milk into the top of a double boiler.
● Place Irish moss in a square of cheesecloth (a piece about 12 inches square). Tie up the ends and suspend the bag in the milk. Simmer for 30 minutes. Press the bag against the side of the pan occasionally to release the gel. Stir continually.
● Remove from heat. Discard the spent bag.
● Add the strawberry preserve, orange juice concentrate, and salt. Stir well.
● Pour the blancmange into the piecrust. Sprinkle the nuts on top. Let stand for 10 minutes, then cover carefully and refrigerate for several hours before serving.
● To serve, set the pie tin in a little hot water for a minute before removing the first slice.

Substitutes

Gigartina (various species)

Gelidium (various species)

South African red ribbons jelly

This food was introduced to the Capetown colonists by their Malay slaves. Although the traditional recipe uses the Red alga Suhria vitata *(red ribbons), the process can be used for making jelly from the fresh or unbleached plants of any of the Gelidium species.*

1 cup dried Gelidium or 2 cups fresh fronds
3 to 4 pints water
spices: cloves, cinnamon, and lemon peel
1 cup honey
2 cups fresh orange juice or fresh lemon juice
½ cup brandy or sherry

- This jelly, when prepared from fresh plants, will have a rank taste. To avoid this, the first cooking of the fresh plant is always rejected. The jelly prepared from dried plants that have been sun-bleached has an agreeable bland taste.
- Wash the fresh or dried plants well before using. Prepare fresh plants by boiling in a lidded pot with enough water to cover for about 15 minutes. Uncover and boil 15 minutes more. This will allow fumes to escape.
- Drain the plants and discard the cooking liquid. Place the plants in a pot, this time with 3 to 4 pints of water.
- Tie the spices in a square of cheesecloth and suspend this bag in the liquid.
- Cover pan and boil the algae to a pulp. Remove from heat. Discard spent spice bag.
- Put the mixture through a sieve and discard the spent algae.
- Add the honey, fruit juice, and liquor. Stir well.
- Place the liquid in a mold that has just been dipped in cold water. Allow to set. Cover tightly and refrigerate until chilled. Unmold. Serve.

Gelidium (various species)
Gracilaria (various species)

Fluffy snow agar

4 SERVINGS

Up until 1875 in Japan, the twentieth year of the Emperor Meiji, one could see men pulling wagons through the streets calling out "kanten," "tokoroten"! Affixed to the carts were glass screens, picturing the beautiful seascapes where the gel-producing plants were harvested.

1 stick kanten (½ ounce)
1½ cups water
12 ounces honey
2 egg whites
½ teaspoon grated lemon rind
1 tablespoon lemon juice
4 fresh strawberries (optional)

- Wash the kanten and squeeze out the water. Place in a saucepan and soak for 30 minutes in 1½ cups water. Then begin to cook over low heat until the kanten has melted. Strain through a fine sieve into another saucepan.
- Add honey and cook over medium heat until liquid is reduced by half. Remove any film that rises to the top.
- Beat the egg whites until stiff. Add lemon rind and juice and beat this gradually into the warm kanten liquid. Mix well and let stand until it begins to thicken.
- Pour into a wetted or lightly buttered 6-inch square mold and allow to set. Chill well.
- Turn out and cut into 8 pieces. Place half a strawberry on each piece. Serve.

Gelidium (various species)
Gracilaria (various species)

Homemade yokan

YIELDS ABOUT 1½ POUNDS

Any cooked pureed beans can be substituted for the limas. Frozen beans work as well as fresh. Traditional Japanese recipes call for red adzuki beans.

1 cup (loosely packed) strand kanten, washed
2 cups cooled pureed lima beans
1 cup honey

- Take a handful of kanten strands and rinse them under lukewarm running water. Squeeze out the water and rinse again. Squeeze gently.

- Measure out 1 cup of loosely packed moist strands. Place in a saucepan with the pureed lima beans and heat to boiling. Boil gently, stirring continually until the kanten is completely dissolved. Remove from heat. Let cool for 5 minutes.
- Add honey. Stir well.
- Pour into low flat mold that has just been dipped in cold water. Let cool at room temperature. Cut into small squares. May be served with tea or given to the children as a wholesome snack.

Variation
- Add well-cooked chopped chestnut meats to the hot liquid just before it is poured into the mold.

Chondrus crispus

Skim milk and apple blancmange

8 SERVINGS

Sea vegetable extracts supply bulk and nourishment without accompanying calories.

¾ cup dried Irish moss
1 quart skim milk
½ cup honey
juice of ½ lemon
2 large apples, peeled, cored, and minced

- Soak Irish moss for 30 minutes in enough cold water to cover. Wash well. Drain. Pick it over to remove any foreign matter.
- Pour the milk into the top of a double boiler.
- Place sea vegetable in a square of cheesecloth (a piece about 8 inches square). Tie up the ends and suspend the bag in the milk. Simmer for 30 minutes. Press the bag against the side of the pan occasionally to release the gel. Stir continually.
- Remove from heat. Discard the spent bag.
- Add the honey, lemon juice, and apples. Stir well.
- Pour the mixture into a lightly buttered mold. Cover tightly and refrigerate for several hours before serving.

Substitutes

Gigartina (various species)

Gelidium (various species)
Gracilaria (various species)

Lime agar dessert

In Japan, before the age of mechanical refrigeration, the liquid agar gel was manufactured high up in the mountains. It was solidified, cut into strips, frozen in the snow, then allowed to thaw, releasing its acrid pink liquid. Then it was dried to form kanten.

1 stick kanten (½ ounce)
1½ cups water
¾ cup freshly squeezed lime juice
1½ cups honey
2 egg whites
1 cup whipping cream

- Wash the kanten and squeeze out the water. Place in pan with 1½ cups cold water and soak for 30 minutes. Cook over medium heat until kanten has dissolved completely. Strain through muslin (optional). Cook until liquid is reduced by half. Remove any film as it rises.
- Remove from heat and allow to cool until it is just warm. Add lime juice and honey. Mix well.
- Beat the egg whites until they form stiff peaks. Fold the egg whites into the warm kanten liquid.
- Pour into low rectangular dish that has just been dipped in cold water. Allow to set. Cover tightly and refrigerate.
- When ready to serve, cut into ½-inch squares. Pile into dessert glasses. Top with whipped cream.

Gelidium amansii

Tokoroten

6 TO 8 SERVINGS

Agar is a sea vegetable gel extracted from certain members of the Rhodophyceae *(Red algae), principally species of* Gelidium *and* Gracilaria. *It is available in powdered form. Tokoroten can also be made from commercially sold agar powder. Proportions of ½ to ¾ tablespoon per 2 cups water produce a delicate gel.*

1 quart water
½ cup dried gelidium plants (tengusa)

JAPANESE SWEET PASTE
½ cup raw sugar
½ cup fresh orange, lemon, or lime juice,
    strained
Mix to the consistency of paste.

JAPANESE PIQUANT PASTE
½ cup rice vinegar
½ cup raw sugar
1 tablespoon soy sauce
Mix to the consistency of paste.

SWEET SYRUP
¾ cup pureed fresh pear
¼ cup honey
Mix well.

Substitutes

Gelidium (various species)
Gracilaria (various species)

● Dried Gelidium plants are sold bleached (white to yellow in color) or unbleached (pink in color). To ensure a pleasant-tasting jelly, unbleached plants of this genus are usually soaked in several changes of fresh water before use, until almost all of their pink coloring is gone. Then they are drained and picked clean of any foreign matter. The dried bleached plants are soaked in fresh water for about 30 minutes, drained, and also picked clean. (Most Gelidium is dried and packaged unwashed, with whatever crustaceans, shells, sand, etc., might be clinging to it.) At this point either product is ready for boiling.

● Boil over moderate heat for 30 minutes to 1 hour or until all of the plant is dissolved. Remove from heat. Allow liquid to cool for 5 minutes.

● Pour into low flat pan or dish that has just been dipped in cold water. The liquid will set at room temperature, forming agar. When it has jelled, cut into 2-inch squares. The traditional method of preparation is to extrude these jelled agar squares or cakes through a device called a tokoroten tsuki (pusher) that transforms them into spaghetti-sized "noodles."

The dish is then dressed with a sweet paste or syrup.

Gelidium (various species)
Gracilaria (various species)

Shimmery apple cider gel

4 TO 6 SERVINGS

Agar, unlike other gels, will set at room temperature, so sweetened desserts will keep without refrigeration.

2 cups apple cider
1½ teaspoons agar powder

- Boil the apple cider. Remove from heat.
- Dissolve the agar powder in the hot liquid. Let cool for 5 minutes.
- Pour into a low flat dish that has just been dipped into cold water. The gel will set at room temperature but should be chilled before serving.
- Cut the gel into small squares and pile into dessert glasses. Top with whipped cream if desired.

Porphyra suborbiculata

Korean kim candy

Children love these sweet but healthful and nutritious candies!

2 cups glutenous rice
1 cup sesame seeds
1 tablespoon sea salt
10 sheets dried kim
peanut oil

- *Sweet rice paste:* Cook the rice. Mash into a homogeneous paste.
  Dry roast the sesame seeds for a few minutes in a heavy frying pan. Then mix with salt and pulverize them in a blender or use a mortar and pestle.
- *Candy:* Lay the kim sheets out on a board and spread them with a very thin layer (about $1/16$ inch) of rice paste. Sprinkle with a fine layer of the ground sesame seed mixture.
- Sun dry these for one day, then cut into bite-sized pieces with a pair of scissors.

• Fry them in a little peanut oil for about 15 minutes or cook over a barbecue fire or oven-broil. During cooking, the candy must be turned constantly until done to avoid burning or scorching.

• These "rock candies" may be served with hot chocolate as a winter treat. Prepared, they will keep for six months or so.

Substitutes

Porphyra (various species)

Beverages

Korean spice tea
Hot dulse lemonade
Lynn's Bloody Mary with kelp seasoning
Bladderwrack tea
Yogurt drink
Glanville Penn's Tortola Iron Jack cocktail

Codium fragile

Korean spice tea

Chonggak is available dried (imported from Korea) for use as tea in Korean markets in major cities.

● Collect fresh growing chonggak from its place of attachment. Wash in cool to lukewarm water. Several washings will be necessary to remove all the sand and clinging chips of rock, shell, or coral. Remove the holdfast and any hardened sections. Chop into pea-sized pieces.

● Dry the chonggak thoroughly in strong sun and a good breeze. Then pulverize into a powder using mortar and pestle. The collecting, washing, and drying of chonggak must be done on a sunny breezy day to ensure speed in drying and avoid decomposition.

● Store the prepared tea powder in an airtight container and use as required. This species will produce a spicy tea. Simply use the dried powder as you would use tea leaves.

Palmaria palmata

Hot dulse lemonade

1 SERVING

This drink is an old New England treatment for coughs and colds. A little rum transforms it into an excellent "hot toddy."

● Soak dulse for 20 minutes in enough cold water to cover. Wash well. Drain.

● Mix lemon juice and honey in a tall glass.

● Boil the handful of dulse in the water for 20 minutes. Pour this liquid through a fine sieve to remove the dulse.

● Fill the glass with the strained liquid. Drink while hot.

Macrocystis (various species)

Lynn's Bloody Mary with kelp seasoning

YIELDS 4 COCKTAILS

Professional guides in the mountains of Tibet always travel with a supply of powdered kelp. They say the strength of the gods is in the plant. As they mount the heights where the air is thin these men ingest a pinch of kelp to relieve muscle strain and feel a burst of new energy.

Powdered kelp is available under several brand names in natural food stores. The species from which most commercial preparations are made is Macrocystis pyrifera.

1 teaspoon powdered kelp
1 quart unsalted tomato juice
juice of ½ lemon
⅛ teaspoon celery salt
1 teaspoon soy sauce
4 dashes hot red chili sauce (optional)
4 ounces vodka (optional)
cracked ice

● Shake all ingredients together until they are well mixed and chilled. Pour into tall glasses. Serve.

Fucus vesiculosis

Bladderwrack tea

YIELDS 4 CUPS DRIED MATERIAL

Bladderwrack tea is available packaged, in natural food stores. Over a period of time Fucus is said to be an arterial cleansing agent normalizing the function of body organs by aiding circulation of blood through the tissues.

8 cups fresh bladderwrack

● Gather fresh bladderwrack at low tide. Cut lateral branches from the hard stipe section. Wash them well in cold fresh water. Drain. Chop coarsely.
● Spread out on a clean surface to sun dry in a good breeze. Then oven dry at 100 degrees for 20 minutes.
● Place in a sealed container. Use 1 to 1½ teaspoons to a cup of boiling water. Let steep 3 to 5 minutes. Sweeten to taste.

Substitutes

Fucus (various species)

Palmaria palmata
Porphyra (various species)

Yogurt drink

1 SERVING

Powdered kelp is thought to be an arterial cleansing agent. Dr. H. E. Kirchner, M.D., health food pioneer, recommends adding kelp to salads, cottage cheese, soups, fruit juices, breads, cookies, and cooked potatoes.

¼ teaspoon powdered kelp
1 tablespoon dried dulse, chopped fine
1 tablespoon dried laver, chopped fine
½ cup yogurt
½ cup tomato/vegetable juice

● Place all ingredients in a blender and liquefy for about 1 minute. Serve chilled or place the blended liquid in the top of a double boiler and heat. Serve hot.

Gracilaria (various species)

Glanville Penn's Tortola Iron Jack cocktail

8 TO 12 SERVINGS

Throughout the Islands, people will tell you, jokingly, that large families are a direct result of the Jamaican affinity for sea moss cocktails.

¼ cup dried sea moss
1 quart water
1 teaspoon allspice
1 teaspoon almond extract or other flavoring
1 quart milk
4 tablespoons honey
¾ ounce Jamaican rum per cocktail (optional)

● Soak sea moss overnight. Wash. Remove any foreign matter. Pour the water into the top of a double boiler. Place the sea moss and the allspice in a square of cheesecloth (about 8 inches square). Tie up the ends and suspend the bag in the liquid.
● Bring the mixture to a boil. Reduce the heat to low and cook for 30 minutes. Press the cheesecloth bag against the side of the pan occasionally to release the gel. Stir continually. Bring to a boil. Remove from heat. Discard bag.
● Add almond extract. Allow the liquid to cool slightly.
● Add milk, honey, ice, and rum, and place in a blender at high speed. Serve icy cold.

Pickles, Preserves and Condiments

Jarred limu oki oki
Ogo kim chee (pickled ogo)
Sweet Irish moss jelly
Nereocystis sweet pickles
Laminaria and cauliflower pickle
Hawaiian Ulva
Kombu no tsukudani (simmered in soy sauce)
Dulse condiment
Hot Ulva relish
Hawaiian Porphyra
Muck a Muck's Porphyra condiment
Hawaiian Sargassum
Japanese sea vegetable condiment (sake ocha-zuke nori)
Hawaiian Gracilaria
Hawaiian Ahnfeltia
Hawaiian Codium
Hawaiian Enteromorpha
Rich man's laver

Gracilaria (various species)

Jarred limu oki oki

YIELDS ABOUT 1 QUART

This Hawaiian relish is extolled as tasting like Russian caviar! It is most often made with limu huluhuluwaena, Grateloupia filicina, *though Gracilaria is a popular substitute.*

4 cups prepared Gracilaria
1 cup chopped kukui nut kernels (*Aleurites moluccana*), finely chopped
1 tablespoon sea salt

- Prepare the limu. Add roasted kukui nut kernels and salt. Mix well. Spoon into a glass jar. Cover. Refrigerate and use as needed.
- The jarred preparation will keep for several months and can be eaten with bread and butter, cold or roasted meats, raw or cooked fish, pasta, or boiled root vegetables.

Gracilaria (various species)

Ogo kim chee (pickled ogo)

YIELDS ABOUT 1 QUART

This dish is prepared in Korean coastal communities all over the world.

2 pounds fresh ogo, chopped into 2- to 3-inch pieces
½ cup sea salt
2 cloves garlic, chopped, per quart of wilted sea vegetable
1 to 2 chopped onions or ½ cup chopped scallions
1 teaspoon chopped red chilies or ½ teaspoon cayenne powder
½ teaspoon paprika

- Wash and clean the ogo. Salt and wilt by allowing it to stand overnight.
- Next day, drain off any liquid that has formed. Add garlic, onions, chilies (or cayenne), and paprika. Toss to coat the ogo. Pack tightly into jars. Seal and refrigerate.
- Let stand for a few days before using.
- Small amounts of Codium and Ulva may be added to the ogo. Hardened portions of the Codium plants must be trimmed off, but otherwise preparation of these three algae is identical to that for the ogo. The *Codium* adds a "just picked" freshness to the mixture.

Chondrus crispus

Sweet Irish moss jelly

YIELDS 1 QUART

This festive jelly makes a lovely holiday gift.

1½ cups dried Irish moss
1 quart water
juice of 2 lemons
1½ cups port wine
¼ teaspoon cinnamon
¼ cup honey

- Soak Irish moss for 30 minutes in enough cold water to cover. Wash well. Drain. Pick it over to remove any foreign matter.
- Pour the water into the top of a double boiler. Place the Irish moss in a square of cheesecloth (a piece about 12 inches square). Tie up the ends and suspend the bag in the water. Simmer for 30 minutes. Press the bag against the side of the pan occasionally to release the gel. Stir continually.
- Remove from heat. Discard the spent bag. Add lemon juice, port wine, cinnamon, and honey. Stir well. Pour the mixture into jelly jars. Cover. Store in the refrigerator.

Substitutes

Gigartina (various species)

Nereocystis luetkeana

Nereocystis sweet pickles

YIELDS 18 TO 20 PINTS

approximately 1 large Nereocystis (stipe portion only) per 1 pint of pickles
2 pints cider vinegar
1 pint water
3 pounds raw sugar (or honey)
3 large onions
8 slices lemon
6 sticks cinnamon
2 tablespoons whole cloves
1 tablespoon mace
1 jarred pimiento, sliced

- Pare off outer skin of the plant with a potato peeler. Rinse the peeled stipe (stem) in cold water. Cut into rings or rectangles ¼ inch in thickness.
- Soak the cut pieces in fresh water for 3 days, changing the water several times to remove bitter sea salts. (Ask everyone in the house to drain the water from the plants and replace it with fresh water as they pass by the pan.)
- On the fourth day, place the rings in cold water to cover. Bring to a boil and simmer 12 to 14 minutes. Drain and measure out 10 pints of rings.

● Combine the cider vinegar, water, sugar (or honey), onions, lemon slices, cinnamon, cloves, mace, and pimiento slices. Bring to a boil and simmer for 5 to 10 minutes. Pour this hot syrup over the rings and let stand overnight.

● Next day, drain off (and reserve) the syrup. Heat it to the boiling point. Again, pour it over the rings. Let this stand another night.

● On the sixth day, drain off (and reserve) the syrup. Bring the syrup to a boil. Fill hot (sterile) jars with the rings; cover with hot syrup and seal. Let stand at least a month before serving.

Substitute

Postelsia palmaeformis (stipes)

Laminaria (various species)

Laminaria and cauliflower pickles

YIELDS 1 PINT

1 cup dried Laminaria
5 umeboshi plums
several chiso leaves
2 cups cauliflower

● Soak the Laminaria for 1 hour in enough cold water to cover. Reserve soaking water. Cut into 1-inch squares. Boil uncovered for 1 hour. (Adjust time according to the thickness of the fronds.) Remove. Drain.

● Boil several umeboshi plums with the chiso leaves in water to cover. Boil until the plums are soft. Remove the plums for use in another recipe. Reserve the juice.

● Break the cauliflower into small flowerets. Pack the Laminaria and cauliflower tightly in a jar and fill the jar with the plum juice. Seal jar. Refrigerate and let stand for 2 or 3 days before eating.

Substitutes

Pleurophycus gardneri
Kjellmaniella gyrata

Ulva (various species)

Hawaiian Ulva

1 cup fresh Ulva
1 tablespoon sea salt

- Wash the sea vegetable thoroughly in lukewarm water. Be sure to remove all sand and crustaceans. Soak in several changes of fresh water, each soaking lasting about 15 minutes. Drain. Sprinkle with salt.
- Now the algae may be either refrigerated for 1 day in a tightly covered container or kept at room temperature if a stronger flavor is desired. It will keep under refrigeration for a week or 10 days, gradually developing a fermented odor.
- It may be used as needed in stews (a small amount will flavor a large stew) or eaten with soft-fleshed raw fish chunks or mixed with mashed soft-fleshed raw fish.

Laminaria (various species)
Kjellmaniella gyrata

Kombu no tsukudani simmered in soy sauce

YIELDS 3 CUPS

Dried slivered kombu made from the Laminarias and related genera like Kjellmaniella *is available commercially as kizami kombu.*

Prepared tsukudani of various sea vegetables is available, imported from Japan, in Japanese markets in major cities, and from mail-order sources.

¾ cup kizami kombu
1 tablespoon fresh ginger, slivered
¼ cup rice vinegar
¼ cup honey
4 cups water
1½ cups soy sauce

Substitute

Homemade slivered alaria (page 257)

- Soak the kizami kombu in water to cover for 1 hour.
- Add the remaining ingredients and cook uncovered at a low heat for 1 hour or until there is very little water left and the sea vegetable is tender.
- Place in lidded jars and store in the refrigerator. This will keep for about a month.
- Serve as an accompaniment to rice or other bland foods.

Palmaria palmata

Dulse condiment

YIELDS ABOUT 1 CUP

This novel condiment can be used much the same way in which "pesto" is used in Italian cooking.

1 cup dried dulse
1 cup spring greens, washed and drained

- Roast dried dulse in a 250-degree oven until it becomes crisp but not bitter (about 45 minutes).
- Pulverize the roasted dulse with a mortar and pestle. Grind this powder with the chopped spring greens to form a paste.
- Serve with rice, as a filling for ravioli, or spread on crackers.

Ulva lactuca

Hot Ulva relish

YIELDS 2 QUARTS

Red chilies against a background of emerald green sea vegetable makes this relish an especially beautiful condiment and a perfect holiday gift.

3 cups fresh Ulva
4 tablespoons sea salt
2 cups fresh hot chili peppers, chopped
2 cups onions, chopped
6 teaspoons honey
1 cup soy sauce

- Wash the Ulva well in lukewarm fresh water. Remove any sand or small snails that might be feeding on the blades. Drain. Cut the sea vegetable into 1-inch squares.
- Combine with the chili peppers and onions. Pack into jars.
- Combine the honey and soy sauce. Pour over the vegetables. Cover jars.

    Let stand 1 day before using. Serve with rice.

Substitutes

Ulva (various species)

Porphyra (various species)

Hawaiian Porphyra

1 cup fresh Porphyra
½ tablespoon sea salt

- Wash the Porphyra carefully in seawater to remove sand and small animals. Drain. Cut into small pieces. Sprinkle lightly with salt. Let stand for 2 to 4 hours before eating.
- This preparation will not keep well, so it must be eaten the same day. Serve with a delicately flavored soft-fleshed raw fish such as bass or bream.

Porphyra (various species)

Muck a Muck's Porphyra condiment

YIELDS ABOUT 1 CUP

A chef like George at Muck a Muck in Vancouver not only creates his own sea vegetable recipes but forages his own fresh plants, to the delight of his patrons.

¼ cup peanut oil
1 cup dried Porphyra, chopped coarsely

- Heat the oil and fry the Porphyra pieces for a few seconds on each side until they are crispy. Use in place of catsup on meats, potatoes, eggs, etc.

Sargassum (various species)

Hawaiian Sargassum

1 cup fresh Sargassum (tender young leaves only)
1 tablespoon sea salt

- Wash the Sargassum well in fresh water, removing all sand, bits of coral, or clinging algae. Remove the leaves from the stipes and soak them overnight in cold fresh water. Remove. Drain. Use as a stuffing for baked fish.
- The Sargassum blades may also be used without

soaking. Chop finely or grind, salt, and refrigerate for future use in soups, etc. Salted, they will keep for long periods.

Porphyra tenera

Japanese sea vegetable condiment sake ocha-zuke nori

YIELDS 2 CUPS

½ cup dried nori, torn into flakes
½ cup dehydrated bonito flakes
½ cup dehydrated salmon flakes
1 tablespoon dashi powder
8 tablespoons soy sauce
water

Substitutes

Porphyra (various species)

Gracilaria (various species)

● Combine the measured ingredients with enough water to make a thick paste. This condiment is sprinkled over hot rice. Then, sometimes, hot Japanese green tea is poured over the rice and condiment and the dish is eaten as a thick soup.

Hawaiian Gracilaria

1 cup fresh Gracilaria
½ tablespoon sea salt

● Rinse Gracilaria in seawater to remove clinging algae, bits of coral, and small animals. Rinse in cold fresh water. Drain. Chop finely. Use immediately or salt lightly to refrigerate or freeze.
● It is best to freeze this sea vegetable in small portions because once it is defrosted it should not be refrozen.
● It is served mixed with other sea vegetables—then eaten with fish or meat. It may be added to chicken stew along with grated coconut. The algae will act as a gel to thicken the stew.

Ahnfeltia gigartinoides

Hawaiian Ahnfeltia

- Wash the Ahnfeltia thoroughly in seawater to remove small crabs and clinging algae. Wash in fresh water. Drain. Chop finely.
- This may be eaten with raw limpets or added to cooking chicken, beef, or pork for flavor and thickening. Traditionally, it was used to wrap around chicken or fish baked in a pit. The pieces of sea vegetable that were covered with drippings were considered a special treat.
- Ahnfeltia was also wrapped in *ti* leaves and baked.

Codium (various species)

Hawaiian Codium

1 cup fresh Codium
1 tablespoon sea salt

- Wash the Codium well in cold water to remove sand or coral chips. Cut off hardened places of attachment. Chop or pound the plants and sprinkle with salt. Mix thoroughly.
- One of the following may now be added: a small amount of chili pepper, some raw cleaned octopus, or other similarly prepared sea vegetables.
- Refrigerated, this mixture will keep indefinitely but is tastiest when eaten within 10 days.

Enteromorpha (various species)

Hawaiian Enteromorpha

1 cup fresh Enteromorpha
1 tablespoon sea salt

- Wash the sea vegetable well in lukewarm fresh water and remove any small snails that may be feeding on the blades. Drain. Cut the algae into pieces less than 1 inch square. Mix with other similarly prepared algae. Sprinkle with salt. Combine with firm-fleshed fish that has been prepared in either of the following ways: mashed lightly together with its own raw liver or torn into chunks and mixed with the raw liver of other fish, then fermented for a few days at room temperature.

Porphyra umbilicalis

Rich man's laver

2 TO 4 SERVINGS

Subtle variations of this nourishing dish are common throughout Europe, with names like slook, sloak, sloke, and marine sauce.

1 cup fresh or ½ cup dried laver
2 cups water
juice of ½ lemon
10½-ounce can beef consommé
sea salt and cracked pepper to taste
butter

- If fresh laver is used, rinse it quickly but thoroughly in cold water to remove all sand. Place fresh or dried laver in a saucepan with 2 cups of water. Bring to a boil. Reduce heat. Simmer until tender.
- Remove from heat and beat into a pulp.
- Add the lemon juice and consommé. Reheat. Season with pepper and salt to taste. Top with a pat of butter.
- Serve on plain toast or biscuits as an accompaniment to roast meat, especially mutton.

Variation
- Just before serving, squeeze the juice of a Seville orange over the laver. Top with butter.

Substitutes

Porphyra (various species)

Seasonings and Staples

Tai tyau feen (sea vegetable powder)
Powdered green sea vegetable seasoning (aonoriko)
Homemade dulse plugs
High-protein Porphyra flour
Laminaria seasoning
Homemade laver plugs
Homemade slivered Alaria
Salt substitute

Enteromorpha intestinalis

Tai tyau feen
sea vegetable powder

● Wash the algae in fresh water. Sun dry completely. Pulverize with mortar and pestle. Then store in a tightly sealed vessel.
● A well-produced powder will have a pleasing aroma. Use as needed. Add to savory oils (sesame is good) for addition to noncooked dishes.
● For a sweet powder, cut the sea vegetable powder half and half with raw sugar.

Substitutes

Enteromorpha (various species)
Chaetomorpha crassa
Chaetomorpha (various species)

Enteromorpha (various species) # Powdered green sea vegetable
seasoning Aonoriko

Aonoriko is available packaged in Japanese markets. Fresh powder has a rich nutty aroma.

● Take fresh foraged fronds of Enteromorpha and wash them quickly in cold water. Drain. Spread or hang the fronds out in the sun and breeze until they are dry and crisp. Toast the dried fronds by holding them a few inches over a flame for two or three seconds. Take care not to scorch them.
● Pulverize or crumble the sea vegetable and put it in a shaker for use as a seasoning for soups, salads, seafoods, vegetables, rice, cereals, etc.

Substitutes

Monostroma (various species)
Ulva (various species)

Palmaria palmata

Homemade dulse plugs

- Dulse doesn't harden or become crisp on drying as do most other sea vegetables. Wash the fresh foraged fronds in sand-free seawater. Drain. Spread them out in the sun and breeze until they are dry but pliable. Then press a handful of the soft pieces together to form a "cake" or "plug." This plug can be wrapped and kept in the refrigerator for a month or more.
- To use, simply turn the plug on edge and slice it into slivers with a sharp knife. Add the slivers to salads and coleslaws.

Porphyra (various species)

High-protein Porphyra flour

YIELDS 1 BATCH OF FLOUR

Flour can be made from any one of a number of edible sea vegetables or combinations thereof.

- Wash 5 to 10 pounds freshly collected Porphyra in fresh water to remove sand and crustaceans. Do not soak!
- Hang the Porphyra on a clothesline or spread it out to dry for a day or two on towels in strong sunlight and a good breeze. Be sure it is thoroughly dry. It may be put in a low oven (150 degrees) for 10 or 15 minutes to ensure crispness.
- Grind the dried algae in a food blender to produce a "flour." This flour may be used as a substitute for wheat flour in any standard bread recipe or may be substituted half and half with wheat flour.
- For best results: replace the milk called for in the recipe with water and add 1 tablespoon of butter.

Laminaria digitata

Laminaria seasoning

Species of Laminaria that contain taste-producing mucilage make the most delicious seasoning.

● Use the scraps and trimmings of Laminaria that are left over after squares have been cut out for addition to soup, etc.
● Place the Laminaria pieces in one layer on a heat-proof tray and roast in the oven at 250 degrees until they are very crisp but not bitter to the taste (about 30 minutes). Then grind them into a fine powder, using a mortar and pestle.
● Place the seasoning in a shaker and use as a substitute for sea salt.

Substitutes

Laminaria ochotensis
Laminaria (various species)
Kjellmaniella gyrata

Porphyra (various species)

Homemade laver plugs

● Wash the fresh foraged laver fronds quickly in cold water. Do not soak! Spread them out in the sun and breeze until they are dry but still soft enough to be pliable (they must bend without breaking). Then stack them one on another and press them into "cakes" or "plugs." Wrap tightly and refrigerate.
● These plugs can be turned on end and sliced as needed for addition to soups. They should be used within 4 weeks.

Alaria esculenta

Homemade slivered Alaria

Alaria foraged and sold commercially in North America is often labeled wakame.

● Take the lateral, ribless fronds of Alaria and dry them thoroughly in the sun. Blanch in boiling water for a few seconds to soften and make pliable. Spread the fronds and stack them on a wooden chopping board. Place another chopping board on top. Weigh the top board down to press the Alaria and to squeeze out all the excess water.

● Remove the resulting "sea vegetable cakes" and place them in an oven set at 150 degrees. Leave the oven door ajar to allow the moisture to escape and to avoid cooking the cakes.

● When they are thoroughly dry, remove and cool. Then shred them finely with a sharp knife and pack the shredded Alaria loosely into fruit jars. Set the jars in the oven until they are warm and then seal them.

● Prepared in this manner, the sea vegetable will stay fresh indefinitely. It can be used in soups, as a vegetable, or crumbled as a seasoning.

Substitutes

Alaria (various species)

Macrocystis pyrifera

Salt substitute

YIELDS ABOUT ¼ CUP

3 tablespoons powdered greens
5 tablespoons powdered kelp
2 to 5 teaspoons powdered aromatic herbs
Sift together and place in a shaker.

Powdered kelp is available under several brand names in natural food stores. The species from which most commercial preparations are made is Macrocystis pyrifera.

● Most fresh herbs and greens (including vegetable tops) will powder easily after drying. These can be readily collected and prepared by hanging in a warm, dry, airy place, or they can be oven dried at a low temperature (100 degrees). Sassafras leaves and bark, spearmint leaves, shepherd's purse, peppermint leaves and fruit, young tansy leaves, nettle leaves, wild carrot leaves, lamb's-quarters fruit, yellow dock fruit, and masterwort leaves are just a few of the many usable wild plants. Carrot, beet, and radish tops can also be used. Aromatic herbs such as celery seed, basil, thyme, summer savory, marjoram, or dillseed can be included in small quantities for added flavor. A combination of 2 or more works well. Sun-dried Macrocystis or other kelp fronds can be further cured by low-temperature oven drying. Heating time will depend upon thickness (up to 45 minutes). Powder the dried greens to a fine consistency in a blender or with mortar and pestle. Sift out coarse pieces of stem, etc.

Cooking on the beach

Tossed seaside salad with edible kelp
Limpets Klallam, Indian style
Oulachen (candlefish) in sea lettuce, Makah Indian style
Stuffed king salmon baked in kelp, Indian style
Grunting fish wrapped in sea vegetable, Indian style

Alaria esculenta **Tossed seaside salad with edible kelp**

2 TO 4 SERVINGS

The sweet taste of the kelp midrib is a nice complement to the more piquant greens.

1 cup chopped midrib edible kelp
2 cups fresh spinach. (If you are a wild greens forager, use 1 cup scurvy grass, _Cochlearia,_ and 1 cup goosetongue, _Plantago oliganthos_ and _P. juncoides._)

DRESSING
6 tablespoons olive oil
1 clove garlic, crushed
6 tablespoons fresh lemon juice
sea salt and cracked pepper

- Wash and drain the fresh Alaria fronds, then cut out the large center midrib and chop it finely.
- Toss this chopped kelp with torn pieces of goosetongue and scurvy grass.
- Toss with olive oil to coat all leaves. Add garlic and lemon juice. Season to taste. Toss lightly. Serve.

Monostroma (various species) **Limpets Klallam, Indian style**

- Find a large intertidal rock that is covered with limpets.
- Lay a blanket of carefully rinsed (in sand-free seawater) sea vegetable over the rock and cover the sea vegetable with hot stones. The tiny mollusks will loosen their holds as they become cooked. Eat them on the spot or take them home.
- The steamed layers of sea vegetable might then be gathered and eaten as a side dish with butter, sea salt, and cracked pepper to taste

Substitutes

Porphyra (various species)
Ulva (various species)

Porphyra (various species)

Oulachen (candlefish) in sea lettuce, Makah Indian style

Since the Porphyras were also called sea lettuce by many Indian tribes, it is hard to reconstruct historical recipes. The genus most tender at any given season should be the one used in cooking.

- Oulachon is an extremely oily West Coast fish. Traveling in schools, it can be scooped up in a net while you are standing knee-high in the sea.
- Soak the fish for about 2 hours in 4 parts salt water to 1 part vinegar. Add garlic or spices to the solution if desired.
- Dry the fish thoroughly and wrap it in a piece of sea lettuce.
- Dip in batter for frying or deep fry without batter.

Substitutes

Ulva (various species)
Monostroma (various species)
Porphyra (various species)

Laminaria (various species)

Stuffed king salmon baked in kelp, Indian style

The Indian tribes of the Pacific Northwest prepared king salmon in this fashion. The thin delicate kelps are best suited to this recipe.

2 or 3 fresh kelp fronds
1 21-pound king salmon

- Wash the freshly foraged fronds in sand-free seawater. Cut off the stipes (stems) and chop them into pea-sized rounds.
- Mix ingredients for the stuffing well.
- Scale the fish, slit the fish on the underside, and remove the guts. Pack the stuffing in, and tie the fish securely with twine. Wrap the stuffed fish in a layer of

STUFFING

2 cups chopped kelp stipes
10 cups dry whole wheat bread chunks
3 medium onions, chopped
2 eggs, beaten
6 cloves garlic, chopped
½ cup melted butter
1 tablespoon sea salt
1 tablespoon cracked black pepper
½ teaspoon mace
½ teaspoon turmeric

kelp fronds. Then wrap again in foil to ensure slow cooking and protection from the ashes.

● Bury the fish in hot coals of the fire. Then cover over with a 4-inch layer of earth. Let the fish bake for 2¾ hours.

● Remove the foil, but don't unwrap the kelp. Cut the kelp-wrapped stuffed salmon into pieces and serve.

The fire

● Layer dry stones and driftwood logs in a pile about 4 feet square. Light the fire and allow it to burn for 2 hours or until the stones are properly hot. Then rake away any pieces of burning wood, leaving only the white-hot embers.

Substitute

Pleurophycus gardneri

Ulva lactuca

Grunting fish wrapped in sea vegetable, Indian style

The West Coast Indians have long considered the grunt (Porichthys notatus) *a delectable sweet treat! These fish are running during late spring and early summer in the intertidal zone from Alaska to southern California.*

● Wash the fish thoroughly. Remove the head and slit the underside to remove the internal organs. Wash again. Pat dry with a clean cloth.

● Wrap in fresh sea vegetable fronds that have been washed in sand-free seawater and drained.

● Bake over hot coals until flesh flakes easily. Serve.

Substitutes

Monostroma (various species)
Ulva (various species)

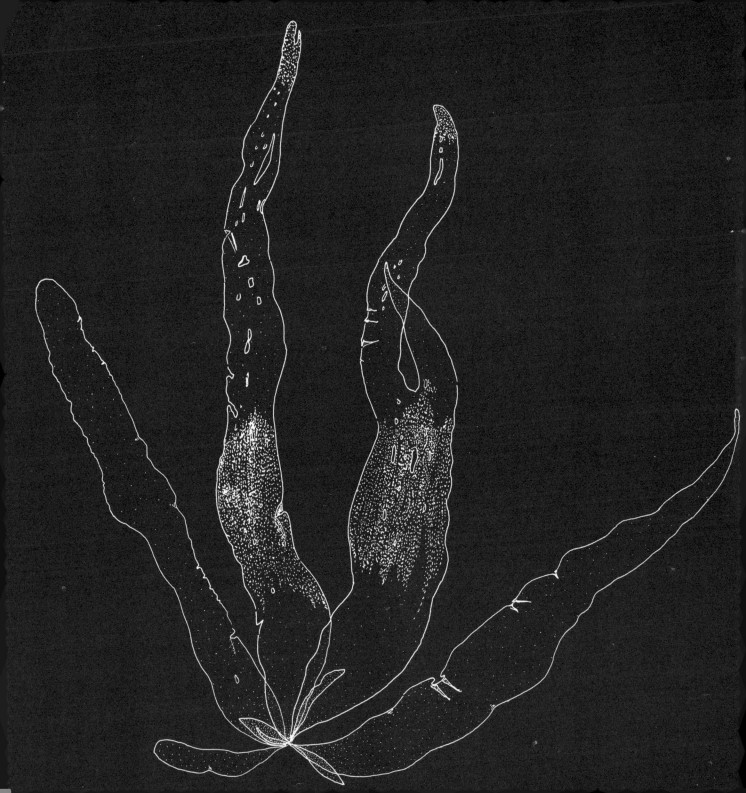

Additional sea vegetable information

Menus

Sometimes family members, especially children, will be resistant to unfamiliar foods such as sea vegetables. If the hurdle can be overcome, that is, if you can entice them to taste what is new to them, then the rest is easy since no one can help but enjoy a well-prepared sea vegetable dish. Young children will often become absorbed in sprinkling sea vegetable seasoning on their favorite foods, older children find sea vegetable sweets hard to turn down, while adults are most often impressed with the subtly spiced, sophisticated main course or a perfect soup or salad.

After incorporating a few sea vegetable recipes into your culinary repertoire, you will see that it is possible not only to complement but to enhance almost any meal with an algal dish, and your family will come to demand them.

Menu 1 has been written to show how the flavors and textures of a few different sea vegetables might highlight an ordinary day's fare.

Menus 2, 3 and 4 are intended as guides to meal planning and contain a variety of sea vegetable recipes to indicate which dishes are compatible. In all four menus, the cook should feel free to substitute either sea vegetable or non-sea vegetable recipes wherever desired, using the sample menus to suggest, not dictate, choices.

I can assure the reader that if he feels ambitious enough to try an all-algal meal for a special occasion, in which each course contains a dish prepared with sea vegetables, he will find the meal a real showstopper.

Menu 1

BREAKFAST

beverage: Tea, coffee, fruit or vegetable juice
pastry: Whole wheat muffin or toast
main course: Laver and plain or pork omelet sprinkled with salt substitute

LUNCH

beverage: Fruit juice, milk, tea, coffee, cocktail or wine
soup: Mackerel soup or beef barley soup
main course: Hamburger served with muck a muck's
Porphyra condiment
side dish: French fried potatoes or potato salad
salad: Spinach salad or wakame, cucumber and
Radish salad
dessert: Egg custard, brown rice pudding, half a
Grapefruit

COCKTAILS

beverage: Warm sake (Japanese rice wine)
snack: Sushimaki

DINNER

beverage: Burgundy wine or vegetable juice served with salt substitute
appetizer: Creamed cheesed stuffed celery sticks,
Deviled eggs with salt substitute
soup: Jellied madrilène or Irish moss tomato aspic
main course: Roast leg of lamb with potatoes and carrots
side dish: Rich man's laver
salad: Tossed green salad
dessert: Fresh fruit and assorted cheeses

Menu 2

beverage: Bladderwrack tea
pastry: Carrot cake with nori flakes
main course: Baked dulse salmon loaf or laverbread

LUNCH

beverage: Yogurt drink
soup: Split pea and wakame soup
main course: Hijiki al burro
side dish: Ham and Laminaria rolls
salad: Chicken and kanten salad
dessert: Shimmery apple cider gel

COCKTAILS

beverage: Lynn's Bloody Mary with kelp seasoning
snack: Porphyra chips or toasted kim

DINNER

appetizer: Shanghai spring rolls
soup: Sargasso Sea soup
main course: Korean rib stew with tasima
side dish: Hiziki vegetable sauté
salad: Dulse and goat's cheese salad
dessert: Irish moss blender pudding

Menu 3

BREAKFAST

beverage: Korean spice tea
bread: High-protein Porphyra flour toast
main course.   Laver and pork omelet

LUNCH

beverage: Yogurt drink
soup: Dulse miso soup
main course: Pork-stuffed Pleurophycus fronds
side dish: Ineh's matsumae (vegetables with tangle) or gluckaston
salad: Hijiki salad with tofu dressing
dessert: Tokoroten (Japanese agar jelly dessert)

COCKTAILS

beverage: Glanville Penn's Tortola Iron Jack cocktail
snack: Korean kim candy

DINNER

appetizer: Kazunoko kombu (herring roe on tangle)
soup: Porphyra soup
main course: Fillets in nori wrappers
side dish: Wakame in sweet and sour sauce
salad: Kanten salad
dessert: Lime agar dessert

Menu 4

beverage: Yogurt drink
main course: Skim milk and apple blancmange

LUNCH

beverage: Lynn's Bloody Mary with kelp seasoning (no vodka)
soup: Sea vegetable soup with bean curd
main course: Sashime (raw seafood) or fillet of sole, Ningpo style
salad: Irish moss aspic
dessert: Homemade yokan

SNACK:

Hot dulse lemonade

DINNER

soup: Alaria miso soup
main course: Stuffed Porphyra fronds
side dish: Stir-fried Irish moss
salad: Beets in Irish moss jelly
dessert: Fluffy snow agar

Glossary of ingredients

Most of the dried or canned items are also available through mail-order sources.

adzuki bean powder: Sold in Japanese and American markets. Substitute cooked pureed lima or other beans.

adzuki beans: Sold dried in Japanese and American markets. Substitute other dried beans.

agar: A sea vegetable gel extracted from certain members of the *Rhodophyceae* (Red algae), principally species of Gelidium and Gracilaria. Powdered form is available in health food stores.

bamboo shoots: Sold canned in Chinese and American markets. No substitute.

bean curd cake (tofu): Sold fresh or canned in Japanese and American markets. No substitute.

bean curd skin: Sold dried in Japanese markets. No substitute.

bonito: Sold fresh in Japanese and American fish markets. Substitute fresh tuna fish or canned tuna packed in water.

Chinese hot chili oil: Sold bottled in Chinese markets. Substitute peanut oil sautéed with hot dried red peppers.

Chinese mushrooms: Sold dried in Chinese and American markets. Substitute Japanese dried shiitake mushrooms.

Chinese mustard: Sold in Chinese markets. Substitute dry mustard mixed with a little gin.

Chinese rice noodles (be-fun): Sold in Chinese and American markets. No substitute.

chiso leaves: Sold in Japanese markets. No substitute.

coriander leaves: Called *cilantro* in Spanish. Mexican and American markets. No substitute.

dashi powder (dashi no moto): Dehydrated dashi stock. Sold in Japanese markets. No substitute.

dashi stock (kombu dashi): Soup stock made with kombu. No substitute.

dehydrated bonito flakes (hamaka katsuo): Sold in Japanese markets. No substitute.

dehydrated salmon flakes (sake): Sold in Japanese markets. No substitute.

dehydrated vegetable powder: Sold in health food stores.
  Substitute fresh vegetable broth.
dried sardines (gomame): Sold in Japanese and American markets.
  Substitute other similar dried fish.
dried shrimp: Sold in Oriental and American markets.
  No substitute.
dried squid: Sold in Oriental markets.
  No substitute.
fried bean curd (aburage): Sold dried in Japanese markets.
  No substitute.
ginger root: Sold fresh in American and Oriental markets.
  No substitute.
ginkgo nuts: Sold in Chinese markets.
  No substitute.
glutenous rice (sweet rice): Sold in Oriental and American markets.
  No substitute.
Japanese chili powder (shichimi togarashi): Sold in Japanese markets.
  Substitute cayenne pepper.
Japanese powdered green horseradish (wasabi): Sold in Japanese and American markets.
  No substitute.
kanpyo (dried gourd): Sold in Japanese markets.
  No substitute.
kanten: Dried-frozen agar, a sea vegetable extract (gel).
kukui nut kernels: Sold in Hawaiian markets.
  No substitute.
lotus root: Sold boiled and canned in Chinese and American markets.
  No substitute.
mirin (sweet rice wine): Sold in Japanese and American markets.
  Substitute dry sherry and honey at 2:1 proportions.
miso: Sold in health food stores and Japanese markets.
  No substitute.
mung beans: Sold dried in Chinese and American markets and in health food stores.
  Substitute small dried peas.
pine nuts (pignola nuts): Sold in American and Italian markets and in health food stores.
  Substitute sunflower seeds.
raw sugar (unrefined): Available in health food stores.
rice vinegar: Sold in American and Oriental markets and in health food stores.
  No substitute.

sake (rice wine): Sold in Japanese markets.
Substitute dry white wine.

sea salt: Sold in American markets and health food stores.
No substitute.

sesame oil (Oriental variety): Sold bottled in American and Oriental markets and in health food stores.
No substitute.

sesame salt: Sold in Oriental markets and health food stores.
No substitute.

sesame seed paste (tahini): Sold in health food stores and Japanese markets.
Substitute cashew butter.

shiitake mushrooms: Sold dried in Japanese and American markets.
Substitute dried Chinese mushrooms.

snow pea pods: Sold frozen in American and Chinese markets.
No substitute.

soy sauce (shoyu): Light and dark varieties sold bottled in American and Japanese markets.
No substitute.

sprouts (alfalfa, mung bean, etc.): Sold fresh in American and Oriental markets and in health food stores.

taro: Sold boiled and canned in Chinese markets.
Substitute small boiled potato.

tiger lily buds (golden needles): Sold dried in Oriental markets.
Substitute fresh day lily buds.

tofu: Sold fresh or vacuum sealed in health food stores, supermarkets, and Japanese markets.
No substitute. (See bean curd cake.)

tortillina powder: Sold in American and Mexican markets.
Substitute cornflour.

tree ears (edible fungus): Sold in Chinese markets.
No substitute.

umeboshi plums: Sold dried in Japanese markets.
No substitute.

vegetable steak: Sold packaged in Chinese markets.
No substitute.

water chestnuts: Sold boiled and canned in Chinese and American markets.
No substitute.

Commercial sea vegetable products

JAPAN

Kombu, konbu, kobu (vernacular)

KOMBU VARIETIES

makombu (Laminaria japonica): used to flavor soup stock and to make sweetmeats.

Mitsuishi kombu (Laminaria angustata): for use as a boiled vegetable and also for flavoring soup stock.

naga-kombu (Laminaria longissima): for use as a boiled vegetable and also for flavoring soup stock.

Rishiri kombu (Laminaria ochotensis): the best dashi kombu for making soup stock.

tororo kombu: (Kjellmaniella gyrata) used for shredding and for making soup stock.

KOMBU TYPES

dashi kombu: refers to any species of kombu primarily suitable for making soup stock. The more delicate types can be prepared as a vegetable after they have been used to create the stock.

aoita kombu = blue-board kombu: a dashi kombu for use in making soup stock and for shredding.

PREPARED KOMBU

kizami kombu = slivered kombu and *aokizami kombu* = blue slivered kombu: kombu to be cooked in water, seasonings (soy sauce or broth, pepper and salt) and sesame seeds = *omusubi kombu* or with sugar, soy sauce, dried fish, salt and pepper = *ochazuke kombu.* Hot green tea is then poured over the *ochazuke kombu. Omusubi kombu* is used as filling for rice balls.

shio kombu: salt-dusted kombu for cooking with soy sauce.

nekombu: dried kombu stipes (stems) for use in preparing various cooked condiments.

sukombu = vinegared kombu: kombu processed with rice vinegar.

oboro kombu or *musubi kombu* = kombu veils: hand-shaved kombu prepared with vinegar and eaten as a snack or wrapped around rice balls in place of nori or added to soups, salads, or used as a garnish for rice

dishes. White shavings = *shiro oboro* and darker, greenish
shavings = *kuru oboro.*

tororo kombu = kombu shreds: machine-cut green kombu shreds for use in
clear or miso soups or for wrapping around rice balls.

suki kombu = slivered kombu sheets: thin-sliced kombu used in place of nori
for wrapping around rice balls.

Hidaka kiri kombu = kombu squares: dried cut squares of kombu processed
with rice vinegar. Prepared by cooking in water until tender.

nishime kombu: precooked salted kombu vegetables for use in one-pot
cookery.

matsumae zuke: semidried pickled vegetables with kombu, prepared by boiling in sweetened water.

chikuwa: fish cake wrapped in kombu.

kombu takuwan: pickled radish cooked with kombu, salt, and sugar.

APPETIZERS AND ACCOMPANIMENTS TO RICE

kakugiri kombu: kombu cooked in soy sauce and sugar.

karashi kombu: kombu cooked in mustard, soy sauce, and sugar.

shiitake kombu: kombu cooked with Japanese mushrooms, soy sauce, and
sugar.

sansho kombu: kombu cooked in Japanese pepper, soy sauce, and sugar.

kombumaki: rolled kombu cooked in soy sauce, sugar, and millet jelly.

shiso kombu: kombu cooked with sesame seeds, sugar, and soy sauce.

shiso iri kombu: kombu cooked with soy sauce, sugar, and beefsteak plant.

komochi kombu tsukudani: kombu cooked with codfish roe, sugar, and soy
sauce.

tarako furikaki: kombu cooked with codfish roe, sesame seeds, rice, and salt.

hato kombu: kombu cooked with chili leaves, sugar, salt, soy sauce, and
millet jelly.

seasoned nametake mushroom and tangle: kombu cooked with nametake
mushrooms and soy sauce.

SEASONINGS

sai matsu kombu: kombu powder, usually pressed into cookies.

koiro kombu: charcoal-roasted kombu, which is candied with sugar to make
kuvashi kombu (kombu cake).

TEA

kombu cha or *kobucha:* kombu tea. Served and often packaged with rice puffs.

SOUP STOCK

kombu dashi: soup stock made from water and kombu. Bonito flakes are sometimes added for additional flavor.
dashi no moto or *dashi powder:* dehydrated soup stock made of kombu and bonito flakes.

Nori

NORI VARIETIES

Asakusa nori (Porphyra tenera): plain, dried nori. The best quality of nori used to come from Asakusa, before Tokyo Bay became polluted.
susabi nori (Porphyra yezoensis): plain, dried nori. A high-yield Japanese species soon to be widely available in North America.

PREPARED NORI

hoshi nori: plain dried nori.
ajitsuke nori = seasoned nori: nori, cut into pieces, and prepared with sugar and soy sauce, salt (optional) or chili powder (optional). This is then eaten with raw seafood (sashime) or steeped in clear soup.
yaki nori: toasted nori. Served as a cocktail snack.

CONDIMENTS

nori tsukudani: nori cooked with soy sauce and sugar.
wasabi nori: nori cooked in Japanese horseradish (wasabi), soy sauce, sugar, and salt.
shiitake nori: nori cooked with shiitake mushrooms, soy sauce, sugar, and ginger.

SEASONINGS

katsuo mirin: dried mixed nori, bonito, sesame seeds, eggs, rice, and salt.
shiso chazuke: dried mixed nori, beefsteak plant, sesame seeds, salt, and eggs.

furikaki nori: dried nori, fish meat, sesame seeds, salt, and sugar.
umeboshi chazuke: dried mixed nori, plum, sesame seeds, rice, and egg.
aonoriko: (Monostroma latissimum): dried powdered green nori.

Hijiki

HIJIKI TYPES

fukuro hijiki: the northern variety sometimes with swollen blades.

PREPARED HIJIKI

shio hijiki = salted hijiki: precooked, salted, dried hijiki for use as a cooked
    vegetable. All hijiki is precooked to lessen home cooking time. Whole
    plants may be purchased, and blades ("grains") or stems are available
    separately.
hijiki with dried fried bean curd: for fast cooking as a prepared vegetable
    dish.

Wakame

WAKAME TYPES

Naruto wakame: a type of dried wakame dusted with wood ash, for use in
    soups, etc. (with center vein). The best quality wakame comes from
    Naruto.
ito wakame = thread wakame: slender dried wakame (center vein removed)
    for use in soups.

PREPARED WAKAME

shio wakame: salted fresh wakame, which is sold vacuum-packed then rinsed
    and drained to be used as salad with various dressings.
nama wakame: fresh wakame for use as a cooked vegetable.
yaki wakame: toasted wakame for snacks.

Sea vegetable gelatins

agar or *agar agar:* (powder) sea vegetable extract used for making gelatins.
kanten: (sticks, strands, or flakes) dried-frozen agar used for making gelatins.
tengusa: dried (sometimes bleached) Gelidium plants for making agar
    gelatin.
fruit mitsumame: canned fruit and agar pieces.

Mail order sources

Chico San Company
Chico San, Calif. 95926
Tel. 916-342-6770
Dried sea vegetables, agar, and kanten.

Erewhon Trading Company
342 Newbury Street
Boston, Mass. 02115
Dried sea vegetables, agar, and kanten.

Erewhon
8001 Beverly Boulevard
Los Angeles, Calif. 90048
Dried sea vegetables, agar, and kanten.

Infinity Company
173 Duane Street
New York, N.Y. 10013
Tel. 212-966-3241
Dried sea vegetables, agar, and kanten.

Japan Food Corp.
P.O. Box 6096
Long Island City, N.Y. 11106
Wide range of sea vegetables, sea vegetable products, and Oriental food items.

Nichols Garden Nursery
1190 North Pacific Highway
Albany, Oreg. 97321
Dried sea vegetables and a wide range of spices, herbs, and Oriental food items.

The Shepards
Franklin, Maine 04634
Dried dulse.

Products by Muso, Lima, Chico San, Infinity, The Shepards, and Erewhon, available in most stores, are completely organic. The Japan Food Corp. declined to give product information.
Health food stores found in most North American towns are too numerous to list. The majority of these stores carry dried sea vegetables, agar, and kanten, and many will fill mail orders. Local store listings can be found in the yellow pages of your telephone book under "Health Foods."

Bibliography

Abbott, I. A., and Williamson, E. H. *Limu an Ethnobotanical Study of Some Edible Hawaiian Seaweeds.* Hawaii: Pacific Tropical Botanical Garden, 1974.

Algae and Man. Sponsor: Scientific Affairs Division, NATO Advanced Study Institute, 1962.

"Algae, Man, and the Environment." *Proceedings of an International Symposium.* Syracuse, N.Y.: Plenum Press, 1967.

Arnold, A. F. *The Sea Beach at Ebb Tide.* New York: Dover Publications, 1901, 1968.

Bardach, J. E.; Ryther, J. H.; and McLarney, W. O. *Aquaculture—the Farming and Husbandry of Freshwater and Marine Organisms.* New York: John Wiley & Sons, 1972.

Bersamin, S. V., et al. "Some Seaweeds Consumed Fresh in the Philippines." *Technical Paper of the Indo-Pacific Fisheries Council* 2 (1961).

Black, W. A. P. "Seaweeds and Their Value in Foodstuffs." *Proceedings of the Nutrition Society* 12 (1953):32.

Blasdale, W. C. "A Description of Some Chinese Vegetable Foods." *Office of Experiment Stations Bulletin—U.S. Department of Agriculture* 68 (1899):1–48.

Boney, A. D. "Aspects of the Biology of the Seaweeds of Economic Importance." *Advances in Marine Biology* 3 (1965).

Botanical Catalog. Hammond, Indiana Botanic Gardens.

Brook, A. J. "The Seaweeds and Their Uses." *New Biology* 7 (1949):89–103.

Chapman, V. J. *Seaweeds and Their Uses.* London: Methuen & Co., 1950, 1970.

———. "We All Eat Seaweeds." *The Explorer* 11, no. 3 (1969):4–8.

Chase, F. M. "Useful Algae." *Smithsonian Institution, Annual Report* (1941):401–52.

Cheng, T. "Production of Kelp—A Major Aspect of China's Exploitation of the Sea." *Economic Botany* 23, no. 3 (1969).

Chiang, Y. M. "The Uses of Seaweeds." *Food Industry, Taiwan* 5, no. 8 (1973):8–9. (In Chinese.)

Chiu, B. T. "Seaweeds of Economic Importance in Hong Kong." *Hong Kong University Fisheries Journal* 2 (1958):132–33.

Collier, A. "The Significance of Organic Compounds in Sea Water." *Transcript of the North American Wildlife Conference* 18 (1953):463–72.

Collins, H., and Setchell, W. A. *Phycotheca Boreali-Americana.*

"Composition of Foods." *Agriculture Handbook #8, Agricultural Research Service.* Washington, D.C.: U.S.D.A., 1975.

Cribb, A. B., and Cribb, J. W. *Wild Food in Australia.* Sidney: Collins, 1975.

Dawson, E. Y. *How to Know the Seaweeds.* Dubuque, Iowa: Wm. C. Brown Co., Publishers, 1956.

———. *Marine Botany.* New York: Holt, Rinehart and Winston, 1966.

Fan, K. "A List of Edible Seaweeds in Taiwan." *Taiwan Fisheries Research Institute,* 1953.

Fenical, W. "Polyhaloketones from the Red Seaweed Asparagopsis taxiformis." *Tetrahedron Letters,* no. 51/52 (1974):4463–66. New York: Pergamon Press.

Fogg, G. E., et al. *The Blue-Green Algae.* New York: Academic Press, 1973.

Gillespie, G. J. "Dulse Harvest." *Canada Department of Fisheries Trade News* 13 (1960):6–7.

Gunther, E. *Ethnobotany of Western Washington.* Seattle: University of Washington Press, 1974.

Hanguk tongsingmul togam. Issued by the Ministry of Education, Korea.

Hanic, L. A. *A Guide to the Common Seaweeds of Prince Edward Island, Canada.* Charlottetown, Canada: Marine Science Club, University of Prince Edward Island, 1974.

Harris, B. C. *Eat the Weeds.* Barre, Mass.: Barre Publishers, 1972.

Hild, J. "Marine Algae as Food and Raw Material." *Kosmos* 61 (1965):181–84.

Hill, J. *Wild Foods of Britain.* London, 1941.

Hoppe, H. A. "Industrial Uses of Algae." *Botanica Marina,* vol. 3. Hamburg: Cram De Gruyter & Co., 1962. (In German.)

Industrial Gums. R. L. Whistler, ed. New York: Academic Press, 1959.

Johnson, A. "Algae and Man." Kuala Lumpur: University of Malaya, 1969.

Koidzumi, G. "On *ajitsuke* nori = Nostoc verrucosum." *Botanical Magazine* 33:263–64. Tokyo.

Kugo tae sajon. (Dictionary.) Y. Huisun, ed. Korea, 1961.

Kurogi, M. "Recent Laver Cultivation in Japan." *Fishing News International,* July-September 1963.

Lapointe, B. E., et al. "The Mass Outdoor Culture of Macroscopic Marine Algae." Contribution #3609—*Woods Hole Oceanographic Institution;* Contribution #47—*Harbor Branch Foundation, Inc.*

Lee, K. "Some Studies on the Marine Algae of Hong Kong I-Cyanophyta, Chlorophyta and Phaeophyta; II-Rhodophyta." *New Asia College Academic Annual* 7 (1965).

Lessico Universale Italiano. Instituto dell' Enciclopedia Italiana, 19th edition, vol. 1 (1968):395–96. Rome. (In Italian.)

Levring, T. "Seaweeds for Food for Man." *Botanica Marina,* vol. 9 (supp.). Hamburg: Cram De Gruyter & Co., 1966. (English summary.)

———, et al. *Marine Algae—A Survey of Research and Utilization.* Hamburg: Cram De Gruyter & Co., 1969.

Lewin, R. *Physiology and Biochemistry of Algae.* New York: Academic Press, 1962.

Lewis, J. R. *The Ecology of Rocky Shores.* London: English University Press, 1964.

Makino's New Illustrated Flora of Japan. Dr. Tomitaro, ed. Tokyo: The Hokuryukan Ltd., 1961.

Marine Food Chains. J. H. Steele, ed. Edinburgh: Oliver and Boyd, 1970.

Mifune, M. "Nostoc verrucosum Vaucher." *Bulletin of the Japanese Society of Phycology* 5 (1957):83–84, 1f.

Miller, C. D. "Food Values of Poi, Taro, and Limu." *Bulletin of the Bernice P. Bishop Museum,* no. 37 (January 25, 1927):1–25. Kauai.

Miyabe, K. "On the Laminariacae of Hokkaido." *Journal of the Sapporo Agricultural College* 1 (1902). Sapporo, Japan.

Montagne, M. C. "Chinese Nostoc edule." *Revue Botanique* (ed. P. Ducharte) 2 (1846–47):365–66.

Newton, L. *Seaweed Utilization.* London: Sampson Low, 1951.

———. "Uses of Seaweed." *Vistas in Botany* 2 (1963):325–55.

Ohmi, H. "Edible Seaweeds in Chile." *Bulletin of the Japanese Society of Phycology* 16, no. 1 (1968):52–54. (In Japanese with English summary.)

Okamura, K. *Icones of Japanese Algae.* Tokyo: Published by the author, 1909–32.

———. "On Chinese Edible Nostoc (fah tsai) Identified by Professor Setchell as Nostoc commune var. flagelliforme." *Botanical Magazine* 27 (1913) Tokyo.

———. "Taste and Classification." *Journal of Japanese Botany* 5, no. 7 (1928). (In Japanese.)

Okazaki, A. *Seaweeds and Their Uses in Japan.* Tokyo: Tokai University Press, 1971. Available Maruzen Co., New York and Tokyo.

Okuda, Y., and Eto, T. "On the Form of Iodine in Marine Algae." *Tokyo University Faculty of Agriculture Journal* 5 (1916):341–53.

Palmer, E. L. "The Marine Algae—In the Sea's Weeds May Lie the Future's Insurance against Starvation." *Natural History* 70 (1961):34–43.

Porterfield, W. M. "References to the Algae in the Chinese Classics." *Bulletin of the Torrey Club* 49(1922):297–300.

Proceedings of the First International Seaweed Symposium. Edinburgh, 1953.

Proceedings of the Second International Seaweed Symposium. Trondheim. Braarud, et al., eds. New York: Pergamon Press, 1956.

Proceedings of the Third International Seaweed Symposium. Galway, 1958.

Proceedings of the Fourth International Seaweed Symposium. Biarritz. A. D. Davy de Virville and J. Feldman, eds. New York: Pergamon Press, 1961.

Proceedings of the Fifth International Seaweed Symposium. Halifax. New York: Pergamon Press, 1966.

Proceedings of the Sixth International Seaweed Symposium. Santiago de Compostella. R. Margalet, ed. Subsecretaria de la Marina Mercante, Direccion General de Pesca Maritima. Madrid, 1968.

Proceedings of the Seventh International Seaweed Symposium. Trondheim. New York: John Wiley & Sons, 1974.

Proceedings of the Thirteenth Pacific Science Congress. Vol. I. Vancouver, B.C., Canada, 1975.

Processed Plant Proteins. A. M. Alschul, ed. New York: Academic Press, 1958.

Sanford, F. B. "Seaweeds and Their Uses." *Fisheries Leaflet* No. 469. *U.S. Department of the Interior,* 1958.

Sauvageau, C. *Utilization des Algues Marines.* Gaston Dion, ed., Encyclopédie Scientifique Bibliothèque de Botanique Appliquée. Paris, 1920.

Scagel, R. F. *Guide to Common Seaweeds of British Columbia.* Handbook #27. British Columbia Provincial Museum, Victoria, Canada, 1972.

Schwimmer, M. *The Role of Algae and Plankton in Medicine.* New York: Grune and Stratton, 1955.

Sea Frontiers, Supplemental Magazine of the International Oceanographic Foundation 17, no. 1–6 (1971):344. Miami, Florida.

"Seaweed for Food—South Wales Laverbread Industry." *Food Manufacture* 34, no. 2 (1959):443–44.

Setchell, W. A. *Limu.* University of California Publications. Botany. Vol. 2, no. 3 (1905):91–113.

Shen, Y. (Chen, Y.), and Fan, K. "Edible Marine Algae of Taiwan." *Quarterly Journal of the Bank of Taiwan* 4, no. 3 (1951):39–46. (In Chinese.)

————. "Edible Seaweeds in Taiwan." *Taiwan Research Bulletin* 13 (1951):42–49. (In Chinese.)

Smith, C. A. *Common Names of South African Plants.* Department of Agricultural and Technical Services. Pretoria, 1966.

Smith, G. M. *Marine Algae of the Monterey Peninsula.* Stanford: Stanford University Press, 1969.

Smith, J. *Dictionary of Popular Names of Economic Plants: Their History, Products, and Uses.* London: Macmillan, 1882.

"Systematic List of Economic Plants in Japan." *General Headquarters for the Supreme Allied Powers. Natural Resources Section Report.* #121. Tokyo, 1949.

Tamiya, H. "Role of Algae as Food." *Proceedings of the Symposium on Algology. Indian Council of Agricultural Resources,* pp. 379–89. New Delhi, India, December, 1959.

Taylor, W. R. *Marine Algae of the Eastern Tropical and Sub-Tropical Coasts of the Americas.* Ann Arbor, Mich.: University of Michigan Press, 1960.

———— *The Marine Algae of the Northeastern Coast of North America.* Ann Arbor, Mich.: University of Michigan Press, 1972.

The Domestic Dictionary and Housekeeper's Manual. 1842.

"The Provision of More Adequate Supplies of Edible Protein." *F.A.O. Report* #60451-65-WM. 1965.

Tiffany, L. H. *Algae: The Grass of Many Waters.* Charles C Thomas, 1938.

Tilden, J. *The Algae and Their Life Relations.* Minneapolis: 1935.

Tokida, J. "On Some Edible Seaweeds Utilized Among a Native Race 'Ami' of Formosa." Collected by N. Nakanome. *Zoology and Botany* 7, no. 9 (1934).

——. "The Marine Algae of Southern Saghalien." *Reprinted from the Memoirs of the Faculty of Fisheries,* Vol. 2, no. 1. Sapporo, Hokkaido University. Japan: December 1954.

Tressler, D. K. *Marine Products of Commerce.* New York: Reinhold Co., 1923, 1951.

Triffitt, J. T. "Binding of Calcium and Strontium by Alginates." *Nature* 217 (1968):457. London.

Tseng, C. K. "Economic Seaweeds of Kwangtung Province, South China." *Lingnan Science Journal* 14 no. 1 (January 1935). Canton, China.

——. "Notes on Some Chinese Marine Algae." *Lingnan Science Journal* 17, no. 4 (October 1938).

——. "Notes on the Marine Algae from Amoy." *Chinese Marine Biological Bulletin* 1 (1936):1–86. Amoy, China.

——. "Studies on the Marine Chlorophyceae from Hainan." *Chinese Marine Biological Bulletin* 1, no. 5 (1936):129–200.

Turner, N. C. "Notes on Haida Indian Edible Seaweeds." Victoria, B.C.: *Provincial Museum,* 1974.

——, and Bell, M. A. M. "The Ethnobotany of the Southern Kwakiutl Indians of British Columbia." *Economic Botany* 27 (1973):257–310.

Uphof, J. C. *Dictionary of Economic Plants.* Weinheim: H. R. Englemann (J. Cramer), 1959.

Usher, G. *Dictionary of Plants Used by Man.* London: Constable, 1974.

Weiner, M. A. *Earth Medicines—Earth Foods.* New York: Collier Books, 1972.

Whistler, R. L. *Industrial Gums.* New York: Academic Press, 1959.

Yendo, K. "Uses of Marine Algae in Japan." *Postelsia* 1 (1902):1–18.

Zaneveld, J. S. "De Economische Betekensis Van Zeewierenen De Mogelijkheid Tot Hun Exploitatie In De Maieise Archipel." *Overdruk Uit Chronica Naturae.* 1949. (English summary.)

——. "Economic Marine Algae of Tropical South and East Asia and Their Utilization." *Special Publication* #3, *F.A.O. Regional Office.* Bangkok, 1955.

——. "The Economic Importance of Seaweeds and the Possibility of Their Exploitation in the Malay Archipelago." *Chronica Naturae* 105, no. 1 (1949). (In Dutch.)

——. "The Economic Marine Algae of Malaysia and Their Applications I-Cyanophyta and Chlorophyta." *Indo-Pacific Fisheries Council Proceedings,* 1950.

——. "The Economic Marine Algae of Malaysia and Their Applications II-Phaeophyta." *Indo-Pacific Fisheries Council Proceedings,* 1951.

——. "The Economic Marine Algae of Malaysia and Their Applications III-Rhodophyta." *Indo-Pacific Fisheries Council Proceedings,* 1952.

——. "The Utilization of Marine Algae in Tropical Southeast Asia." *Economic Botany* 13, no. 2 (1959):89–131.

BIBLIOGRAPHIES

A Bibliography of Eastern Asiatic Botany. Baltimore, Md.: Lord Baltimore Press, 1938.
A Bibliography of Eastern Asiatic Botany. Supplement: E. H. Walker, ed. American Institute of Biologic Sciences, 1960.
Medicinal and Food Plants of the North American Indians, A Bibliography. L. Lynas, ed. New York Botanical Gardens, 1972.

Index

Boldface numbers refer to sea vegetable data pages and illustrations.